STRANGE BEDFELLOWS

STRANGE BEDFELLOWS

*How Late-Night Comedy Turns
Democracy into a Joke*

RUSSELL L. PETERSON

RUTGERS UNIVERSITY PRESS
NEW BRUNSWICK, NEW JERSEY, AND LONDON

Library of Congress Cataloging-in-Publication Data

Peterson, Russell Leslie.
Strange bedfellows: how late-night comedy turns democracy into a joke /
Russell L. Peterson.
    p. cm.
Includes bibliographical references and index.
ISBN 978-0-8135-4284-3 (hardcover : alk. paper)
    1. Television comedies—United States—History and criticism.   2. Television talk
shows—United States.   3. Television broadcasting of news—United States.   I. Title.
PN1992.8.C66P48   2008
791.45'6170973—dc22   2007026812

A British Cataloging-in-Publication record for this book is available from the British
Library.

Visit our Web site: http://rutgerspress.rutgers.edu
Manufactured in the United States of America

For Becky

CONTENTS

STRANGE BEDFELLOWS

INTRODUCTION

It's a chilly night in late February 2006. Slide under the covers, fluff up your pillow, and grab the remote. (Click.) "The White House has given permission for a company owned by the government of Dubai [United Arab Emirates] to run six U.S. ports, including the Port of New York," says Jay Leno. "What's next, we'll put Mexico in charge of immigration? How about Dick Cheney in charge of gun safety? Courtney Love in charge of Olympic drug testing?"[1]

Turn the channel. (Click.) David Letterman says letting Dubai run the ports is "like telling Kirstie Alley to keep an eye on the buffet."[2]

(Click.) CNN's Anderson Cooper is soliciting the opinion of Congressman Peter King (R, NY), who finds himself in the awkward position of opposing a president of his own party. While King is careful to say "a full investigation may show the company can be trusted" (as President George W. Bush has been insisting), he can't help noting that the UAE was, "you know, one of only three governments in the world to recognize the Taliban."[3]

(Click.) Stephen Colbert says Bush supported the Dubai deal—which, while at least arguably sound policy, was politically tone-deaf—because he was thinking with his brain rather than his "gut." "We all know he's not a brain thinker," Colbert explains. "He doesn't make decisions based on facts." ("Makes Facts Based on Decisions," a bullet point on the right side of the

(Click.) Chris Bury begins *Nightline*'s port report by noting that the "controversial deal to sell the American port operations of a British company to one owned by the government of Dubai may mask far more serious risks."[5] (Off.) Time to go to sleep (if you can).

———

Politics, says the old cliché, makes strange bedfellows. So too with comedy and news; yet in the bleary late-night haze the twenty-four-hour urgency of CNN, Fox, and MSNBC blurs into the bubbling frivolity of Jay and Dave and *The Daily Show* in a strangely intimate way. It would be too glib simply to say that you can no longer tell where the news leaves off and the comedy begins, though in fact there are plenty of people saying just that. A survey conducted by the Pew Center for the People and the Press in 2004 found that 61 percent of people under the age of thirty got some of their political "news" from late-night comedy shows.[6] This survey (which the Pew people have conducted in each presidential cycle since 1996) has provided the premise for a number of news stories raising concerns about the younger generation's information diet: by getting information directly from topical comics, the metaphorical argument goes, they are skipping their spinach and going straight for the pumpkin pie.

At the same time, the nutritional value of the news itself has come into some doubt. News programming is, according to the consensus, becoming almost indistinguishable from entertainment programming. With its snappy theme songs, soap-operatic continuities (Laci Peterson, runaway brides, the life and death of Anna Nicole Smith), and a cast of characters ranging from photogenic newsreaders to egomaniacal pundits, contemporary television journalism rivals, in its shallowness and sensationalism, the finest works of the late Aaron Spelling. From the parapets of the Pew Center and other such watchtowers of serious discourse, the prospects for maintaining an informed electorate look bleak indeed. On the one hand, it's terrible how people choose entertainment over the news; on the other hand, *what* news?

The individual viewer, however, might see the blurring of the info/tainment boundary from a different perspective and ask: what difference does it make? The news says the system is broken, our leaders are crooks, and there's not a damn thing I can do about it. Comedians tell me the same thing, but at least they do it in a funny way. A vicious cycle of trivialization and cynicism is set in motion: people are focusing on the wrong things (Tom Cruise's sex life, high-speed car chases, *American Idol*), but the things they should be paying attention to (global warming, the trade deficit, the terrorist threat) are so beset by special-interest influence, partisan gridlock, and leaders who put their political survival ahead of the public good—that knowing about them wouldn't help anyway. Hell, we might as well laugh—gimme that remote.

Yet late-night comedy does more than simply induce apathy and dumb down our discourse. It adds its own dimensions to the interpretation of current events, even as it shuts out others. Turn back to the Dubai port story—which, while it has been superseded by other insomnia-inducing threats, was a major scandal at the time—and consider the varying perspectives behind the responses. Take Letterman: by invoking Kirstie Alley, the formerly svelte star of *Fat Actress,* he gives the somewhat abstract notion of port security a recognizable shape and offers the audience a laughable absurdity in place of a maddening one. Leno's joke is similar, but it also relates the port controversy to an array of other contemporary issues—or media obsessions.

Colbert contextualizes the story in a more explicitly political manner, framing Bush's port position in a way that raises larger questions about his approach to governing and his relationship to the conservative media Colbert pretends to represent. Leno and Letterman give shape to the public's rage; Colbert offers incisive analysis, though it is coated with a layer of silliness.

Meanwhile, though they are richer in factual detail and thoroughly serious in tone, it is far from clear that the news accounts serve their audience better. Cooper's CNN segment does little beyond allowing Congressman King a bully pulpit from which to delineate (carefully) his differences with the president, while *Nightline*'s "hidden threat" approach puts fear-mongering ahead of any higher journalistic purpose. News informs, yes, but it also spins and sensationalizes. Comedy trivializes, but it also offers catharsis and, occasionally, insight.

Topical comedy, in short, is not simply an inadequate substitute for the news; for good and for ill, it adds something of its own to our understanding of current events. Moreover, the problem is less that we pay it too much attention than that we don't pay it enough; after all, a joke—as Aristotle, Sigmund Freud, Henri Bergson, and the myriad other "serious" thinkers who have turned their minds to such matters would tell you—is rarely just a joke. On the one hand, not all late-night political humor deserves to be called "trivial." On the other hand, not all of it deserves to be called "political." (Some of it doesn't even deserve to be called "humor.") We ought to consider the subject in all its complexity. Above all, we ought to understand it for what it is, not just for what it isn't. Rather than simply dismissing this phenomenally popular genre as a symptom of civic decay or a cause of electoral apathy, we ought to be asking: what are we laughing at, and why?

CHAPTER 1

LOSING OUR RELIGION

Fast-forward to a few weeks after the Dubai debacle. On the second Saturday after Easter, the city of Washington, D.C., witnessed a miracle of sorts. The president of the United States appeared before the assembled members of the White House Correspondents Association accompanied by an uncanny doppelgänger. This apparent clone, who stood stage right of the commander in chief at a matching podium, not only looked and sounded like George W. Bush, he seemed to give voice to the president's subconscious thoughts: "Here I am at another one of these dang press dinners. Could be home asleep, little Barney curled up at my feet. Nooo. I gotta pretend I like being here. Being here really ticks me off. The way they try to embarrass me by not editing what I say. Well, let's get things going so I can get to bed."[1]

The president's double, actor Steve Bridges, did a heckuva job reproducing his voice and gestures, and the crowd loved it. The members of the media elite erupted in laughter when George W. Bush's "inner voice" pronounced the first lady "*muy caliente.*" It was the funniest and most elaborate presidential comedy routine since Bill Clinton's "Final Days" video, back in 2000.

But this wasn't the miracle, just a clever bit of stagecraft. The miracle came after the Dueling Bushes routine, when Comedy Central's faux pundit Stephen Colbert stepped up to the lectern. What he said was not in itself so remarkable; the content of his routine was very much of a piece with the tongue-in-cheek right-wing pontificating seen four nights a week on *The Colbert Report*—a few of the jokes were even recycled from the show. What made his monologue startling—even awe-inspiring—was the fact that although the primary target of Colbert's ironic attack, the president of the United States, was sitting not six feet away from him, he pulled nary a punch. "The greatest thing about this man is, he's steady," proclaimed the comedian, with his impenetrable mock-sincerity. "You know where he stands. He believes the same thing Wednesday that he believed on Monday, no matter what happened Tuesday. Events can change; this man's beliefs never will." The president squirmed, his mottled face betraying the effort behind a strained smile. The audience, who had greeted the Bush/Bridges act with full-throated laughter, now sounded subdued, lapsing at times into uncomfortable silence. Colbert appeared undaunted. It was a brave and bracing performance, demonstrating what the comedian would call (in character) *muchos huevos grandes*.

That we live in a country where one can publicly criticize the head of state is of course a kind of miracle in itself, one we perhaps too often take for granted. But to see *this* president—whose administration has specialized in intimidating critics and marginalizing dissent—mocked so mercilessly, to his face, in front of a cozy gathering of Washington insiders (who would suffer their own share of Colbert's satirical punishment that night), was like witnessing Moses calling down a plague of frogs on Pharaoh and his courtiers. That is, if Moses had been funny.

Yet the mainstream media, whose shindig this was, appeared to leave all memory of Colbert's astonishing performance in the banquet hall, along with the parsley on their plates. Monday morning's *New York Times* ran a bubbly account of the president's "double" routine without so much as mentioning Colbert's name. Television news, both network and cable, followed suit, fawning over the video of the Bush "twins" as if it were the latest baby panda footage but avoiding any reference to the evening's controversial headliner.[2]

While the diners and the media corporations they represented seemed to be experiencing selective amnesia, though, the Internet was going Colbert-crazy. Liberal blogs sang his praises, while conservative commentators condemned him for disrespecting the nation's chief executive (something most of them had little problem countenancing when that office was held by Bill Clinton). Someone launched a "Thank You, Stephen Colbert" Web page, which in no time had registered the gratitude of thousands of netizens who felt that President Bush had for too long been treated far too gently by the main-stream press.[3]

When this cyber-rumbling began to grow too loud to ignore, a few members of the diners' club decided they had better say something. But they succeeded only in proving their critics right: the mainstream media's belated response to Colbert was characterized by groupthink and a preoccupation with style over substance. (Sure, his jokes pointed out some unpleasant truths, but did he have to be so blunt about it?) "The only thing worse than the mainstream media's ignoring Stephen Colbert's astonishing sendup of the Bush administration and its media courtiers," wrote *Salon*'s Joan Walsh, "is what happened when they started to pay attention to it." Indeed, from *Hardball*'s human airhorn Chris Matthews—who began his Siskel-and-Ebert bit with fellow irony-challenged critic Mike Allen of *Time* magazine by asking, "Why was he [Colbert] so bad?"—to Lloyd Grove of the *Daily News* to the *New York Observer*'s Christopher Lehman to alternative-media-emeritus Ana Marie Cox (formerly of the Wonkette blog, now safely ensconced in the media mainstream as a Time-Warner columnist, cable news bloviator, and, incidentally, Mrs. Christopher Lehman), the pundit establishment seemed to be on the same page. "The dreary consensus," noted Walsh, was that "Colbert just wasn't funny."[4]

What is and isn't funny is of course a subjective judgment, but there may have been more to this near-unanimity among the top tier of television and print journalists—who happen to comprise most of the guest list at events like the White House Correspondents Dinner—than the fact that they all share remarkably similar tastes. "Why so defensive?" asked the *Washington Post*'s media critic, Dan Froomkin.[5] Perhaps it was because a mere comedian had not only embarrassed the press corps's guest of honor but had also shown up his hosts by beating them at what was supposed to be their own game: speaking truth to power. The Fourth Estate is called that because it is meant to act as an extragovernmental check on the judicial, legislative, and executive branches. But the news media's compliant behavior in the wake of 9/11 and the run-up to the invasion of Iraq, their failure to aggressively pursue a raft of administration scandals, and even the cozy ritual of the

Correspondents Dinner itself belie that adversarial ideal. Colbert used the occasion to backhandedly chide the press for their lazy complicity: "Here's how it works: the president makes decisions. He's the decider. The press secretary announces those decisions, and you people of the press type those decisions down. Make, announce, type. Just put 'em through a spell check and go home. . . . Write that novel you got kicking around in your head. You know, the one about the intrepid Washington reporter with the courage to stand up to the administration. You know—fiction!"

It's hard to imagine a sharper critique of the press's failure to act as a watchdog, short of hitting Wolf Blitzer in the schnozz with a rolled-up newspaper. Colbert's real achievement, however, lies not in policing the standards of another profession but in asserting those of his own: for if "speaking truth to power" is part of the journalist's job, it is the satirist's primary mission—a higher calling, in fact, than merely being funny.

But if Colbert was just doing his job, why did it make the audience so uncomfortable? If this was just a case of satire fulfilling its function, why call it a miracle? Because, in spite of the fact that comedy *about* politics is now as common as crabgrass, political comedy—that is, genuine satire, which uses comedic means to advance a serious critique—is so rare we might be tempted to conclude it is extinct. Seeing it right there in front of God, the president, and the press corps was an astonishing moment, which stood out from the mundane rituals of politics and the press commonly seen on C-SPAN, *Meet the Press,* and the nightly news. It was like seeing an ivory-billed woodpecker alight on your satellite dish.

So "miracle" is indeed the word. Though some branded Colbert a heretic (the *Washington Post*'s nominally liberal columnist Richard Cohen called him a "bully" for picking on the poor president), others saw him as a satirical evangelist, a Jonathan Edwards who took his text from the First Book of Jonathan Swift.[6] If the president and the press didn't laugh very much during the course of this sermon, it was because they recognized themselves as the sinners in the hands of an angry comedian.

Of course it is possible that Colbert approached the dais with no mission in mind beyond making 'em laugh—though one suspects he and his writers are smart enough to know what they were getting into. Even if most of its practitioners would be loath to admit it, satire is a moral art. It calls on people and institutions to do their duty, as when Colbert scolded the press for their recent toothlessness: "Over the last five years you people were so good—over tax cuts, WMD intelligence, the effect of global warming," he said, wistfully. "We Americans didn't want to know, and you had the courtesy not to try to find out. Those were good times, as far as we knew."

This is the satirist as revivalist preacher, calling his congregation back to the True Faith. And in America—which, despite the efforts of the Christian Right, remains a secular nation—the name of that Faith is Democracy. Its holy book is the Constitution, its clergy the Supreme Court and our elected representatives, its congregants We the People, its rituals voting and vigilance. Like other faiths—but unlike other governmental systems, which are held in place primarily through the threat of force—democracy depends on the devotion of its followers to sustain it. Some of the people, some of the time, must keep on believing that our electoral choices matter, that if we speak out our voices will be heard, that our representatives truly represent our interests. It's a tall order, but if we were to abandon all hope that democracy could endure—if democratic apathy reached the point of democratic atheism—our national faith would go the way of the cults of Baal, Zeus, Quetzalcoatl, and other unemployed divinities.

Thankfully, our civic religion has not yet reached its moment of Nietzchean doom. But its tenets—equal justice for all; government of, by, and for the people—have been subjected to a subtle yet constant and corrosive barrage of blasphemous derision. It echoes from the office water cooler to the corner bar to the corridors of government itself. Most seductively, it rings out amidst the pealing laughter that emanates from millions of Americans' televisions each night.

The Lesser of Two Weasels: Anti-Political Comedy

While genuine satire arises from a sense of outrage, the topical jokes heard in mainstream late-night monologues are rooted in mere cynicism. Unlike satire, which scolds and shames, this kind of comedy merely shrugs. Unlike Colbert, whose appearance at the Correspondents Dinner evoked a democratic revivalist, Jay Leno, David Letterman, and Conan O'Brien are evangelists of apathy.

The difference is easier to discern if we go back to a presidential election year. So pick up that remote, hit rewind, and keep going, all the way back to 2004:

> Political pundits are saying President George W. Bush has made gains in two key states: dazed and confused. (Letterman)
>
> You see the pictures in the paper today of John Kerry windsurfing? . . . Even his hobby depends on which way the wind blows. (Leno)
>
> Earlier today, President Bush said Kerry will be a tough and hard-charging opponent. That explains why Bush's nickname for Kerry is "Math." (O'Brien)
>
> Kerry was here in Los Angeles. He was courting the Spanish vote by speaking Spanish. And he showed people he could be boring in two languages. (Leno)[7]

A larger sampling would prove, as this selection suggests, that the political jokes told by network late-night hosts aim, cumulatively, for a bipartisan symmetry. Although election season "joke counts" maintained by the Center for Media and Public Affairs do not show a perfect one-to-one balance of jokes aimed at Democratic and Republican nominees, as the election got closer, a rough equity emerged, suggesting that George W. Bush was no more or less dumb than John Kerry was boring.[8] So it is in every presidential election year. Even in between, care is taken to target the abuse at "both sides," even if, during the Bush years, it has often meant resorting to time-worn Monica Lewinsky jokes. Maintaining this equilibrium is understood as one of the ground rules of the genre—a tenet so well established that an industry-specific cliché has arisen to describe those who embrace it: "equal-opportunity offenders."

The phrase, or the ideal it expresses, is typically brandished by late-night comics as a shield against charges of bias. But it is a paradigm embraced even more fervently by journalists who write about comedy. Bill Maher, Robin

Williams, and Carlos Mencia—even an Israeli/Lebanese comedy team who bill their show as "The Arab-Israeli Comedy Hour"—have been celebrated in press accounts as equal-opportunity offenders. Being branded an EOO by the journalistic establishment is something like getting the Good Housekeeping Seal of Approval, though the honor is bestowed with some subjectivity. Sarah Silverman is praised by the *Milwaukee Journal Sentinel* for being one, and criticized by the *Houston Chronicle* for not being enough of one.[9]

To offend unequally, on the other hand, is offensive indeed. Page one of the August 22, 2004, *New York Times* Arts and Leisure section features a telling juxtaposition of two articles concerning topical comedy. At the top of the page, the *Times* frets that a few of those making jokes about President Bush have transgressed the boundaries of "just kidding" and crossed the line into genuine (gasp!) satire. Though Jon Stewart, for example, "has repeatedly insisted that he's nonpartisan," his jokes about the incumbent "have started to seem like a sustained argument with the president." A comedian using humor to express an opinion? *J'accuse!* Yet below the fold, the *Times* toasts *South Park* creators Matt Stone and Trey Parker's upcoming film, *Team America,* which promises to "take aim at sanctimonious right-wing nutjobs and smug Hollywood liberals alike." Parker takes the opportunity to assert his EOO bona fides: "People who go [to the film] will be really confused about whose side we're on. That's because we're really confused." Ah, that's what we like to see—fair and balanced comedy.[10]

Journalists' peculiar devotion to the equal-opportunity offender ideal results from a tendency to project their own profession's standards of objectivity onto comedians. Expecting Jay Leno to play by the same rules as Anderson Cooper is a bit like squeezing apples to get orange juice, but conventional wisdom seems to take this conflation of journalistic and comedic ethics for granted—the Pew poll, after all, asks its respondents to consider *The Tonight Show* and CNN side by side. Comedians' own reasons for maintaining balance, however, have little to do with abstract notions of fairness; it's more a matter of pragmatism than idealism. As Jay Leno put it, once a comedian takes a political side, "you've lost half the crowd already."[11] These guys are in show *business,* after all, and it doesn't pay to alienate 50 percent of your potential viewers. Such bottom-line considerations, incidentally, help explain why *The Colbert Report* and *The Daily Show* can afford to be more politically "risky" than Leno's: a little over a million viewers—a narrowly interested but loyal core—amounts to a pretty respectable audience for a cable show like the *Report,* but for *The Tonight Show,* which averages six million viewers nightly, it would be a disaster.[12]

The bigger difference between the network and cable shows' humor has to do with what the jokes say, not how many of them are aimed at Democrats versus Republicans. On closer examination, the only political thing about the mainstream jokes quoted above is that they happen to be about politicians. They are personality jokes, not that different from the ones those same comedians tell about Paris Hilton or Ozzy Osbourne—just replace "dumb" and "boring" with "slutty" and "drug-addled." And unlike Colbert's jokes about Bush's inflexibility or his tendency to think with his "gut," the jokes told on the network shows rarely transcend the level of pure ad hominem mockery to consider how such personal traits might manifest themselves in terms of policy.

The bottom line of all the jokes about Bush's dumbness, Kerry's dullness, Al Gore's stiffness, Bob Dole's "hey-you-kids-get-outta-my-yard" crankiness, and so on is that all politicians are created equal—equally unworthy, that is—and that no matter who wins the election, the American people lose. Thus, despite their efforts to play it safe by offending equally (and superficially), the mainstream late-night comics actually present an extremely bleak and cynical view of American democracy.

What, then, is the secret of their appeal? Why do millions of us tune in, night after night, to be told—not overtly, but insinuatingly and consistently—that our cherished system of self-government is a joke? Perhaps because this confirms what we have always suspected: democracy is a nice idea but not, ultimately, a practical one. And if Americans doubt democracy, we hate politics. Politics is treated like an infection, or a tumor. It is to be avoided if possible, and when found lurking—in a sitcom writers' room, in an Oscar acceptance speech, in the funnies (*Doonesbury* has been exiled to the editorial pages of many of the papers that carry it)—it must be excised before it can infect the nation's body non-politic. Politics is *icky*.

Even our politicians disdain politics. A candidate can't go wrong by running against Washington, D.C., and all that it supposedly stands for. George W. "I'm from Texas" Bush successfully campaigned as an anti-establishment "outsider"—and his dad was the president! Ronald Reagan got applause when he proclaimed that government was not the solution, but the problem—though he himself had just campaigned for, and achieved, the government's top job.[13]

Most Americans see nothing strange in this; for as much as we like to wave the flag, and pledge our allegiance to the republic for which it stands, as a people we regard our government, its institutions, and its representatives (save those who take care to inoculate themselves with anti-political rhetoric) with contempt. This feeling is reflected not only in our appallingly low voter turnout rates but also in our culture—particularly in our humor.

Which is why most of this country's "political" humor—from Artemus Ward to Will Rogers, from Johnny Carson to Jay Leno, from Andy Borowitz to JibJab.com—has in fact been *anti*-political. "All politics is applesauce," Rogers once said, by which he did not mean that it was a tasty side dish with pork chops.[14] He meant that progress was the opposite of Congress, that the Democrats were worse than any other party except for the Republicans and vice versa, that six of one was half a dozen of the other. Will Rogers was an equal-opportunity offender.

Rogers's observation that "both parties have their good and bad times . . . they are each good when they are out, and . . . bad when they are in" reappears almost seventy years later as Jay Leno's characterization of the 2000 election as a choice between "the lesser of two weasels." It appears again, in an "edgier" guise, when the *South Park* kids are given the opportunity to learn about democracy by nominating and voting for a new school mascot: "We're supposed to vote between a giant douche and a turd sandwich," Stan tells his parents, "I just don't see the point." His parents react with shocked sanctimony: "Stanley," scolds his mother, "do you know how many people died so you could have the right to vote?" Mom just doesn't get it.[15]

Whether the metaphor describes electoral choice as a contest between a pair of rodents or between a feminine hygiene product and a piece of excrement, it's the same old joke. Anti-political humor is everywhere; clean or dirty, hip or square, as told by professionals over the airwaves and amateurs over the cubicle divider. In fact, what I think of as the quintessential anti-political joke is one I heard not from any television show but from my dad— and although this version dates from 1980, all that is necessary to make it work in any other presidential election year is to change the names:

> Q: If Jimmy Carter, Ronald Reagan, and John Anderson [that year's third-party threat] were all in a rowboat in the middle of the ocean, and the boat flipped over, who would be saved?

> A: The United States.

WHAT IS GOVERNMENT FOR? WHAT ARE JOKES FOR?

The implications of the rowboat riddle are fairly grim: no choice would be better than the choices we have, and anyone who would presume to be worthy of the people's vote deserves to drown like a rat. Yet this nihilistic punch line is no more than a crystallization of the message repeated night after night, joke after joke, by Jay, Dave, and Conan. Late-night's anti-political jokes are implicitly anti-democratic. They don't criticize policies for their substance, or leaders for their official actions (as opposed to their personal quirks, which have little to do with politics per se); taken as a whole, they declare the entire system—from voting to legislating to governing—an irredeemable sham.

To understand the appeal of such anti-democratic heresy, it is helpful to start with a couple of fundamental questions. First, what is government for? The answer, according to the framers of the Constitution, is to provide for the common defense, to promote the general welfare, and so on. Or as Abraham Lincoln more succinctly put it, our government is for the people— as well as by and of them. We, the people, choose our government and therefore—indirectly, at least—are the government. The U.S. is "us." Most of us learned this in elementary school.

When we grow up, however, this naïve faith in representative democracy joins Santa Claus and the Easter Bunny on the scrap heap of our childish beliefs. Even if we continue to believe, we tend to be a little bit embarrassed about it. The majority of voters, in most election years, would probably tell anyone who asked that they were holding their noses as they entered the voting booth. We participate in the political process in only the most minimal ways: we ignore local elections, few of us attend caucuses or work as campaign volunteers, and between the first Wednesday of November and the kickoff of the next season of attack ads, we pay little attention to what our representatives do (unless there's a sex scandal, of course). We treat democracy, our civic religion, only about as seriously as what so-called C-and-E Christians (for Christmas and Easter—the only occasions they bother to show up in church) treat theirs. And of course the majority of those eligible to vote don't even bother.

Even lapsed voters may still profess faith in the democratic ideal, but are likely to consider it lost to some more perfect past—before Watergate, Irangate, or Monicagate; before PACs and lobbyists; back in the days when politicians were statesmen, not these clowns you see running for office nowadays. In just a century and a half, this version of the anti-political argument goes, we've gone from Lincoln versus Douglas to a douche versus a turd.

Of course, this is nostalgic nonsense; American leaders have been failing to live up to their predecessors since Adams succeeded Washington. The problem with the democratic ideal—with any ideal—is that reality will always fall short. Our candidates can never measure up to the Founding Fathers' patriarchal nobility, nor can our day-to-day experience of liberty, equality, and justice live up to the ringing words of the Declaration of Independence. Some years ago, Professor Louis Rubin dubbed the gap between the City on a Hill of our star-spangled dreams and the somewhat less utopian actualities of the nation we actually inhabit "the Great American Joke": "On the one hand there are the ideals of freedom, equality, self-government, the conviction that ordinary people can evince the wisdom to vote wisely, and demonstrate the capacity for understanding and cherishing the highest human values through embodying them in their political and social institutions. On the other hand there is the *Congressional Record*."[16] When you live in a country founded upon ideals—rather than the mere commonalities of tradition, language, and culture that formed the basis of older nations—you are doomed to perpetual disappointment.

But before further considering America's strained relation with its founding principles, let us turn to the second question: what are jokes for? This seemingly trivial query has in fact tested the cognitive powers of some pretty heavy-duty thinkers, from Aristotle to Immanuel Kant to Thomas Hobbes. Sigmund Freud provided one of the most useful contributions to this body of inquiry a century ago, in a book entitled *Jokes and Their Relation to the Unconscious*.[17] The purpose of joking, he theorized, is to help individuals cope with societal repression. At the core of all of Freud's work lies the assumption that even the most well adjusted of us are carrying a heavy burden of hostility and sexual aggression. Bottling all that up can make us crazy, but if we allowed ourselves to express these impulses in an open and straightforward way, civilized society would be impossible—day-to-day life would resemble some unholy double feature of *Mad Max* and *Animal House*. So how do we get through the day? Freud identified a number of ways— many of which don't cost a hundred dollars an hour—including telling, and laughing at, jokes. Laughter is a safety valve for our anti-social drives. The rules of polite society (and the need to keep your job) prevent you from acting on your intensely felt desire to punch your boss in the teeth, but you can safely express that hostile impulse by imitating his stupid, jackass laugh for your coworkers during happy hour at the local bar.

Thus, laughter helps the individual cope with society. But might it also help society cope with the individual? According to Freud's contemporary the philosopher Henri Bergson, the principal function of laughter is not so much to keep people sane as to keep them in line. "By laughter," he wrote, "society avenges itself for the liberties taken with it."[18] Whenever we laugh at someone whose comportment or behavior is somehow "wrong"—whether he or she is a nerd, a klutz, a pervert, a ninny, or a fanatic—we reinforce what we consider to be "normal," non-laughable behavior. Laughter enforces conformity; it's the border collie that helps maintain the herd mentality.

How do these turn-of-the-twentieth-century Continental theories apply to contemporary American political comedy? First, and most obvious, laughing at political big shots is satisfying in the same way as laughing at your boss (because you can't punch the president, either). In fact, says Freud, if the target is big and important enough, the joke doesn't even have to be that good, "since we count any rebellion against authority as a merit" (a loophole *Saturday Night Live* has been exploiting for years).[19] Add to this basic truth the fact that America was born in rebellion and celebrates anti-authoritarianism in any form, from the Boston patriots' dumping tea in the harbor to Elvis's hip-swiveling impudence, and it's not hard to see how this point resonates with particular force in our culture.

Bergson's argument about laughter and social conformity speaks to one of the main sources of our democratic skepticism. If we take the idea that "all men are created equal" to be a fundamental American "norm" (and there is no principle we claim to hold dearer), then grasping at political power—seeking, that is, to escape the very equality that allows any one of us to run for office in the first place—is a violation of that norm. A fella (or even a gal) would have to think he's pretty hot stuff to sit in the House or Senate—to say nothing of the White House—and round these parts we don't cotton to folks what's too big for their britches. This is the central paradox of American representative democracy: the egalitarian idea that anyone can grow up to be president is inseparable from the notion that none of us deserves such an honor. This is why potential leaders of the free world go to such absurd lengths to look like someone you'd like to have a beer with: *I guess it's okay he wants to be president, as long as he doesn't think he's any better than us.*

Oddly enough, our devotion to the principles on which our government is founded—liberty (no one can tell me what I can and cannot do) and egalitarianism (none of us is any better than anyone else)—makes it impossible for us to believe in government itself. Government makes all kinds of demands on our liberty—we must pay our taxes, obey the laws, serve on juries, or even, at various points in our history, serve in the military. Moreover, it derives its authority to do all of this based on the unacceptably contradictory principle that our elected representatives, who supposedly serve at our pleasure, are also somehow the boss of us.

We carry this paradox, and the resentment that goes along with it, in the backs of our minds, even as we cast our ballots, salute the flag, or send our children off to war. It is the shadow side of our patriotism; the doubt at the heart of our devotion; our secular, civic version of original sin. It's the small, insistent voice that grumbles, even as we recite the Pledge of Allegiance or sing "The Star-Spangled Banner," *Yeah, right.* It is the voice of anti-political, anti-democratic heresy, echoing down the centuries, and from all across the political spectrum. It is the common complaint of left-wing anarchists like Abbie Hoffman (author of *Revolution for the Hell of It*), right-wing libertarians like anti-tax crusader Grover Norquist, civilly disobedient dropouts like Henry David Thoreau—even anti-state vigilantes like Timothy McVeigh.[20] In their own lighthearted way, late-night comics are torchbearers in this same anti-political parade. Unlike McVeigh, the damage they do is merely insidious, and largely invisible; but unlike Hoffman, Norquist, and Thoreau, they reach tens of millions of Americans each night.

DEFENDING THE FAITH: A PLACE FOR SATIRE?

In spite of its anti-democratic implications, anti-politics (and anti-political humor) is itself a bedrock American tradition: a contrarian habit as old as the republic itself. Atop this foundation of anti-political disdain, we have in recent decades been building a towering Fortress of Irony, reaching, by the turn of the twenty-first century, a point where it seems as if every communication is enclosed in air quotes. In contemporary America, sincerity is suspect, commitment is lame, and believing in stuff is for suckers.

Late-night comics did not invent the air-quote culture, anymore than they invented our anti-political sentiments, but they have played a leading role in proselytizing this cynical message. Election after election, night after night, joke after joke, they have reinforced the notion that political participation is pointless, parties and candidates are interchangeable, and democracy is futile.

This is not to suggest that comedy that takes politics as its subject matter is inherently destructive. Mocking our elected representatives and our institutions is an American birthright, and exercising that right is worthwhile, if only to maintain it. The problem is not the presence, or even the proliferation, of political comedy per se. The problem is that too little of it is actually "political" in any meaningful way. Genuine political satire, like good investigative journalism, can function as democracy's feedback loop. It can illuminate injustices, point out hypocrisy, and tell us when our government is not living up to its ideals, thereby raising the awareness that is the first step toward alleviating any of these problems. Real satire—such as Colbert's excoriation of the press and the president—sounds the alarm: something is wrong, people must be held to account, things must be made right. Anti-political humor—the far more common kind, practiced by Leno, Letterman, and O'Brien, among others—merely says, resignedly, "Eh, what are you gonna do?"

Yet the public, and especially the press, are so blinded by anti-political disdain and unblinking devotion to the equal-opportunity offender idea, that we have difficulty distinguishing genuine satire from the ersatz kind, even when we see it. In a feature on *The Colbert Report* (published several months before the Correspondents Dinner), *Newsweek* stubbornly hangs on to the news media's beloved apolitical paradigm: "[Though his] character is clearly a parody of God-fearing, pro-business, Bush-loving Republicans . . . Colbert guards his personal views closely, and if you watch the show carefully you'll see subtle digs at everyone on the political-media map." With what seems like willful naiveté, the magazine seizes on the host's rote disclaimer that his show is strictly for laughs: "Despite the fact that politics is a primary inspiration and target, Colbert isn't interested in being political."[21]

Whether he's interested or not, though, Colbert's show *is* political, in a way that the more traditional late-night programs—and, even for all their enthusiastic offensiveness, the works of Stone and Parker—are not. *The Colbert Report* is not an equal-opportunity offender. Neither is *The Daily Show*. Nor, for that matter, is Bill Maher, who has definitely met a man (or two) he didn't like. This is not to say that the *Report* is liberal propaganda, nor to deny that Colbert, Stewart, and Maher take satirical shots at "both sides"—though perhaps it is worth considering what would be so terrible about comedy that expresses a consistent point of view. But the important difference between the smallish vanguard of cable comics and the late-night mainstream is not so much a matter of taking political sides as of taking politics seriously. It is the difference between engaging with the subject and merely dismissing it. Satire, at its best, is not just a drive-by dissing but exactly what the *Times* accuses Jon Stewart of presenting: "a sustained argument."[22] Consider the way Colbert deconstructs Bush's fetish for "resolve." Watch how *The Daily Show* analyzes official rhetoric, as when Stewart goes sound bite for sound bite with a videotaped politician, calling attention to every outrage and evasion. Left or right, right or wrong, fair or unfair, this is comedy that engages us in politics, instead of offering us an easy out. It is a form of debate, not just entertainment; and as such, it should be welcomed, not treated as "rude," or inappropriate.

Undoubtedly, many of the guests at the Correspondents Dinner—including the president—would have had a more pleasant evening listening to the inoffensive humor of, say, Jay Leno. There's nothing wrong with innocent laughter, of course. But insofar as our appetite for the dismissive, plague-on-both-their-houses, progress versus Congress, Tweedledum versus Tweedledee, pot-calling-the-kettle-black variety of "political" humor reflects our fundamental doubts about the value of political participation, and the viability of democracy, it is no laughing matter.

CHAPTER 2

"SHOWMEN IS DEVOID
OF POLITICS"

THE ROOTS OF PSEUDO-SATIRE
AND THE RISE OF THE COMEDY-
INDUSTRIAL COMPLEX

What do you think of when you think of Bob Dole? His twenty-seven years in the Senate? His opposition to the family and medical leave bill? His position on affirmative action? (Come on; he was the Republican presidential nominee only a few years ago!) How about "old guy who refers to himself in the third person"? Yeah, I thought so.

Okay, let's see if you can identify the following: a) Liked jelly beans, and began every sentence with "Well . . ."; b) Enjoyed McDonald's french fries, and had an eye for the ladies; c) Could not spell "potato"; d) Screamed like a madman after coming in third in the Iowa caucus.

If you answered a) Ronald Reagan; b) Bill Clinton; c) Dan Quayle; and d) Howard Dean, you are correct—but it's entirely possible you haven't read a newspaper in the last twenty years.

Most Americans don't spend a lot of time informing themselves about politics, but we absorb a great deal from the media, not least from late-night comedy. I recall a conversation with a co-worker back in 1992. A newspaper in the break room featured a headline about the North American Free Trade Agreement, and I took the opportunity to say that I thought it was a bad idea. My co-worker replied by breaking into an impression of Ross Perot (or an approximation of Dana Carvey's impression), the eccentric Texas billionaire who had made opposition to NAFTA a central theme of his third-party presidential bid.[1]

Unless you work at the Brookings Institution, the break room is no place to launch into a learned treatise on international labor and environmental standards, but I was somewhat taken aback by this response. My co-worker, though he was by no means a news junkie, was certainly no dummy, but what he knew about NAFTA was this: Ross Perot was against it. And since Perot was kinda kooky, opposition to NAFTA was kinda kooky, too—and so, therefore, was I.

Years later, a reasonably bright student of mine asserted that Democratic presidential contender John Kerry did not deserve to be taken seriously, because he had "married into ketchup"—a reference to the fact that his wife, Teresa, had inherited a large dollop of the Heinz Ketchup fortune upon the death of her first husband, Senator John Heinz.[2] While there were certainly more substantive reasons one could find to oppose Kerry, his wife's tomato-based millions were a favorite topic of late-night jokes, which was enough to convince this young voter—who was, in fact, a journalism major.

College kids too young to remember any of the details of his administration can approximate Carvey's impression of George H. W. Bush, and some can even do a pretty fair Nixon. Most of us can repeat, verbatim, Bill Clinton's denial of having had sexual relations with "that woman" (a clip David Letterman, among others, liked to run again and again), even if we don't remember which woman he appointed to the Supreme Court. Voters who understand dangerously little about Social Security can laughingly recall Darrell Hammond's Al Gore droning on about a "lockbox"—just don't ask them to explain what he meant.

Maintaining an informed electorate is one of democracy's most daunting challenges. Arguably, topical comedy makes matters worse, if not by misinforming us exactly, then by encouraging us to focus our attention on the wrong things. Basing one's view of NAFTA on Ross Perot's perceived mental health, or picking a president based on the source of his wife's inheritance, or even his tendency to speak in sentence fragments, as the elder President Bush was known to do, wouldn't, as he might put it, be prudent.

Genuine satire can give us information and insight that enhances our ability to fulfill our roles as citizens in a democracy. But the easy, EOO type of topical comedy that dominates late-night's network mainstream fills our heads with trivia and anti-political disdain. Satire nourishes our democracy, while the other stuff—let's call it pseudo-satire, since it bears a superficial resemblance to the real thing—is like fast food: popular, readily available, cheap; tasty in its way, but ultimately unhealthy.

SATURDAY NIGHT AND *TONIGHT*

"Satire," George S. Kaufman once quipped, "is what closes Saturday night."[3] As the co-author of several of the American stage's most successful comedies, Kaufman presumably knew what he was talking about. The folks who buy the tickets just want to laugh, not think.

But if satire closes Saturday night, how do we explain *Saturday Night Live*'s thirty-two-year run? And what about the rest of the week's late-night lineup? Don't Jay, Dave, Conan, Kimmel, and what's-his-face with the Scottish accent joke about current events? Don't they regularly make fun of Republicans, Democrats, Congress, the president? Isn't *that* satire?

Not necessarily. The critical distinction between genuine satire and pseudo-satire has less to do with content than with *in*tent. To put it another way, while the genuine satirist and the pseudo-satirist are both joking, only one of them is kidding. Real satire means it. The problem with this definition is that there is no way to objectively measure sincerity—the Mean-It-o-Meter has yet to be invented. And simply asking is no good: a professional comedian, whether he is a satirist or not, will deny having a "message" as a matter of course—it's part of the code.

Since intent is difficult to verify, let's start with some examples and work backward from there, to see what characteristics tend to separate real satire from the ersatz stuff (table 2.1). Note that these distinctions have nothing necessarily to do with quality: some genuine satire is preachy and dull, and some of the pseudo stuff is gut-bustingly funny.

Determining whether a given piece of comedy falls into column A or column B may be a somewhat subjective process, but it is not arbitrary. To qualify as satirical, a comedian, a sketch, a cartoon, or a movie must have a

TABLE 2.1

GENUINE SATIRE	PSEUDO-SATIRE
The Daily Show with Jon Stewart	The Tonight Show with Jay Leno
Al Franken	Andy Borowitz
Doonesbury	The Capitol Steps
Letterman's "Great Moments in Presidential Speeches"	Pretty much all the other political stuff Letterman does
www.whitehouse.org	www.jibjab.com
Tom Toles, Tony Auth	Most other contemporary editorial cartoonists
Wag the Dog, Bulworth	Legally Blonde II: Red, White & Blonde
SNL's 1988 debate sketch, featuring Dana Carvey as George H. W. Bush, and Jon Lovitz as Michael Dukakis	SNL's 2000 debate sketch, featuring Will Ferrell as George W. "Strategery" Bush, and Darrell Hammond as Al "Lockbox" Gore
Stephen Colbert	Rich Little*

* Little, whose career as an impressionist-comedian peaked during the 1970s, was the White House Correspondents Association's choice to perform at their 2007 dinner.

message (other than the easy, anti-political "all politics is applesauce" kind) and mean it. In a few cases, the presence or absence of intent is obvious: Al Franken is interested primarily in making a point, and only secondarily in entertaining—see especially his latest book, aptly titled *The Truth, with Jokes.* Andy Borowitz, on the other hand, wants only to make you laugh—his book could be called *The Jokes, with More Jokes.*[4]

Equally obvious about their intent are the two Web sites cited. The White-house.org site is a scathing, often obscenely juvenile assault on the Bush administration, its policies, and its personalities. A typical item is titled "President's Ruminations on the Three Year Anniversary of America's Super-Successful Freedomizationizing of Vietraq." Jibjab.com is mildly irreverent but has no axe to grind. Its most popular feature is still the 2004 animated music video featuring Johns Kerry and Edwards, George W. Bush and Dick Cheney, singing and dancing their way through a parody of "This Land Is

Your Land." It's all very good-natured and nonpartisan, and about as sharp as a rubber ball.[5]

The two *Saturday Night Live* examples present a more subtle distinction:[6] Though a couple of the show's writers have been upfront about their politics (including longtime contributors Franken, a liberal, and Jim Downey, a conservative), there is no single "author" to whom we can ascribe intent. Moreover, *SNL* is, generally speaking, a pseudo-satirical, EOO show. But, perhaps because the polls were predicting a lopsided win for Bush Sr. in 1988 (as opposed to the photo finish everyone expected—and got—in 2000), a bit of satire was allowed to sneak through. (What difference could it make?) Though both candidates come in for some ribbing, the defining moment of the earlier sketch arrives when Bush Sr. tries to skate through the debate by reciting his emptiest clichés ("read my lips," "a thousand points of light"), only to be told by the moderator that he still has two minutes to fill—thus setting up Dukakis's devastating punch line, "I can't believe I'm losing to this guy." Carvey's impression is funny (as is Lovitz's super-dull Dukakis), but the sketch is not just a showcase for mimicry; it makes a clear, polemical point: the presumptive president-elect is a man with nothing to say. The 2000 sketch, by contrast, is content to focus on the personal quirks and characteristic phrases and gestures of each man without using them to make any larger point—except to reiterate the anti-political mantra that debates are dumb, elections are pointless, and all candidates are the same. The sketch revolves around nothing more profound than the meeting of two cartoonish, funny characters—it might just as well be a face-off between Emily Litella and Master Thespian.

Though both use impersonation, only the 2000 sketch relies upon mimicry as its main source of humor—and, indeed, its reason for being. One of the telltale characteristics of pseudo-satire is a focus on personalities to the exclusion of policies and issues. Another distinction—subtle but detectable in this pair of sketches—is tone: there is a hint of exasperation in Dukakis's punchline that reflects not just the candidates' but the writers' frustration. Genuine satire expresses this sort of meaningful indignation. Pseudo-satire, by contrast, is simply dismissive. *What a couple of goofballs these guys are! Choosing the leader of the free world is so lame!*

Sometimes the clearest clue to the intent behind a piece of topical comedy is the reaction it provokes. Genuine satire often causes its targets to take umbrage (or to adopt a studied silence, as in the mainstream media's response to *l'affaire Colbert*); but pseudo-satire is often embraced by its supposed victims, who are eager to get credit for their good sportsmanship and to show they are impervious to such "criticism." For instance, what is officially known as the Office of Strategic Initiatives is, thanks to *SNL*'s Bush-Gore debate sketch, referred to around the Bush White House as the "Office of Strategery." *Strategery* is also the title of a book by conservative writer Bill Sammon praising Bush's political acumen. Guess the president and his supporters weren't too threatened by that particular piece of hard-hitting topical humor.[7]

Finally, as Kaufman's remark suggests, real satire is commercially risky, and thus relatively rare. If we were to continue charting *SNL* sketches, late-night shows, editorial cartoonists, and so on, we would soon have a very lopsided table, with column B stretching out for many pages after we had run out of examples of genuine satire. To understand this imbalance—to which late-night TV has contributed significantly—and to further clarify the distinction between genuine satire and pseudo-satire and why it matters, it will be helpful to look briefly at the place of both forms in American comedic history. We'll begin with a pair of examples that date from a time before television or the Internet, before the current crop of comedians and politicians—even Bob Dole—were born.

"I Hev No Politics"

Artemus Ward was the Jay Leno of the Civil War era; Petroleum V. Nasby, its Stephen Colbert. Both were popular comic writers who also performed their works on the lecture circuit—stand-up comics before the term (and the two-drink minimum) had been invented. Both used pseudonyms for their comic works and deliberately wrote in a way that made them seem less literate than they really were. Both were great favorites of Abraham Lincoln. Only one, however, was a genuine satirist.

Like Leno, Ward, whose real name was Charles Farrar Browne, parlayed a workmanlike mastery of joke-craft and a calculated, nonpartisan approach to politics into broad popularity and commercial success. In terms of his comedic persona, however, Browne was less like Leno than like Larry the Cable Guy (real name: Dan Whitney). Following what was already a well-established tradition in American humor, he delivered his comic observations in the guise of a "wise fool." Like Mr. Cable Guy, he affected a folksy pseudonym, a dialect calculated to evoke rustic, rural origins (despite his Ozarks twang, Mr. Cable Guy hails from Omaha), and a lack of book learnin' (Mr. Cable Guy attended a rather prestigious private high school, which, oddly enough, lacked a vocational program for would-be cable technicians).[8]

In fact, Americans' affinity for hick shtick from this sort of character dates back to Revolutionary times. Our earliest comic hero was the Yankee, whose rough edges and homespun sincerity set him (and, by implication, us) apart from those phony, fancy-talkin' Brits. Later, when New England—with its Ivy League schools and its old-money snobbery—started to look a little too much like Old England, plain talkers from farther west rose up to reassert the common wisdom of simple folk. Messrs. Cable Guy and Ward in fact share a lineage not only with other rustic comedians, such as Will Rogers, Minnie Pearl, and the pre-Mayberry Andy Griffith, but with "plain-talking" politicians ranging from Congressman Davy Crockett to President George W. Bush.[9]

Because Artemus Ward reached his largest audience on the printed page, Browne relied on comic misspelling to convey his character's educational status. The logic behind this is somewhat problematic, as E. B. White noted ("Who ever wrote 'uv' for 'of'? Nobody. Anyone who knows how to write at all, knows how to spell a simple word like 'of'"), but the folks seemed to like it.[10] The character debuted in the *Cleveland Plain Dealer*, where, following the lead of his editors, he supported Stephen A. Douglas's Democrats, who were willing to tolerate the expansion of slavery to save the Union. But Ward's popularity soon led Browne to leave both Cleveland and partisan politics behind.[11] In his dispatches to the old *Vanity Fair* (always opening with the salutation, "Dear Mr. Fair"), Ward did his best to claim the apolitical middle ground—a tough trick to pull off when the country was headed into civil war.

Two pieces published on the eve of the conflict give a good indication of Ward's even-handedness. He begins his 1860 "Interview with President Lincoln" by declaring, "I hev no politics. Nary a one." After a few gentle pokes at Old Abe, Ward—who was supposed to be a sort of third-rate Barnum, traveling the country with a collection of "wax figgers" and a menagerie of caged critters—advises the president-elect to fill his cabinet with showmen. "Showmen," he explains, "is devoid of politics"—a motto that, grammar aside, one could easily imagine being recited by contemporary late-night hosts.[12]

Ward followed up with a piece in which he interviewed Jefferson Davis, employing the same kid-glove, good-natured approach in dealing with the Confederate president he had used with Old Abe. Hevin' no politics allowed Browne's character to get along with anybody. If television had been around in the 1860s, Lincoln and Davis might have appeared as guests on *Late Show with Artemus Ward*—though probably not on the same night. (Lincoln's Top Ten list would probably have been pretty funny.) Talk about being an equal opportunity offender—here the country was literally being torn apart by a political argument that had been brewing for four score and seven years, give or take, and Ward dismisses the whole dispute as nothing but a lot of "fussin." His only beef with Davis is that, in firing on Fort Sumter, the South has shown disrespect for "the piece of dry-goods called the Star-Spangled Banner."[13]

Unlike Ward's creator, Charles Farrar Browne, David Ross Locke was not one to dismiss the most important debate of the day in favor of safe, patriotic bromides. His creation, Petroleum V. Nasby, bore a superficial resemblance to Artemus Ward (a stylistic debt Locke acknowledged), but he was not content to play the role of the anti-political observer. Locke was in the fight; so was Nasby, but on the opposite side.[14] As Stephen Colbert would later do, Locke developed an alter ego to give voice to ideas with which he himself disagreed—the better to expose their sinister illogic.

One of the bitterest Nasby pieces appeared soon after Lincoln's assassination—his Swiftian irony is still shocking, 140 years later. "The nashen mourns! The hand uv the vile assassin hez bin raised agin the Goril—the hed uv the nashen," Locke, in character, proclaimed. (Lincoln's enemies commonly referred to him as a "gorilla" or "baboon.") "Hed it happened in 1862, when it wood hev been uv sum use to us, we wood not be so bowed down with woe and anguish. . . . But alas! The tragedy cum at the wrong time!"[15]

Locke was no mere showman—he hed politics. A fervent abolitionist, Locke had helped several slaves escape to freedom in Canada in the years leading up to the war. Unlike Stephen Colbert, however, who—at least before his Correspondents Dinner appearance—apparently had some rather dim conservative fans who didn't understand that he was not one of their own, Locke left little doubt as to where he stood in relation to his alter ego.[16] In his personal appearances, Locke would "open" for himself as Nasby, delivering a comic prelude to a serious and sincere speech in which he would, as himself, disavow the words he had just spoken "in character."[17]

If this seems like unusual behavior for a professional mirth-maker, it is because the mainstream of American political comedy has followed the example of Artemus Ward. It's hard to imagine Petroleum V. Nasby having a television show (well, maybe on HBO). Ward's heirs, on the other hand, have proliferated across the comedic landscape, especially in the last thirty-odd years. While Nasby's satirical path is open only to those who, like Locke himself, are motivated by strong views, Ward showed how one could make a career out of joking about politics without ever taking much of a political stand—even when the pressure to choose up sides is at an absolute maximum. (You may think stem-cell research is a divisive issue, but so far, no army of embryonic-rights secessionists has fired on UCLA Medical School.) Those who follow Locke's example are choosing the path of the iconoclast—with a cult following, at best. Those who take Ward's way can take their place as part of a large, efficient, and profitable industry.

THE COMEDY-INDUSTRIAL COMPLEX

For political humor to reach beyond an elite audience of movers and shakers (such as Mr. Lincoln), and that portion of the citizenry sufficiently literate and politically interested to appreciate something like Petroleum V. Nasby, a mass media would have to be invented. By the last half of the nineteenth century, improvements in printing technology had already allowed political cartoonists to connect with an audience unreachable by purely literary efforts. New York's notorious Boss Tweed was justifiably nervous about Thomas Nast's worth-a-thousand-words caricatures—or, as Tweed described them in three, "them damn pictures!" Tweed professed not to be worried about what the papers wrote about him, since "my constituents can't read."[18] Still, cartoons like Nast's demanded a fair degree of political literacy (and, despite Tweed's exasperated cry, regular literacy—all those labels!).

Even with pictures, the print media required too much from its audience to be a really good platform for pseudo-satire. What spoon-fed cynicism really requires is a passive public, and that's where twentieth-century technology steps in. Movies opened up new possibilities for mass-audience comedy—and most of the time you didn't have to think too much, just watch. But with a few important exceptions, American movies in the studio era steered clear of even anti-political political humor. The Hollywood moguls feared government interference in their business and were acutely sensitive to political pressure. Besides, the journey from script to screen is so long that by the time the satire hit the screen, things in the real world might already have changed substantially.

Radio offered the virtue of timeliness: news could, for the first time, reach the masses instantaneously—even fake news, as Orson Welles's *War of the Worlds* would demonstrate, long before *The Daily Show* came along. It also accustomed the public to the idea of hearing the same performer on a very regular basis. You didn't have to wait for Jack Benny to appear at the local vaudeville house or cinema—he came into your house every week.

Radio's immediacy and its ability to turn regular performers into the audience's intimate friends were well suited to Will Rogers's folksy and (mostly) anti-political style. His Sunday night broadcasts, in addition to his newspaper column, gave him perhaps the largest audience for any political commentator, humorous or serious, up to that time. Another of the medium's notable, if minor, contributions to pseudo-satire was Senator Claghorn, a lovable blowhard of a character, featured on Fred Allen's popular show. Claghorn had no real political identity beyond a rather disturbing devotion to the old Confederacy—he was sort of a cuddly Strom Thurmond. He lives on, stripped of his senatorial rank and turned into a chicken, as the Warner Bros. cartoon character Foghorn Leghorn.[19]

But most of the new mass-comedy—which by the 1930s and '40s had made it possible for millions of people to laugh at the same jokes, characters, and clichés, at roughly the same time—was not satirical, pseudo-satirical, or political in any way (though much of it was very funny). The burgeoning mass media courted consensus and steered clear of controversy. This suited them commercially, and—considering the large role government played in keeping the studios and networks afloat, and facilitating their profitability— it also suited them politically.

The society that emerged after World War II, however, was beset by worries about the conformity of the Organization Man in the Gray Flannel Suit. When dissenters began to speak out in the 1950s, many of them chose humor as their weapon. Mort Sahl was comedy's Jack Kerouac; he reinvented the comedic monologue, turning it from the vaudevillian recitation of jokes into a scat-sung philosophical solo. His impact would be felt not only on the artistic but also on the commercial side of comedy. He recorded the first comedy album and made the comedy club a viable venture.[20] Lenny Bruce, Second City, and *MAD* magazine were among the other voices questioning authority, long before the sixties' long-haired kids made it the new national pastime.

While a more irreverent form of comedy was exploding on the page, stage, and long-playing record, the newest member of the mass media family was treading cautiously. The establishment of television as a feature of everyday American life took place in a fraught climate: the postwar commie-hunt had reached Hollywood, and soon television was purging left-leaning performers and writers from its ranks. At the same time, all the anxiety about conformity-producing mass culture gave critics a platform from which to lash out at "the box." Considering how obnoxious it has since become, it's hard to believe how sensitive television once was to such concerns, with performers politely thanking us for inviting them into our homes.

Much of the new comedy of the fifties was too hot for TV. Though he made a bit of a splash as part of NBC's 1960 coverage of the political conventions, as far as television stardom was concerned, Mort Sahl couldn't get arrested. Lenny Bruce, on the other hand, could do nothing *but* get arrested after a while (racking up several busts for drugs and "obscenity" before he died in 1966), but then he was never suitable for family viewing.

Early television comedy consisted mainly of "vaudeo" shows like Milton Berle's and Sid Caesar's. Later, sitcoms (many of them adapted from already long-running radio shows) took over the schedule. In 1954, though, a new kind of show came along, not quite like anything borrowed from other media. *The Tonight Show* marked the birth, for all intents and purposes, of "infotainment"—though the word had yet to be invented. *The Tonight Show* was in fact conceived of as a companion to *The Today Show,* which looked pretty much the same then as it does now, if you just substitute Matt Lauer for J. Fred Muggs (Lauer's the tall one). Original *Tonight Show* host Steve Allen was more culture vulture than political animal, but Jack Paar introduced an element of topicality, which was carried on by Johnny Carson when he took over in 1962.[21]

The infrastructure was in place for a massive new comedy-industrial complex. An irreverent new attitude was in the air. But it was not yet *on* the air. TV was still a nervous guest in America's living rooms, and political humor was still confined mostly to the margins. What's more, bringing the message to the medium would get harder before it got easier. Mort Sahl's anti-establishment 'tude may have been too hot for the tube, but things were about to get much, much hotter.

FIRST THE RAIN, THEN THE FLOOD

As the cataclysms of the 1960s—the Vietnam War and the anti-war movement, assassinations, race riots, generational conflict, cultural and political upheaval—arose to shatter the postwar consensus, television comedy escaped into fantasyland. While the news showed us flag-draped coffins and burning cities, prime time showed us talking horses and genies. It was the age of Unreality TV.[22]

Still, the decade saw a few attempts to secure a place for satire on the tube. *That Was the Week That Was,* a news parody program (best remembered now for Tom Lehrer's brilliantly funny songs) that predates both *SNL*'s "Weekend Update" and *The Daily Show*, aired fitfully on NBC in 1964 and 1965—though the network nervously preempted the show in the weeks leading up to the '64 election (and sold most of the airtime to the Republican Party).

Four years later, *The Smothers Brothers Comedy Hour* became a cause célèbre when CBS, having finally had enough of the brothers' criticism of the Vietnam War, canceled their still-popular show. Though some of their political daring showed up in the program's sketches (faux presidential candidate Pat Paulsen made the network so nervous, they kept him off the air in the weeks leading up to the election for fear the real candidates would demand equal time), what really got them in trouble was musical guest Pete Seeger's performance of "Waist Deep in the Big Muddy," a not-so-veiled shot at LBJ.

Johnny Carson was by this time already well into his reign as the king of late-night, but his monologue had not yet reached the second-take-on-the-news status for which it would become famous. Though quips about politicians were always part of the mix, Carson was careful to avoid the sixties' stickiest controversies, insofar as that was possible. He had particularly little to say about Vietnam, having learned, perhaps, from the Smothers Brothers' cautionary example.[23]

But the tube was loosening up, in fits and starts. Only a little more than a year after the Smothers Brothers' cancellation, *All in the Family* debuted, and before long a whole new range of subject matter was rendered fit for TV consumption: racism, sexism, and, yes, even the war. What appeared to be "progress" was partly a matter of form: *All in the Family* (and the other "relevant" comedies that followed in its wake) benefited from the open-endedness of the sitcom genre. *All in the Family* found a new way to be topical without *really* being political: Mike (a.k.a. "Meathead") may have spoken for producer Norman Lear, but as several contemporary studies showed, plenty of the show's avid viewers agreed more often with Archie.[24] CBS didn't care about mixed messages, though; the network that had booted the Smothers Brothers had discovered that "relevance," handled cautiously, could be more profitable than escapism.

All in the Family's success was in some part also a matter of timing. The public, it seemed, was finally ready to see reality reflected in their living room screens. Too late to help the Smothers Brothers, but just in time for Norman Lear, the tide of opinion had turned definitively against the war. The storms of domestic unrest were at last subsiding, but they left in their wake a more skeptical, cynical nation.

That cynicism was about to get a big boost. On June 17, 1972, five burglars broke into Democratic Party headquarters in the Watergate complex in Washington, D.C.[25] More than thirty years later, we are still, in many respects, living in Watergate's shadow. But less discussed than its effects on public trust in government, the presidency, and the press is the type of comedy that, like a bumper crop of mushrooms, grew and prospered in that shadow.

Watergate was that rare event in which reality literally outstripped satire. But it was tailor-made for *pseudo*-satire. Compared to Vietnam, it was serious but not tragic. Like Monicagate (one of many subsequent scandals to which it bequeathed its suffix), it featured a cast of wacky characters, led by the estimable Richard M. Nixon. And as with the 2000 Florida recount (hanging chads! Katherine Harris's makeup!), its inherent absurdity (G. Gordon Liddy! duct tape! Sam Ervin's eyebrows!) practically dared you to take it seriously. Most fortuitously, Watergate played to Americans' basest anti-political suspicions, revealing corruption so deep and so fundamental as to transcend partisan argument. Though it began as a Republican scandal, by the time the House committee voted for impeachment, the Nixon administration had no defenders on either side of the aisle, and very few anywhere else.

In a way, Watergate democratized political comedy. It turned satire—or rather, what *looked* like satire—from a dish enjoyed only by the cognoscenti into a buffet open to all; from what closed Saturday night into something as inescapable as elevator music. "Comics across the country are milking Watergate for every plausible or implausible laugh that it is worth," *Time* reported in the summer of 1973. "At least a dozen records and albums featuring Watergate humor have already been released, and countless funnymen have built acts around the scandal." Some of the Watergate-inspired humor was genuinely satirical, but most of it was "pseudo," or simply silly. The Second

City alumni team of Burns and Schreiber released an LP titled *The Watergate Comedy Hour* (satire). Deejay Dickie Goodman released a novelty record titled "Watergrate," in which every reportorial inquiry was answered with a sound bite from a popular song: "Mr. Nixon, what will your position be from now on?" elicited Alice Cooper's "No more Mr. Nice Guy, No more Mr. Clean" (pseudo-satire). Those who called a special phone number could hear Congressman William Hungate (D, MO) singing "Down at the Old Watergate." There were Watergate jigsaw puzzles, pins, monogrammed towels and bumper stickers that asked motorists to HONK IF YOU THINK HE'S GUILTY. The "Dirty Time Company" advertised Spiro Agnew and Richard Nixon watches in the backs of comic books. There was even talk that an ice cream company was considering marketing a new flavor, to be called "impeach-mint."[26]

Johnny Carson, sensing a chance to go farther than he had previously dared, seized the moment and fulfilled his destiny as the pace-setter for the new pseudo-satire juggernaut. "When he began making Watergate jokes," wrote the critic John Leonard, "we knew it was permissible to ridicule the President."[27] Mass-marketed irreverence is such a fixture of our contemporary landscape that it is difficult to believe it was not always so common. But it took a change in public attitudes, the construction of a comedy-media infrastructure, and an event like Watergate to definitively prove that topical comedy could be a big, and—if handled in the proper way—not at all risky business. One could imagine the ghost of Artemus Ward, lounging in his I AM NOT A CROOK T-shirt, digging into a bowl of impeach-mint ice cream, watching Carson's monologue, and chuckling approvingly.

LIVE, FROM NEW YORK, IT'S ARCHETYPAL POLITICIAN NO. 7B,
WITH OPTIONAL CATCHPHRASE

A few months after Richard Nixon flashed his final double-V before being whisked off to exile in San Clemente, a late-night show debuted that would help turn the mass production of pseudo-satire into something as routine and reliably profitable as the manufacture of windshield wipers or plastic trash bags.

It started out on a satirical high note, however. *Saturday Night Live*'s first presidential impression wasn't really an impression, in any typical sense. Chevy Chase portrayed Gerald Ford without special makeup and without making any effort to approximate his voice. To evoke the august presence of the thirty-eighth president, Chase simply acted confused and fell down a lot.

Though somewhat crude and ad hominem, it was devastating. In fact, Chase's non-impersonation of Ford may have done more to shape public perceptions than any of *SNL*'s subsequent political portrayals. What's more, the White House knew it. Ford and his press secretary, Ron Nessen, made a concerted effort to co-opt Chase and the show. Nessen went so far as to surprise a young *SNL* writer named Al Franken by accepting his half-facetious invitation to host the show. But Operation Good Sport backfired when Lorne Michaels and his writers conspired to make the material surrounding the secretary's appearances—which he had foolishly neglected to vet—as dirty as they possibly could. It wasn't exactly the sort of thing that would have made Jonathan Swift or Petroleum V. Nasby proud, but it did prove highly embarrassing to the White House.[28]

In the long run, though, this juvenile response, rather than Chase's brash irreverence, would prove typical of *SNL*'s generally anti-political orientation. Like *South Park*'s, its "edginess" has always had more to do with sex, death, and bodily functions than with politics. Even Doug Hill and Jeff Weingrad, whose worshipful history generally takes *SNL* as the satirical milestone it purports to be (TV critic Steven Stark more accurately called it "television's most self-congratulatory show"), concede that with the exception of Chase, Franken, and a handful of others over the years, "the staff of the show was surprisingly apolitical."[29]

Still, the zeal with which *SNL* attacked Ford stands out as one of the few times the show lived up to its stickin'-it-to-the-man reputation. Previous presidents had been subject to impersonations, ranging from Vaughn Meader's good-natured and pseudo-satirical mimicry of JFK on the *First Family* albums to David Frye's more biting portrayals of LBJ and Nixon; Chase's Ford was a recurring comic character in a much-talked-about weekly television show—a figure of fun who returned again and again to be laughed at, like Gilligan or

Archie Bunker.[30] This represented a new level of irreverence in 1975, but as presidential impressions became a regular feature of *SNL* (who do you suppose will play Barack Obama?), they gradually lost their ability to shock.

Chase's technique—or lack thereof—also lent *SNL*'s depiction of Ford a particularly devastating edge. If imitation is, as the old saw has it, the sincerest form of flattery, there was no sign of flattery in this portrayal. Carvey's Bush, Hammond's Clinton, and even Dan Ackroyd's Nixon, are—because of the care and study that have obviously gone into them—in some measure tributes to their originals. Chase's non-impersonation, on the other hand, suggests that Ford was not worth the trouble. Moreover, freed of the technical demands of portraiture, Chase's performance is directed entirely toward defining its target as an addle-brained klutz, with no residual effect of making him seem endearing. (Isn't it cute how Will Ferrell says "strategery"?)

Chase left in the middle of the second season, and whatever anti-establishment "edge" the show may once have had left a few years later (though, like some past cast members, it has returned for the occasional cameo appearances). But since its debut, *SNL* has never been without a designated presidential impersonator. Some have been quite convincing; a few others have relied upon a lot of help from the makeup department. Occasionally, *SNL*'s political impressions have been put to worthy, satirical purposes. More often—especially in later years, as the show's conventions have continued to ossify—the show's political "characters" are as one-dimensional and "lovable" as any of the other catchphrase-spouting mannequins Lorne Michaels might hope to spin off onto the big screen (Jason Sudeikis as George W. Bush and Darrell Hammond as Dick Cheney in—*Night at the Roxbury II*).

How Do We Do It? Volume, Volume, Volume!

Johnny Carson had late-night, and its characteristic brand of topical humor, pretty much to himself for a while. In fact, when *SNL* debuted, it replaced a "Best of Carson" weekend rerun.[31] Now *Saturday Night* and *Tonight* are only the most venerable of many outlets in a chain of pseudo-satirical superstores that never close.

Needless to say, proliferation and homogenization go hand in hand; more late-night shows means more of the same jokes and premises. *SNL*'s biggest contribution to the growth of the pseudo-satire industry (other than making the jokes a little raunchier) has been the way its characterizations of politicians have cross-pollinated with those of other late-night shows. Chase's emphasis on Ford's supposed clumsiness, for example, influenced the way Johnny Carson joked about the president. Whatever traits or turns of phrase *SNL*'s political mimics have picked up on will likely be exploited by other topical jokesters. Needless to say, it's a two-way street, with the monologists' choices influencing the sketch artists as well.

As late-night has continued to expand, so has the echo chamber: If Dana Carvey portrayed Ross Perot as a paranoid crank, that was the Perot David Letterman joked about. If Leno's Clinton is more Lothario than Bubba, this is likely to influence what *SNL* emphasizes, and so forth. Without a detailed timeline, it's hard to say whether Norm MacDonald's take on Bob Dole influenced Robert Smigel's (on Conan O'Brien's show), or vice versa (though Dan Ackroyd's impression had them both beat).

The consequence of all this cross-pollination—the way premises for mocking a particular politician or policy migrate from show to show—is that the members of the pseudo-satire gang have developed their own version of conventional wisdom. Like the news media, late-night comedians have frequently fallen prey to groupthink.

The ideas that spread like viruses from show to show also spread to us, the viewers. This makes it difficult to trace a premise back to its source, much less hold it up to the light and decide whether it is fair and true. Who first decided that Hillary Clinton was cold, or that Howard Dean was crazy, or that John McCain was a straight talker? Are these characterizations correct, or in any way sufficient? Why do we know so much about ketchup and "strategery," and so little about what's actually going on in Iraq, or why the trade deficit is going up, or why fifty million of us don't have health insurance?[32]

To paraphrase Will Rogers, all we know is what we see on the TV.

CHAPTER 3

FILM AT 11:00, JOKES AT 11:30

TOPICAL COMEDY AND THE NEWS

DATELINE: The United States of America, any presidential election year, 1992–present:

A new survey reveals that "nearly a quarter of Americans between the ages of 18 and 29 get their campaign news from comedy-TV shows." The poll, conducted by the Pew Center for the People and the Press, shows that members of "the under-30 crowd . . . consider *The Daily Show* and *Saturday Night Live* top sources of campaign news." Unlikely as it sounds, these young citizens get "their core campaign coverage from *Saturday Night Live*'s Tina Fey and Jimmy Fallon, Comedy Central's Jon Stewart and other such smirking sources," and see comedians as the "primary vehicle for getting their news." For some, these shows are "the sole source of election news." "To a young generation of Americans, Jon Stewart may as well be Walter Cronkite." In fact, members of this generation "form political opinions after watching Stewart, instead of making decisions from viewing traditional political reporting," raising the frightening prospect that "young people voting under the influence of humour could very well swing the election."[1]

The quoted passages above are all from major North American newspapers and magazines (the last is from the *Montreal Gazette,* which explains the extra *u* in "humour"). What unites these accounts, and others like them, in both print and broadcast media—aside from the subject matter of the Pew surveys—is a common narrative. In a nutshell: TV comedians, with their cheap tomfoolery and silly japes, have captured the attention of an alarming

number of impressionable young voters, usurping the rightful role of qualified journalists and news organizations. Woe unto our democracy!

The first thing to say about what we will call the Usurper Narrative is that
it simply isn't true—or perhaps more generously, it isn't *simply* true. The Pew
survey actually asks respondents "how often, if ever, you LEARN SOME-
THING about the PRESIDENTIAL CAMPAIGN or the CANDIDATES"
from any of a rather lengthy list of media sources.[2] The 2004 survey, for
instance, found that, of all respondents, 9 percent "Regularly" and 19 percent
"Sometimes" learned something from "Late night TV shows such as David
Letterman and Jay Leno." Among 18- to 29-year-olds the numbers were somewhat higher: 13 percent "Regularly" and 31 percent "Sometimes." For "Comedy
shows such as *Saturday Night Live* and *The Daily Show*," the numbers were 8
percent and 18 percent for all viewers, 21 percent and 29 percent for the
younger group. While such results are hardly insignificant, it should be
noted that the terms of the question do not posit an either/or choice between
different sources of information: the same respondent could "Sometimes"
(or even "Regularly") learn from both Jon Stewart and Brian Williams. In
fact, the survey indicated that network newscasts are still No. 1 on the information Hit Parade, with 35 percent of all respondents "Regularly" and 35 percent "Sometimes" learning something from the big three (23 percent and 41
percent for the youngsters). NPR, PBS, and "Your daily newspaper" also
ranked higher than late-night shows as sources for political information.
Twenty-four hour news outlets "such as CNN, MSNBC, and the Fox cable
news channel" scored 38 percent in the "Regularly" column and 37 percent
under "Sometimes" for all viewers, and 37 percent/41 percent with the
youngsters. For that matter, C-SPAN garnered a total of 8 percent regular
and 21 percent sometime viewers—to date, however, no articles expressing
alarm over C-SPAN's undue influence have appeared.

But of course the late-night comedians are the odd men out on the survey's source list. Never mind that the *Washington Times* qualifies as a newspaper, and Geraldo Rivera as a "journalist." Forget the mainstream news
media's many failings—high-profile plagiarism scandals, the heavy hand of
corporate ownership, the coziness of top reporters and government sources

that gave us the phantom Iraqi WMDs—people should not be getting news from *comedians*. As the *American Journalism Review* explains, the late-night hosts are "gatekeepers without gates," who lack the good judgment and credentials to decide what is newsworthy. "Jay Leno and David Letterman can put a story into play long before it has been checked out," *AJR* editorialized—something a trained journalist, like the *New York Times*'s Judith "WMD" Miller, would never do.[3]

The construction of the Usurper Narrative—which, regardless of its shaky foundation, is the labor of many hands—is clearly a defensive project. From within the Fourth Estate's embattled garrison, the growing ranks of late-night comics appear not so much to be gatekeepers as to be gate-crashers. The Pew survey makes the outlines of this supposed conflict explicit by listing comedy and news shows side by side, but the Usurper Narrative was quickly adopted by a press establishment anxious to defend its domain. It was employed, for example, in the coverage of ABC's attempt to lure David Letterman away from CBS to replace *Nightline* in the spring of 2002: "[ABC] news staffers expressed outrage over the network's plan to bump its groundbreaking news show *Nightline* to make room for stupid pet tricks and top-10 lists," sniffed the *Washington Post*. More recently, an East Carolina University study (*East Carolina?*) gained the media spotlight for its claim that exposure to *The Daily Show* seemed to make young viewers "more cynical." Though the evidence for this conclusion was in fact rather weak—and the authors a little loose in their use of the term "cynical"—it was all *Post* columnist Richard Morin needed to accuse Comedy Central's satirical hit of "poisoning democracy," and all MSNBC's *Scarborough Country* needed to ask, "Is Jon Stewart a Threat?"[4]

Journalistic umbrage flows thickly through the quintessential Usurper article, Marshall Sella's "The Stiff Guy vs. the Dumb Guy," which appeared in the *New York Times Magazine* two months before the 2000 presidential election.[5] Sella's story, heralded by a cover photo of Jay Leno mugging with campaign buttons over his eyes and the caption "The Most Trusted Source for Campaign News (Well, Almost)," relies upon the then-latest edition of the Pew poll to invoke the specter of impressionable young citizens corrupted by comedy. "Alexis Boehmler is a junior studying English at Davidson College,"

Sella begins. "At 20, she is bright and well versed, with strong views on the abortion issue and other political matters." But alas, this paragon turns out to be all too typical of a new generation of voters who prefer jokes to journalism: "Her opinions do not betray a hint of apathy or intellectual lethargy, and she has every intention of voting in November," Sella reports. "And her primary news source—often, her only news source—is *The Daily Show with Jon Stewart*, a parody. 'I've always gotten news through watching comedy shows,' Boehmler says. 'The coverage on CNN is something I honestly find boring. . . . With Leno and Stewart, I can get the news in an interesting format.'"

In case readers fail to find Boehmler's youthful insolence sufficiently shocking, Sella calls to the stand one Wolf Blitzer, who testifies that his own daughter ("Cub" Blitzer?) has informed her bewhiskered patriarch that she decided to vote for Al Gore not because of what she has learned by watching CNN's campaign coverage (which was, no doubt, fair, thorough and untainted by humor), but because "he was cool on *The Tonight Show*." Kids!

The comedians, for their part, are quick to refute any notion that what they do constitutes a suitable alternative to the news. Conan O'Brien shrugged off the Pew results by declaring, "Anybody learning anything from my show would disturb me." In fact, he added, if there was any truth to the notion that the public was turning to *Late Night* for information or political insight, "I would worry grievously for America's future."[6]

Of course, he would say that, wouldn't he? The rote denial of any serious intent is a part of the jester's contract with his audience: a comedian must maintain the illusion that he is "only joking," or he might lose his license—so to speak. Yet knee-jerk disavowals like O'Brien's subtly reinforce the assumptions underlying the Usurper Narrative: "news" is inherently important, and comedy is irreducibly trivial; what NBC, CNN, *USA Today,* and the *Wall Street Journal* do is, in every sense of the word, serious, and what comedians do is—well, not. Anything one might learn while laughing can't be worth knowing. (Apparently, Twain, Swift, Cervantes, and other serious-minded humorists were just wasting their time.)

The biggest problem with the Usurper Narrative, though, is not that it understates comedy's rhetorical value or overstates its influence, but that it sets up a false either/or model of communication in which the under-thirty crowd has rejected its elders' sensible reading and viewing habits, shirking its democratic duty to be informed in favor of a hedonistic desire to be entertained. Alexis Boehmler and her cohort are like those 1920s flappers who threw away Granny's corset and bobbed their hair, and Sella and his fellow finger-waggers are the sober Victorian moralists decrying the evils of gin and jazz.

The Usurper Narrative is clearly an oversimplification of the Pew data, and a rehash of an older and even sillier recurring story, "These Kids Today Are Ruining America." Moreover, this alarmist perspective fails to account for the real impact and importance of political comedy. The point in debunking the baseless but persistent Usurper myth is not to deny comedy's role in shaping its viewers' political attitudes, or even influencing their decisions regarding voting (or not voting). Rather, it is to argue that topical comedy's real-world effects must be considered within the larger context of what Americans hear, say, and think about government, elections, and issues—as a part of our political discussion, not a replacement for it.

Secondhand News

Once upon a time, there were only three TV networks, and—for all practical purposes—one late-night comic. Any story makes more sense if you start at the beginning, so let's rewind to that simpler time—say, about 1975—when it was Johnny Carson rather than Jon Stewart who was sometimes compared, albeit with a notable lack of hysteria, to Walter Cronkite. (If Cronkite was "the most trusted man in America," Carson was perhaps the most trusted funnyman.)[7] This will also allow us to put aside, for the moment, the Usurper Narrative's collapsing of the distinctions between news parody shows (like *The Daily Show* and *Colbert*) and "traditional" late-night fare.

Even without taking the "fake news" subgenre into account, we can see some striking similarities between the roles of news anchor and late-night host, or, to put it more archetypically, Walter and Johnny. Both appeared on television every night, Monday through Friday, making them familiar in a way prime-time characters, who only visit our living rooms weekly, could never be. Both Cronkite and Carson were allowed to address the audience directly, giving them a kind of authority vis-à-vis their relationship to the home viewer not extended to J. R. Ewing or the Fonz.[8] And of course, both Walter and Johnny depended upon the events of the day for "material," though they presented it differently. Cronkite left off with "that's the way it is," whereas Carson picked up with "and here's why it's funny."

While the Usurper Narrative suggests that comedy competes with news—as if anchor and host were participants in a footrace—the better metaphor would be a relay. Without the handoff from journalists, topical comedians would be left empty-handed, and with nowhere to go. Without "Film at 11:00," there could be no jokes at 11:30.

The news has its basis in the real world of events; a topical monologue, like Carson's, has its basis in the news. But what is "news," exactly? Like history, it is not simply a record of everything that has happened, presented in exhaustive and unmediated detail. The work of the historian or the journalist is not simply transmitting information but translating it: imposing order on the chaos of events, in a way that makes them understandable and meaningful. Although this can—and does—present a somewhat distorted picture of reality, it is nonetheless an essential service. You may not need a weatherman to know which way the wind blows, but you can't look out your window to see what's going on in Baghdad or Washington, D.C.

Still, news is less a window on the world than a lens: it has a limited field of view; it may make some things seem larger and others smaller than they really are; it may pull some details into focus even as it blurs or distorts others. But given a certain level of competence and the absence of any deliberate desire to mislead—neither of which can be taken for granted, by the way—the news presents a "true," if necessarily incomplete, picture of what is going on.

Comedy gives us its own picture of reality, but it is a view heavily indebted to that provided by the news. Following both Cronkite's *CBS Evening News* and Carson's *Tonight Show* from real-world input to broadcast output makes this clear.

The news biz assembles its picture of the world in three stages: *gathering* facts, *sorting* them to make stories (and sorting those stories to make a newscast), and *evaluating* the material in a manner that explains its significance.[9] In the gathering phase, it would be safe to say that Johnny and company would have been operating at a considerable disadvantage to Walter's crew. Cronkite was the front man for an operation that employed a host of reporters, camera operators, sound-recordists, producers, and editors, stationed all over the world—a vast, fact-gathering army, standing at the ready wherever there was a quote to be gotten or a gale-force wind to lean into.

Carson and his writers had access only to the facts already gathered (and selected) by CBS and the rest of the news media—a wealth of material, to be sure, but all of it obtained secondhand, by perusing newspapers, magazines, and television. This is still basically true for contemporary late-night hosts, though arguably *The Daily Show*'s correspondent field interviews and Leno's Jay-Walking segments constitute a form of "independent reporting." (The latter routine, in which Jay stumps ill-informed pedestrians with the simplest of questions, *does* bear some resemblance to a presidential news conference, but that is largely an accident of recent history.)

The sorting stage encompasses two processes. At the story level, it means deciding which facts must be included, which can be excluded, and the relative emphasis the facts within a story should be given: if the president had dinner with the Chinese premier, is it more important that their table talk broached the subject of tariffs or that they had duck? Once these determinations have been made, there is a second round of sorting, in which the anchor/editor determines which stories should appear in the newscast and which are the most important. Newspapers indicate stories' relative urgency with their physical placement (the "top" story goes on page one, above the fold), headline size, and length. In broadcast news, a story's importance is conveyed by the amount of airtime it's given and its placement relative to the beginning of the newscast—those first few minutes being TV's equivalent of a newspaper's front page.

With no independent ability to gather facts, the comedian is obliged to follow journalism's lead in the first phase of sorting (arranging facts into "stories"), but in deciding which events to "cover" and how prominently they should figure in that night's monologue, Johnny would be less beholden to

Walter's judgment. As editor in chief, Cronkite was largely responsible for the second-phase sorting that turned the work of those various reporters, photographers, and so on into a half-hour nightly newscast. On a given night he might have to decide, for example, whether the latest news from Lebanon (yes, there was trouble in Lebanon even back then) should take precedence over what the Apollo-Soyuz astronauts were up to that day. Such decisions, subjective though they inevitably were, would be based on the principle that the presentation of stories should reflect their relative importance.

Yet on that same hypothetical date Walter was weighing détente in space against violence on earth, Carson might have opted for a different "lead" altogether—say, Liz Taylor's latest divorce (or his own). Unlike the anchor-man, the late-night host is under no ethical obligation to accentuate the consequential and eliminate the trivial. His organizing principle is not "What is most important?" but "What will get the biggest laugh?" Still, if he is going to maintain his relevance as a current-events commentator, the topical comedian can ill afford to ignore major events. Though Carson did, as noted, ignore much of the news about Vietnam, the comedy-industrial watershed of Watergate, the arrival of *SNL,* and television's belated embrace of "relevance" has raised new expectations for topical comedy since then.

Needless to say, the necessity of dealing with "big" stories can put a late-night host in a difficult position at times: it's hard to be funny when tragedy looms or the world seems on the brink of disaster. A *Tonight Show* monologue from the eve of the 1991 Gulf War (prequel to our current quagmire) illustrates how Carson learned to balance the dueling demands to be funny yet relevant. On January 11, 1991, as the clock ticked down to President George H. W. Bush's ultimatum demanding Iraqi troops withdraw from Kuwait, the first joke out of Johnny's mouth was about Doc Severinsen's jacket ("Does Crayola make that color?"). After that ice-breaker, he was free to address a few jokes to the tense situation abroad, but skillfully kept the tone from getting too bleak by weaving these around references to such trivial matters as actress Delta Burke's salary dispute with the producers of the sitcom *Designing Women.*[10] (Carson's skill as "editor" of his monologue is evident when comparing this performance to guest-host Jay Leno's monologues during the same period (January 20–25). During his late-night apprentice-ship, young Jay rigidly followed the journalistic "inverted pyramid" form, starting with the day's "top story"—no matter how grim—and gradually working through to the "Lifestyle Section.")

The topical comedian is utterly dependent on the news establishment's fact-gathering and must also, to a certain extent, take his cues from their sorting decisions. But the third step in the communication process, evalua-tion, is where the divergent goals of anchor and comedian come most tellingly into play. The difference between what Johnny and Walter (or, if you like, Jay and Brian, Jimmy and Charles, Dave and Katie) do at this stage of the game can be summed up in a single word: *judgment.*

Here Come the Judge

One of the great frustrations of watching, reading, or listening to "objective" journalism is the lack of what we might call "closure." It's not just that war, scandal, greed, and deceit are stories that never reach a conclusion, it's that journalists are so often unwilling to *draw* conclusions. Are we winning the war? Were any laws broken? Should we believe Congressman So-and-So's story? What does this have to do with the price of eggs?

Good luck getting any answers from the news. Are we winning the war? "Republicans say yes; Democrats say no. One thing remains certain: the con-troversy will continue." Are health-care costs out of control? "Patient-advocacy groups say yes; insurance industry representatives say no. One thing remains certain. . . ." Is the sky falling? "Chicken Little says yes; Henny Penny could not be reached for comment." You get the idea. In journalistic practice, "objec-tivity" is often an obstacle, rather than a pathway, to truth. If anything, this bal-ancing act has gotten more mindless since Cronkite's day—after all, when his need to tell us "the way it is" outweighed his objective credo, Uncle Walter *did* tell us we were losing in Vietnam. But thanks to increasing corporate control of the media, and ever-more-sophisticated spin techniques on the part of politi-cians, reporters and news organizations have come to think of the "he said/she said" approach as a safe and easy way to achieve the appearance of balance.

"Objective" journalists, you see, are not supposed to pass judgment—even if what "he said" is factually correct and what "she said" is unmitigated spin (or, to use an older and more accurate term, bullshit). Comedians, on the other hand, are under no obligation to shy away from making judgments—in fact, they might as well sport black robes and gavels. Are we winning the war? "The general election's taking place today in Iraq. So I guess that means we're one step closer to being there for another ten years," says Letterman. Is Congressman So-and-So guilty as charged? "Tom DeLay announced he will not run for reelection. However, he will still continue to serve the people of his state by making them license plates," quips Leno.[11]

Fair? Maybe not. Satisfying? Oh, yes. And if you're looking for what "bright and well-versed" viewers like Alexis Boehmler get from comedy that they don't get from the news, there's your answer. (It is also what a less "bright and well-versed" segment of viewers gets—in spades—from such non-objective pundits as Rush Limbaugh and Sean Hannity, but we're getting ahead of ourselves.) Objective journalists are supposed to tell us only the facts (or more often, what some official or spokesman *says* are the facts) without coming to any conclusions of their own. Comedians can throw caution aside and tell us what they think (and what we suspect) it all means: *Screw "he said/she said," here's what I say—are you with me, people?* Journalists report; comedians decide.

Mainstream late-night comics have their own version of "objectivity" (the equal-opportunity offender business), which we've already discussed; but the difference in how comedians and journalists evaluate (or fail to evaluate) information is less a matter of taking sides than one of drawing conclusions. The problem with "objectivity" is that it offers no opportunity for catharsis. Comedy, on the other hand, trades in catharsis. Consider this Jay Leno joke, which aired two weeks after the 2001 World Trade Center attack: "I'm watching our local news, and they said, 'America continues to search for alleged terrorist Osama bin Laden.' Alleged? We already said we want him dead or alive. Do we have to keep saying 'alleged'? Apparently, it's okay if we kill him, [but] God forbid he sues us for libel."[12] Journalists convey allegations. Comedians indict and convict.

This is not to say that journalists merely pass along information without interpreting it. As we have already seen with the construction of the Usurper Narrative out of a few flabby facts and a lot of knee-jerk defensiveness, turning events into "stories" involves a certain amount of evaluative license. The fact that the news media's judgments take shape behind a skein of objective disinterest—as opposed to the verdicts comedians render in "open court" — only adds to their insidious power. Narratives constructed in the press— characterizations and paradigms that coalesce around persons, institutions, and events—exert considerable influence over how the public is likely to think about those same subjects. And given the relay relationship between news and comedy, they also have considerable influence over how comedians are likely to joke about them.

In a very narrow sense, of course, news and comedy *are* in competition with one another—but then, so are *Wheel of Fortune* and *Masterpiece Theater.* Ignoring or downplaying the hand-me-down nature of late-night's relationship to news, as the Usurper Narrative does, reduces a complex communicative web of information, interpretation, emphasis, and reinforcement to a simplistic absurdity. Although topical comedy assuredly affects our political discourse, it is dependent upon not only the resources but also the institutional practices (and prejudices) of the news media, and could no more usurp their functions than a barnacle can steer a ship.

Channeling the Flow

Fast-forward back to the present. Why does the news media seem so much more threatened by the idea of Jon Stewart as a surrogate Walter Cronkite than it ever did by Johnny Carson? Why did the Pew results, the *Nightline* debacle, and the East Carolina University's *Daily Show* study touch such a nerve amongst the thin-skinned ladies and gentlemen of the press?

One reason, surely, is that the media environment has undergone a drastic transformation since the days when Walter and Johnny ruled the earth. We have seen how anti-political humor—already a well-established presence on the American ideascape—found fertile ground to grow in on late-night television in the 1970s. But if Watergate and the debut of *SNL* made televised topical comedy into a cash crop, the coming of cable helped it to spread like kudzu.

By 1989, after twenty-seven years in which he fought off challenges from Merv Griffin, Joey Bishop, and Dick Cavett (among others), Johnny Carson had what looked to be a real ratings challenge in Arsenio Hall, and a pair of dueling heirs apparent in David Letterman and Jay Leno. After Carson retired in 1992, Hall soon faded, but Leno and Letterman split what remained of his 11:30 audience, and the networks' late-night offerings soon expanded to include Conan O'Brien, Craigs Kilborn and Ferguson, Jimmy Kimmel, and, last (and definitely least), Carson Daly. And that was just on the broadcast side; cable offered *The Daily Show,* Bill Maher, Dennis Miller, Chris Rock—all, in varying degrees, more political than Carson, but all undeniably influenced by him. There was even, for a few brilliant seasons, a *Tonight Show* parody, *The Larry Sanders Show,* on HBO.[13]

But if there were more places to see a comic perspective on the world of events, there were also more places to see those events presented and discussed "seriously"—and often very loudly. CNN had introduced twenty-four-hour news programming in 1980 and was joined by MSNBC and Fox in 1996. Whether this improved the quality of television journalism is debatable, but the increase in volume (in both senses of the word) was undeniable.

It's important to bear in mind that while more channels has meant more programming, it has not meant more viewers—adjusting for the overall increase in population, cable proliferation has basically meant more competition for the same number of eyeballs. Network news and comedy shows have both lost viewers to cable. While Walter Cronkite's audience reached twenty million viewers at its peak, CBS's network newscast now draws only about seven million nightly. (The three network newscasts net between twenty and thirty million viewers overall.) Carson's late-night audience reached fifteen million, but Leno leads the current late-night pack with just six million. *The Daily Show* draws a measly 1.6 million, Colbert a little less, and cable news's biggest (shudder) hit, *The O'Reilly Factor,* is seen by an average of two million viewers nightly (and that's not counting the later rebroadcast).[14]

It doesn't seem too far-fetched to suggest that the guardians of the "traditional" media (including newspapers like those quoted at the beginning of the chapter, besieged not only by cable, but by television generally, and now the Internet), were backed into a corner and primed to pounce when the Pew poll suggested they had not only cable but comedy to fear. After all, it's one thing losing audience share to Anderson Cooper—but Jimmy Kimmel? While the Usurper model's suggestion that comedy and news are direct competitors is silly, there is no denying that the exponential increase in the choices available to viewers has made the entire medium more competitive.

More important, though, the proliferation of channels and programs and the dawn of "new media" have altered the structure of the overall communications universe. It's easy enough to visualize a relay between shows like Cronkite's and Carson's, when there was likely to be, on any given weeknight, a fair amount of overlap between their audiences; but how to trace the path of communications now, with so many voices, coming in from so many directions?

Television programs are not so differentiated to begin with, and one of the ways news shows have responded to the competition (such as it is) from entertainment shows is to become more entertaining. Consider the fact that Keith Olbermann has incorporated a fair amount of Letterman-style comedy into MSNBC's *Countdown,* right down to the breaking-glass sound effect. Or the fact that his show and ABC's *This Week* have featured late-night clips on a fairly regular basis.[15]

For that matter, the *New York Times* now devotes a few column inches per week to reprinting late-night jokes.[16] But for television, the blurring of categorical lines is endemic to the medium. TV viewers don't watch sitcoms or dramas or ball games so much as they "watch TV." Fact and fiction, tragedy and farce, program and commercial all blend together into what cultural critic Raymond Williams dubbed "flow." Or as Roderick Hart put it, "A presidential press conference is followed by a tractor pull. A news special on starving Sudanese is interrupted by a Volvo commercial. A comedy channel lampoons the Republican convention, while CBS dutifully covers the real thing. Television's various genres are therefore linked by a Continual *And*."[17]

From this perspective, *everything* that comes out of the box is some permutation of that unholy hybrid, infotainment. No one I know keeps kosher by using one TV for the PBS *NewsHour* and another for *Big Brother*.

Flow is a useful corrective to the Usurper notion that comedy and news represent discrete and mutually exclusive viewing options, but we would be equally mistaken to take this model of indiscriminate viewership too literally. Newspaper readers, after all, are assumed to know when they are reading an op-ed column by David Brooks and when they are reading "Blondie" (for starters, Dagwood has a more nuanced position on Iraq). Is flow such a powerful aspect of the television experience that the same people, when watching TV, can't distinguish between *SNL* and CNN?

Daily Show viewers certainly can. One of the principal shticks of Jon Stewart's fake-news show is its critique of real news. This often entails playing video clips of Fox or CNN—which means, by the way, that even those theoretical viewers who "get their news" from *The Daily Show* also see a lot of real news, if only by default. Moreover, the fact that the audience can easily follow this meta-discourse suggests that the flow idea, like the Usurper Narrative, gives the viewing public too little credit. It also points to the possibility—borne out by yet another survey (which, though less often cited than the Pew Center's, bears the stamp of the equally prestigious Annenberg Public Policy Center) —that *Daily Show* viewers get a more complete picture of current events than those who watch the news without a Jon Stewart chaser.[18]

The communications stream travels neither in discrete channels springing from separate sources nor in an undifferentiated flood of flow. Like a river with many tributaries, switchbacks, eddies, and rocks, its currents are complicated, and the path from an event to how it is perceived is difficult to trace. A bit of flotsam picked up by the *New York Times* might be carried downriver by *Meet the Press*, until it spills over the rapids of *The Tonight Show*, trickles through the airwaves, and seeps into our consciousness—or something like that.

The point is that it is difficult to attribute whatever "SOMETHING" we "LEARN" to any particular media source, or series of sources, or to weigh the relative contributions of news and comedy to the impressions we form of politicians, parties, and issues. One way to approach this question is to start with what makes us laugh and work backwards, to determine what we had to know in order to get the joke.

Knowing and Getting

In no previous era of civilization has an age's defining paradigm more thoroughly surrounded its denizens than in the Information Age. Even our Stone Age ancestors could leave the rocky confines of their caves once in a while, but just try finding a camping spot more than a hundred yards from the nearest cell phone, iPod, or GPS device. In an atmosphere where information is as plentiful as carbon dioxide, the notion that a comedy show or shows could be anyone's "sole source" of news strains credulity. "People are getting their news from the tops of taxi cabs, from sluglines on Yahoo and from accidentally stopping on CNN," says former *Daily Show* executive producer Ben Karlin.[19] Indeed, with so much ambient information flying about, one wonders where Leno manages to find so many ill-informed people for his Jay-Walking bit.

It seems most likely that the Jay-Walkers represent a segment of the populace that probably ignores both news and topical comedy. On the other hand, those who appreciate jokes about current events (and laugh at the ill-informed Jay-Walkers) would, you'd think, have to have some idea of what those events *are*, in order to understand the punch lines. Indeed, this is point the late-night comics and their writers often make. "They kind of have to know what's going on already to get the jokes," argues Stephen Colbert. Jay Leno has said, in a similar vein, that in order for a current-events reference to work, "it's got to be in all the papers."[20]

The comedians insist that the audience needs to know what's in the news in order to get topical jokes, while the Pew survey respondents indicate that they sometimes learn something from late-night shows. Again, it is necessary to distinguish (as the survey itself does, but the stories about it fail to do) between Comedy Central's news parody shows, whose format allows them to include a good deal more "straight" information, and traditional, monologue-and-interview late-night shows. It's easy to see how you can get a certain amount of real news from *The Daily Show*'s fake news—just as you can glean the basic plot of a movie you haven't seen from reading the *MAD* magazine parody version. But what, if anything, can you learn from a simple, old-fashioned joke?

There's an old Steve Martin bit in which he shares with his audience a joke he had supposedly prepared for a plumbers' convention. This "joke" is nothing but a long, rambling non sequitur, laced with made-up plumbers' jargon ("... seven-inch Langley wrench ...") and ending in the nonsensical punch line "I said *socket,* not *sprocket!*" Martin's audience laughs—not at the plumbing joke, but at the *meta*-joke—because they understand, instinctively, the point: the success of any given joke depends upon the audience having the proper foreknowledge.

This is why humor usually translates so poorly from one language, one culture, or one era to another. Remember your ninth-grade English teacher trying to explain why Shakespeare's references to cobblers in the opening lines of *Julius Caesar* were supposed to be funny? ("You, sir, what trade are you?" "Truly, sir, in respect of a fine workman, I am but, as you would say, a cobbler." Get it?) Or consider this Russian joke: A professor is lecturing to an audience of three students. Suddenly, five of them stand up and walk out. The professor thinks to himself: "If another two people come in, then there will be nobody listening."[21]

Apparently, the Russians have a greater fondness for absurdity than we do.

Laughter is a reflexive response—it usually has to happen right away, if it's going to happen at all. If a joke has to be explained after the fact, it might be rendered comprehensible, but it's already too late for it to be funny. (See, one who "cobbles" might be construed to be a shoemaker, or merely a shoddy workman—one who "cobbles" things together. What, ho? Ha? Heh? Never mind.)

This does not mean that we can't "learn something" from a joke, only that *what* we can learn within the context of a joke is limited, since the laughter reflex always arises from triggering some mental association already in place. Consider this example, from a 1996 Conan O'Brien monologue

Bob Dole, believe it or not, took a lap around the Charlotte Motor
Speedway. . . You could tell it was Dole because he had his blinker on
the whole time.[22]

It's unlikely many people outside of Charlotte had heard of Dole's race-
track visit, so *Late Night* viewers might have "learned" of that particular
event from Conan O'Brien. But it is not necessary to have known this tidbit
prior to hearing the joke in order to get it. To appreciate the punch line, however, you would need to already know (or believe) the following:

1. Speedways are similar to highways in that cars are driven on them, but
   dissimilar in that they are used for racing.
2. Old people, stereotypically, often drive down the highway unaware they
   have left a turn signal blinking.
3. Bob Dole is old.

Dole's speedway visit, conveyed within the joke's setup, is new information, but it is *joke-irrelevant*. The basic cultural knowledge of what a speedway is, the stereotype about old people, and the strong identification of Bob
Dole with the characteristic "old" are, by contrast, *joke-relevant*, and knowing or believing them is crucial to triggering the reflex upon which the
punch line depends.

Hey, Readers: Watch Me Pull an Analogy out of My Hat

So, although it is possible to "learn something" in the course of hearing
a joke, the new information cannot be joke-relevant, if the joke is to have
any hope of succeeding. For a topical comedian, a nugget of new information, such as Dole's speedway caper, serves much the same purpose as a
magician's use of banter, or misdirection. A typical magic trick follows these
steps:

1. Introduction of familiar object or objects (a carton of milk and a rolled-
   up newspaper), which sets up certain expectations (the milk will make
   the paper wet).

2. Introduction of irrelevant information, or *misdirection* (In ancient Egypt, the pharaohs bathed in milk, which they believed to have age-defying properties . . .).
3. Surprising *frustration* of original expectation (Hey, the paper's dry! And what happened to the milk?).

O'Brien's Dole joke takes a similar path, but with a crucial difference in step 3:

1. Introduction of familiar subject (Dole), which sets up certain expectations (he's old).
2. Introduction of irrelevant information (he took a lap around Charlotte Speedway).
3. Surprising *fulfillment* of original expectation (isn't it funny how old he is?).

In both cases, the irrelevant information serves to distract us from the simple, direct path between expectation and resolution. It is in the *nature* of that resolution that the telling difference lies—the magician plays with our expectations by frustrating them, the comedian by fulfilling them. In an important sense, then, the "surprise" in a joke is actually an *anti*-surprise.

Still, the tricky part of the trick—like the funny part of a joke—must trade upon expectations the audience already holds. Moreover, although some aspects of audience expectation are conditioned by the trick's setup ("My assistant is getting in the box," "I'm putting your card back in the middle of the deck"), to surprise and delight us, an illusion must deal with more *fundamental* and *automatic* expectations: liquids are wet, living people cannot be painlessly sawed in half, cards and other inanimate objects cannot move of their own accord, and so on—beliefs so deeply held as to operate at the level of uncontemplative reflex.

So too with jokes. While a comedic trope like "Bob Dole = old" does not, perhaps, represent such a universal and fundamental belief as "living people cannot be painlessly sawed in half," the late-night comedy audience accepts it on that same reflex level. If they didn't—if they even had to pause long enough to think, "Oh yeah, I guess he *is* kind of elderly" —O'Brien's joke would make as little impression as *Julius Caesar*'s "cobbler" puns. Where do these beliefs originate, and how do they become so deeply ingrained as to operate at this subconscious, reflex level?

LAUGH-ARENDUM

Bob Dole was seventy-three years old when he ran against the fifty-year-old Bill Clinton in 1996. So the first thing we could say about the audience's belief that *Dole = old* is that it had a firm basis in fact.* The same could be said about some of the other joke-relevant tropes on which late-night shows tend to rely: *Tom DeLay = crooked* (the basis of Leno's license-plate joke) reflects the fact that the former Speaker had been indicted for conspiracy, having already been admonished by the House Ethics Committee on three separate occasions. *Bill Clinton = horndog* is a characterization that rests on a firm foundation of having "caused pain in [his] marriage." *Al Gore = stiff* is based on—well, just *look* at him. Even more subjective propositions, such as *Howard Dean = crazy, Dick Cheney = evil,* or *Hillary Clinton = cold,* must reflect perceptions that are widely held (or at least widely known) before comedians can successfully draw upon them. They are not—cannot be— created at the comedian's whim: if a premise works, it is because at least a sizable portion of the audience believes it.

The evidence supporting this line of reasoning is hard to dismiss: why would an audience laugh at a joke unless its premise struck them as true? If a comedian were to tell a joke based on the notion that, say, George W. Bush is a towering intellect, or Al Gore a seething volcano of passion, he would almost certainly be met with silence and uncomprehending stares.

Thus, every joke a comedian tells amounts to a referendum on its premise. The audience is invited to "vote" with their laughter and applause. A premise that meets with such approval will be used again (and again, and again . . .). Comedy is democratic in this sense, but by the same token it can

---

* Though Dole's age was raised as an "issue" in news coverage, since the outward signs of aging are obvious to any observer, it could be argued that the news media had little role in creating the perception that Dole was old through their fact-gathering and selection process. After all, old is old. Still, who provided those liver-spotted pictures to the public?

be said to reflect a kind of conformist, "mob mentality" (something that concerned Bergson when he wrote about laughter as an agent of social control).[23] Though an individual's "sense of humor" is often said to be a matter
of subjective taste, comedy must seek consensus, if it is to succeed. To the
extent a comedian must be a kind of politician himself, he must be a populist, telling people the jokes they want to hear—particularly if he seeks to
please the kind of mass audience a network host is expected to maintain.

Comedians do not have the power to characterize politicians and events in
any old way they see fit—their judgments must comport with beliefs the audience (or at least a laughing majority) already holds. Where could such beliefs
originate, if not in the news media? The audience has witnessed Clinton's
hair-splitting definition of the word "is." They've read about DeLay's ethical
lapses "in all the papers." They come to late-night ready to draw upon these
preconceived notions, part of their reflex-level foreknowledge.

YODEL-LAY-HEE-HA: LAUGHTER IN THE ECHO CHAMBER

Still, we must not fall into the same trap as the Usurper Narrative's assumption that comedy and news travel in discrete, mutually exclusive channels.
The overlapping chatter of information and entertainment, and the mutually reinforcing nature of joke premises and news narratives make for a tangled web indeed. In this media "echo chamber," characterizations of persons
and events ricochet, mutate, and repeat until they become the things that
everybody "knows" —whether they are true or not.

Take the story of Al Gore, Serial Exaggerator. It started during an interview
with CNN's Wolf Blitzer, in which the then–vice president (and Democratic
presidential nominee) remarked that "during my service in the United States
Congress, I took the initiative in creating the Internet." Though awkwardly
stated, Gore's claim had considerable merit: as a member of the House and
later the Senate, Gore took a leading legislative role in transforming the military's Arpanet computer communications network into the household mar-
vel we now use to send e-mails, order books, and otherwise waste time when
we're supposed to be working. But a Republican Party press release seized

upon the comment to claim—inaccurately, and with malice aforethought—
that Gore had claimed credit for "*inventing* the Internet," the suggestion
being that the vice president was so deluded as to think of himself as some
combination of Thomas Edison, Bill Gates, and Alexander Graham Bell.[24]

Turning Gore's justifiable trumpeting of his legislative achievement into
the caricatured ravings of a mad scientist was unfair, to say the least. It would
be a bit like saying President Dwight Eisenhower deserves no credit for the
Interstate Highway Act because he didn't drive the bulldozer. In any event, by
the time the news media picked it up again, the GOP version of what Gore had
said had not only displaced his *actual* words; this "exaggerated" boast somehow became, by consensus of the chattering class, the key to his character.

It also became key to late-night's characterization of Gore. Gore claiming
credit for "inventing" things provided an irresistibly easy and infinitely adapt-
able basis for jokes, a welcome addition to the well-worn "stiff" premise. Late-
night shows were soon reporting that Gore had claimed to have invented the
cue card, the dog, and the phrase "Don't go there, Girlfriend!"[25] Meanwhile,
the real "inventor"—the anonymous author of the GOP press release—must
have felt a little like the proverbial guy who put the "bop" in the "bop shoo-
wop shoo-wop": "invented the Internet" had become a phrase sensation that
was sweeping the nation, thanks to the combined efforts of journalists (who
should have known better) and comedians (what are you gonna do?).[26]

It is worth noting, however, that late-night—though it undoubtedly did
much to keep the misquote alive, and to reinforce its implications, invented
neither the phrase nor the notion that it "summed up" Gore. Like Howard
Dean's "scream," or George W. Bush's "Yo, Blair!" open-mike incident at the
G-8 Summit, both of which got a lot of subsequent late-night exposure,
it was still the sober and responsible "gatekeepers" of the mainstream
press that first defined these incidents as "stories" and validated their
importance.[27†]

[†] And when Gore reentered the electoral fray by endorsing Howard Dean in 2003, Joe
Klein, Jeff Greenfield, and Tim Russert—the latter in an appearance on *Late Show with
David Letterman*—were among the "responsible journalists" who took the opportunity to
resurrect the phony quote.

The Assault of Laughter?

Mandy Grunwald, a former media adviser to President Clinton, expressed a common opinion when she remarked that what late-night comics say "is likely to stick much more solidly than what is in the political ads or in papers like the *Washington Post*."[28] Sure, the news media has its careless moments, and its reductive narratives, but one joke can do more damage than all the Judith Millers and Bob Novaks in the world, right?

But is comedy really such a powerful form of rhetoric? Mark Twain, in one of his more optimistic moods, proclaimed that "against the assault of laughter, nothing can stand."[29] Freud also believed that humor could be especially persuasive: "Where argument tries to draw the hearer's criticism over on to its side, the joke endeavours to push the criticism out of sight," he wrote. "There is no doubt that the joke has chosen the method which is psychologically the more effective."[30]

As one might expect, the late-night comedians deny that they have any such power to persuade. "You don't change anyone's mind with this stuff," says Jay Leno. "You just reinforce what they already believe." Darrell Vickers, once Carson's head writer, agreed: "I don't think what we do sways public opinion. We reinforce what the public already knows."[31]

In an immediate sense, at least, they are right. As we have seen, jokes don't work unless the audience brings some foreknowledge or prior belief to the table. But beyond this, there is also empirical evidence refuting the notion, shared by Twain, Freud, and Mandy Grunwald, that a funny message is a persuasive one. Communications professor Charles R. Gruner gathered the results of various studies, including several of his own, in his book *Understanding Laughter*. In each case, test subjects were exposed alternatively to humorous or straightforward versions of the same (written or spoken) message. Care was taken to minimize all other variables except for the presence or absence of humor. In the experiments that dealt with overtly "political" material, subjects were surveyed before and after exposure to detect possible changes in relevant issue attitudes.

Though Gruner prefaces his conclusions with the usual cautions about the real-world validity of laboratory results, the bottom line of his research is fairly clear. "Perhaps the one conclusion that can be drawn with the most

certainty," he writes, "is that humor fails to increase persuasiveness of argu-
mentative messages."[32] As for explicitly political messages, Gruner found
that "satire has the effect more of a reinforcing of one's attitudes than a
changing of them." Jay Leno couldn't have put it any better.

What's "New"?

Perhaps the most misleading thing about the Pew survey's attempt to gauge
the relative impact of comedy and various forms of news is embodied in the
phrase "how often . . . do you LEARN SOMETHING." We call it "news," but
"learning" isn't all about taking in new information. The things we *really* learn
tend to be the things that are reinforced, over and over again. The things we
know or believe on that deep reflex level have been drummed into our brains,
like the basic rules of speech or the words to the *Gilligan's Island* theme song.

There are bits of political conventional wisdom that are lodged just as
firmly in American brains: bipartisanship is good, "class war" is bad;
Democrats are the tax-and-spend party, Republicans are the party of fiscal
conservatism. Individual politicians get filed away in the same manner:
everyone "knows" about John Kerry's evasive vagueness and Dole's decrepi-
tude. Many of these nuggets of "knowledge" don't bear close scrutiny, but
because they are repeated so frequently and so mechanically—one might as
well say hypnotically—they rarely receive any.

The jokes told on mainstream late-night shows play a part in perpetuating these beliefs. But their persuasive power lies not in the fact that they are
funny but in the cumulative effect of many jokes reinforcing the same premise. Like the journalistic tropes they echo, comic premises become articles of
faith—become, that is, things that everybody "knows"—at the point they
become inescapable. The danger in "LEARNING SOMETHING" from these
echoes bombarding us has less to do with the fact that some of them are
amusing, or irreverent, than that there are just so many of them, coming
from so many more directions than in the days of Johnny and Walter. In such
a noisy environment, where spin and cynicism and comic hyperbole overlap
each other and blur around the edges, half-truths become truisms, and
untruths—if repeated often enough—become "facts."

CHAPTER 4

THE PERSONAL AND
THE POLITICAL

As illustrated by O'Brien's Dole/speedway joke, the "facts" reinforced by late-night jokes usually pertain to the personalities of the people being mocked. Contemporary practices in both news and politics play into this tendency to focus on politicians' characters—or, more appropriately, on politicians *as* characters.

We are often told, nowadays, that "character counts." This is the mantra of political candidates who would prefer voters to focus on their regular-guy likability, their adorable children, their humble faith, their flannel shirts with the rolled-up sleeves, their authentic regional accents, or the cut of their jib than, you know, their voting record, the soundness of their fiscal and foreign policies, or their plans to give tax cuts to their biggest donors. Somehow, the question of whether a potential president might send your kids to war or burden your grandchildren with crippling deficits is less important than whether you would trust him or her to babysit them. Ask not what the candidates would do to your country; ask, "Which of these guys would I rather have a beer with?"[1]

"Character" is at the center of contemporary political journalism, as well. Watching Chris Matthews drool over President George W. Bush's "sunny nobility" (in Matthews's world, Bush's handling of the Dubai controversy made him look like "a wise man . . . and a man of restraint, almost Atticus Finch"), or the *New York Times* obsess over the Clintons' marriage (according to the Paper of Record, the revelation that "since the start of 2005, the Clintons have been together about fourteen days a month on average" was worthy of page-one coverage), one might think that the presidency was a merit badge for good citizenship, rather than a difficult job that carries awesome responsibilities.[2] But that's all right; as the feminists used to say, "the personal is political." (Of course, they meant that such matters as reproductive rights and spousal battery ought to be addressed as issues, rather than mere "social problems," but oh well.)

It's not difficult to imagine why journalism has moved in this direction. In terms of its infotainment potential, the problem with news, in its traditional sense, is that it's simply one damn thing after another. Lacking the coherent and consistently paced (if drawn-out) continuity of a soap opera, the real world of events offers disappointingly few compelling reasons for viewers to "tune in tomorrow" Will the latest scandal result in resignations or impeachments? Will the political tide suddenly turn? Will there be peace in the Middle East? Don't hold your breath.

The solution, especially for the cable news channels, which need to keep viewers glued to their sets 24/7, is to do whatever they can to turn raw reality into a serial. One way to do this is to highlight the elements of drama—suspense, conflict, sex, and violence—wherever they occur, which is why real-life mysteries featuring kidnapped babies and missing brides are so relentlessly covered. Another way is to treat newsmakers not as the subjects of newscasts but as the news's cast. By featuring John McCain as the Maverick, Al Gore as the Robot, Rudy Giuliani as the Serial Groom, and Hillary Clinton as the Ice Queen, journalists (especially TV journalists) have a way to hook viewers used to cop dramas and soaps.

And so instead of analysis of policies and positions, we get Maureen Dowd's armchair psychoanalysis; FOX News's "body language" expert Tonya Reiman finding significance in Senator Hillary Clinton's "little-girl posture" and Senator Barack Obama's downcast eyes during the State of the Union address; story after story about haircuts and "earth tones"; and Elisabeth Bumiller's "White House Letter" about President Bush's feather pillow (actual New York Times headline: "Running on a Campaign Trail Paved in Comfy Feathers").[3] Because the personal is political, and character counts.

The increasing focus on personal style over political substance has hardly been a healthy trend for political campaigning or journalism. But it has been a positive boon to late-night comedians: for however the boundaries of the political have shifted over the past few years, the comic is, and always has been, personal.

WHAT A BUNCH OF CHARACTERS

The personal approach not only provides continuity (something late-night also lacks in comparison to other TV genres), it also allows pundits and comics to talk endlessly about politics without being political—without, that is, the risk of boring the audience with wonky discussions of policy or, worse, appearing to take sides.

The difference between *Hardball* and *The Tonight Show,* then, is little more than the difference between a serial and a sitcom. On Chris Matthews's show, Howard Dean, Rudy Giuliani, and Hillary Clinton are equated with Fox Mulder, J. R. Ewing, and *Dynasty's* Alexis Carrington-Colby; on Jay Leno's, they are more like *Seinfeld's* George, Kramer, and Elaine.

This "character-centered" approach informs not only the way in which politics is discussed but also what is discussed. Take John Kerry's "botched joke"—thirty-nine words from one of dozens of stump speeches on behalf of Democratic congressional candidates the party's 2004 standard-bearer delivered during the 2006 midterm campaign: "You know, education—if you make the most of it—you study hard, you do your homework and you make an effort to be smart, you can do well. If you don't, you get stuck in Iraq."[4]

The written text of Kerry's remarks clearly showed that he intended to say, "Do you know where you end up if you don't study, if you aren't smart, if you're intellectually lazy? You end up getting *us* stuck in a war in Iraq. *Just ask President Bush*" (emphasis added).[5] It was, in other words, a swipe at the president's intelligence, not that of the American troops. Anyone aware of the president's reputation and Senator Kerry's service in Vietnam would have had a hard time misconstruing his words—without doing so deliberately. Of course, plenty of Republicans, including the president, were more than willing to do just that, insisting, with a great display of indignation, that Kerry apologize for "insulting" America's fighting men and women. Perhaps that is to be expected in an era of cutthroat politics; what is harder to understand is why, the following evening, all three network newscasts led off with Kerry's "botched joke." (CBS and NBC led with it two nights running.) Never mind that on the same day (Halloween, appropriately enough), U.S. commanders in Iraq had capitulated to Prime Minister Nouri al-Maliki's demands that they abandon the search for a missing American soldier—in violation of time-honored military tradition. Never mind the suspicions that Maliki was responding in turn to the demands of U.S. arch-foe Moqtada al-Sadr. War, life, and death can wait: John Kerry screwed up a joke. The print media performed no better: the *Los Angeles Times* ran Kerry's "joke" on page one, relegating the abandoned soldier to page ten.[6]

Some liberals and Democrats complained that this was evidence of the networks' conservative bias. But several Republicans, including conservative fire-breathers Tom DeLay and Dick Armey, spoke in Kerry's defense.[7] A more likely explanation of the media's overreaction is that Kerry's fumble fit nicely into his pre-established "character." This media version of Kerry, in turn, was derived from a number of strands, as inscrutably tangled as the Christmas lights in the back of the closet: the '04 "Swift Boat" attacks on Kerry's patriotism; the senator's highly visible leadership of Vietnam Veterans Against the War—which, though it had happened some four decades earlier, still inspired a good deal of resentment; a reputation for inelegant speaking constructed from reporters' and commentators' reviews of his rhetorical style, late-night jokes, and Kerry's own, real-time contributions. In short, the story was a story not because it actually revealed anything about Kerry but because it seemed to confirm what the media already "knew" about him. When it comes to news priorities, "character counts"—more than life and death, apparently.

As usual, late-night followed the "news judgment" of the journalistic mainstream in highlighting this specious "story":

> John Kerry has apologized for saying those who do not study hard and
>   do their homework will get stuck in Iraq. Now, those that do not
>   campaign well and are boring, will end up stuck in the Senate. (Leno)

How about this John Kerry controversy? So he's out there in California,
tells some kind of joke and it backfires. He's saying he botched the
joke. . . . This guy can lose elections he's not even in. (Letterman)
Senator John Kerry is in trouble for making a joke about soldiers being
uneducated. As a result, Kerry promised to stop making jokes and
stick to boring people. (O'Brien)[8]

The Daily Show, showing its typical insight into the ways of the news
media, did manage to point out the disproportionate attention paid to
Kerry's comments. Stewart began with a straightforward account of the
withdrawal of U.S. troops from Sadr City, but was interrupted by the "breaking news" of Kerry's botched joke. Showing clearer insight into the story's
political ramifications than most leading news organizations, Stewart sum-
marized: "After an election season in which the GOP has been beaten up by,
let's say, reality, the party has rediscovered a winning issue: the has-been's
faux pas." Still, in a prime example of having your cake and eating it, too, *The
Daily Show* managed to get in a few jokes that reinforced the *Kerry = dull
and obtuse* characterization, including a sampling from his (fictional) CD
The Botched Comedy Stylings of John Kerry: "Under certain conditions, you
might be a redneck. Unfortunately, I can't think of any at the moment."[9]

But it is the mainstream, network shows that rely on "character" jokes for
the bulk of their material. ("We rarely do ad hominem attacks," Jon Stewart
told *Rolling Stone*—though "Cheney, I guess we do a little bit," and "[colum-
nist Robert] Novak is a douche bag.")[10] For Leno, Letterman, and O'Brien,
members of Congress and the administration comprise a stock company of
buffoons: the D.C. Players. There's Pretty-Boy John Edwards, and Party-
Hearty Kennedy, and of course Dim-Bulb Bush and Mean Old Man Cheney.
It's as colorful an assortment of eccentrics as the cast of the old *Andy Griffith
Show*, except that we only hear of their exploits, instead of seeing for ourselves (and I won't tell you which one's Goober).

The beauty of "character" is that, within the flux of current events, it is a
reliable constant. By returning to the same set of laughable traits, night after
night and joke after joke, late-night comics ensure that the least-informed

viewers will still get the punch lines: *Here comes a joke about Bill Clinton—I don't know what he did today, but I bet it's got something to do with sex!*

> Former President Bill Clinton is telling people that his gut is saying that America is ready for a woman president. And I would say to President Clinton, that's not your gut talking. (Letterman)[11]

Like O'Brien's Dole/speedway joke, this approach doesn't ignore the day's headlines as much as it makes them irrelevant. The timeliness of a particular night's monologue is offset by the timelessness of "character":

> The Senate has voted to approve the building of a seven-hundred-mile fence along the two-thousand-mile border of Mexico. This is what happens when you let President Bush do the math. (Leno)
>
> Happy Birthday to Senator John Kerry. Sixty-three years old today. They threw a surprise party for him. Well, they think he was a surprised. With his personality, it's hard to tell. In fact, instead of blowing out the candles, he just talked to them until all the life just flickered out of them. (Leno)
>
> This year the White House Christmas decorations include a ten-foot-tall nutcracker. Experts say this is the biggest nutcracker at the White House since Hillary Clinton. (O'Brien)[12]

In his book *Story*, screenwriting guru Robert McKee distinguishes between "characters" and real live people by noting that the former are far more consistent in their attitudes and behavior. "[Characters] are designed to be clear and knowable," he writes, "whereas our fellow humans are difficult to understand. . . . I know Rick Blaine in *Casablanca* better than I know myself. Rick is always Rick. I'm a bit iffy."[13] What's true for a character in one movie must be even more so for those that appear in weekly series—or nightly jokes.

WILE E. COYOTE VERSUS HAMLET

Before they had rap lyrics and computer games to fret about, parents groups were given to crusading against violence in animated cartoons. The efforts of these earnest busybodies did little to curb juvenile delinquency, but they did manage to ruin Saturday morning TV.

Henri Bergson, however, would have understood something that the Concerned Mothers of America did not: laughing at Wile E. Coyote falling off a cliff does not make you a sadist. Wile E. Coyote, as even the dimmest child understands, is not *real*—not just because he's made of ink and paint rather than flesh and bone, nor even because he's a six-foot-tall coyote who walks upright and apparently has an inexhaustible line of credit with the Acme Corporation. Wile E. is not real because he is a comic character—like Falstaff, Tartuffe, Laurel, Hardy, Archie Bunker, Charlie Brown, Homer Simpson, and Urkel.

It's not that these characters aren't all brilliant and lovable creations (well, maybe not Urkel), but compared to living, breathing human beings, they are merely two-dimensional—and not only the cartoon ones. They are "human" only in the universal, generic sense, not in any particular, individualized sense. We can "relate" to them, and see in them certain aspects of ourselves and other people we know, but we've never known as thorough a loser as Charlie Brown, or as clueless a bigot as Archie Bunker, or anybody as blissfully dumb as Laurel or Homer.

If characters like *Casablanca*'s Rick Blaine are simpler than real people, comic characters are simpler still. They exhibit a narrow, often obsessive view of the world (wouldn't some other prey be easier to capture, and just as tasty, as the Road Runner?) and behave in predictable ways (doesn't Charlie Brown know by now that Lucy will never let him kick that football?). Comic characters are as reliably consistent as McDonald's hamburgers. What's more, they are "types," rather than utterly unique individuals: the Jolly Libertine (Falstaff) the Guileless Fool (Laurel), the Blustery Egotist (Hardy), the Bigot (Archie), the Loser (Charlie), the Jolly Oaf (Homer), the Nerd (Urkel). This is why, as Bergson explains, we can laugh at such characters without being cruel. Even as we empathize with Wile E.'s frustration, the sight of him having an anvil dropped on his head takes a universal experience to an extreme that anyone with the most basic understanding of gravity or pain recognizes as unreal.[14]

By contrast, characters in drama or tragedy—like real people—are one-offs: three-dimensional, complicated, relatively unpredictable. "Nothing could be more unique than the character of Hamlet," Bergson observes.[15] He earns our sympathy because we believe in him, as an individual. We grow attached to Hamlet, and gasp rather than laugh at his death, because we have come to know him, over the course of a very long play. It takes time to understand Hamlet (Is he mad? Righteous? Does he suffer from an Oedipus Complex?), or Rick Blaine (Is he a romantic? A cynic? Will he get on the plane?), because—although they are "characters,"—they are nonetheless *individuals*, rather than mere "types." Homer Simpson, we recognize right away.

This distinction is apparent, Bergson insists, even in the manner in which tragic and comic characters are referenced: "We say 'a Tartuffe,' but we should never say 'a Phedre' or 'a Polyeucte' "—or, to translate the point from nineteenth-century France to twenty-first-century America, we might say someone was "a Dilbert" (or even "a Bozo"), but not "a Citizen Kane."[16] Indeed, postmodern comedy has taken the notion of generic character types to new heights of self-awareness, with *The Simpsons'* "Comic-Book Guy," not to mention "the Church Lady," and "Opera Man" from *SNL*.

Bergson was not the first to note the generic nature of comic characters. The sixteenth-century commedia dell' arte featured stock characters, each of whom was defined by a mere handful of consistent traits: Pantalone, no matter who played him, was a dirty old man; El Capitan was a reliable braggart; Harlequin a buffoon; and so on.[17] Shakespeare's contemporary Ben Jonson devised his "comedies of humours" based on the old idea that there are four basic personalities, determined by the dominance of one of four "humours": phlegm, yellow bile, blood, and black bile.[18] Though biological science has advanced since then, comedy is much the same. *Seinfeld's* Elaine, Jerry, and George are, respectively, choleric (energetic and temperamental), sanguine (confident), and melancholy. (Kramer's a little too demonstrative to be "phlegmatic" in the classic "unemotional" sense, but he is laid-back, which is in the ballpark.)

Bergson's contribution to the observation that comedic characters tend to types arises from his vantage point at the dawn of the twentieth century. Not only are comic characters something less than fully human, but in their moments of comic *extremis*—when walking off the edge of a cliff, say—they behave like machines, or mere objects.[19] They are carried along by a kind of momentum. They run on autopilot, doing the same silly things over and over. Ralph Kramden's schemes didn't pan out any better than Wile E.'s, but they both kept trying. Emily Littella always heard things just a little bit wrong ("What's all this fuss about presidential erections?") and always ended up apologizing ("Never mind"). Moe, Larry, and Curly are like an assembly line dedicated to the production of mayhem. The predictability of comic characters is often the source of that "anti-surprise" at the end of a comedian's "trick."

It's a simple matter to apply such reductive characterizations to politicians—to turn them into consistent, laugh-producing machines. Malapropisms spring forth from George W. Bush's mouth as regularly a cuckoo springs from his clock. Bill Clinton can go from zero to horny in 4.5 seconds. The late-night version of a politician is only as lifelike as a talking doll: pull the string, and you will hear any of five phrases from each of them.

Yet the targets of late-night jokes—George W. Bush, Hillary Clinton, Dick Cheney, Al Gore—are not pure comic creations, but simplified portraits of real individuals. And though the caricatures used to joke about them do exhibit the narrow predictability of types, Bob Dole is not just "*a* Bob Dole," George W. Bush is not "dumb" in precisely the same way as Dan Quayle, and Democratic party-boys Bill Clinton and Ted Kennedy are not quite inter-changeable. Politicians have always maintained a dual existence as public and private persons; in the age of late-night TV, they also exist as both real people and as cartoon characters as predictable and resilient as old Wile E.

Thus the conundrum of ad hominem political jokes: though the personal is made political, comedy's version of the personal refers not to the actual person but to a mere caricature—which is why even the most mean-spirited such jokes can be plausibly dismissed by both the teller and the target as "nothing personal." Indeed, a politician who has been depicted as a dope, a sneak, or a senile crank might sit down to chat amiably with the very comedians who have made it their business to portray him in this two-dimensional manner; he will probably join in mocking that character himself, acknowledging, in a backhanded way, that it isn't really him.

But, of course, it *is* him (or her), as far as the public is concerned. "Most comedy is based on reducing somebody to one or two basic characteristics and ignoring the rest," *Letterman* writer Gerard Mulligan has observed.[20] Political "character" is constructed on the same simplistic terms. We seem to want our leaders and candidates to be as consistent and predictable as the two-dimensional cartoons late-night gives us—though we might prefer them to be more like Superman than like Opera Man.

If we've pegged McCain as a "straight-talking maverick," we want him to be that, and only that, forever. Once we have convicted Dan Quayle of criminal cluelessness, there is no hope of parole. This is unrealistic, but not unreasonable: since electoral choices so closely resemble consumer choices, it stands to reason that we would like to know what we're buying. While we can appreciate Hamlet as a character, nobody wants to vote for him (so indecisive!).

Our demand for superhuman consistency in our politicians dovetails nicely with the demands of comedy for inhuman, mechanical predictability. Thus, late-night's political targets are cartoons, simply drawn, with a few consistent, endlessly repeatable traits: Hillary Clinton = cold and calculated; Bob Dole = geezer who refers to himself in the third person; John Kerry = windy flip-flopper; and so on. As Mulligan puts it, "We're not trying to catch complexities."[21] Indeed, in constructing a political image, whether it is for electoral purposes or comedic ones, complexities must be stripped away.

IMITATION IS THE SINCEREST FORM OF FLATTENING

There's a great old Bob and Ray routine about impressionist Arch Rolandson (Bob), whose specialty is U.S. presidents of the nineteenth century. The gag is that Rolandson's Polk turns out to be indistinguishable from his Van Buren—and that both are indistinguishable from his regular voice.[22]

The fact that his guest is a fraud only gradually becomes apparent to the interviewer—a nice illustration of how even an inaccurate representation can shape the public perceptions of an individual. Friends of Gertrude Stein were said to have complained that she did not look like the portrait Picasso painted of her. Picasso dismissively replied that it did not make any difference, because in time, "she will."[23] He was right, of course; the famous portrait is how we remember the author, in spite of the existence of photos and other depictions—though Stein may have less to complain about than Shakespeare and Columbus, whose well-known "likenesses" were almost certainly painted by people who had never set eyes on them and may, in fact, have been intended to portray other people altogether. (For that matter, photographic evidence suggests that Picasso's version of Stein was not *that* far off—she's lucky he didn't put both her eyes on the same side of her nose.)

The existence of photography, sound recording, and television limits the license of those constructing portraits of contemporary politicians. But the caricatures employed by late-night comics are nonetheless stylized, exaggerated portraits. What's more, the liberties a comic Picasso might take in constructing these depictions become self-perpetuating and self-reinforcing when the images start passing, as they now invariably do, from performer to performer and show to show. The caricature takes on a life of its own—thus the phenomenon of people too young to remember the presidency of George H. W. Bush still recognizing Dana Carvey's impression of him. A whole generation to whom Manuel Noriega and "voodoo economics" mean nothing still recognize "nah gunna do it" and "wouldn't be prudent." Gertrude Stein would sympathize.

An inevitable note of tribute can be detected in even the meanest impression—at the very least, the fact that *SNL* has assigned someone to imitate you is a sign that you have arrived. Carvey's portrayal of a vapid Bush may have seemed like a devastating critique when it was first performed, but with only the slightest shift in perspective, it could be seen as an affectionate tribute. After his 1992 loss to Bill Clinton, the senior Bush, showing that he was a good sport (a trait that does *not* seem to run in the family) invited Carvey to perform his routine for the staff at the White House Christmas party.[24] One might credit Bush with pulling off the kind of co-optation Gerald Ford hoped to achieve with Chevy Chase—albeit belatedly. But because Carvey's impression, unlike Chase's, attempted to capture its model's actual vocal inflections and physical mannerisms—because, in other words, it was more flattering to begin with—co-optation was a relatively easy matter.

Be that as it may, the intended function of a comic impression, as with a comic caricature, is not flattery but *flattening*. By reducing a living, three-dimensional person to a collection of infinitely repeatable phrases and gestures, the comedian turns his target into what Bergson would have called "something mechanical encrusted upon the living"—a man-machine who repeats these words and motions with clockwork predictability.[25]

Aside from *SNL,* where the reliance on political impressions has kept Darrell Hammond in the regular cast for a dozen years, mimicry has played a relatively minor part in late-night shows. Carson did a passable impression of Reagan, though it was heavily indebted to Rich Little's version. Leno occasionally "interviews" political impressionists in character. Jon Stewart does an admittedly minimalist Bush, consisting of little more than hunched shoulders and "heh-hehs." And of course *Late Night with Conan O'Brien* provides a forum for Robert Smigel and the other "Clutch Cargo" players, whose spirited impressions put comic brio above accuracy.*

Comic impressions are just performative versions of the kinds of caricature late-night monologists rely upon. But they may provide a clearer illustration of the reductiveness and distortion that go into such depictions. Whenever real people are "flattened" into comic characters, some aspects of the real subject are smoothed over or left out. But often something is added as well. The impressionist Will Jordan, whose principal claim to fame in his 1960s heyday was an impression of television host Ed Sullivan, has pointed out that his celebrated portrayal actually bore very little resemblance to the original. "It wasn't anything like the real Sullivan," Jordan told Gerald Nachman. "He never said 'really big,' he never said 'shew,' he never cracked his knuckles, he never rolled his eyes up, he never did spins. . . . I did not exaggerate Ed Sullivan's mannerisms. He didn't have any. I *invented* them."[26]

Yet the humorous appeal of Jordan's "Ed Sullivan" character was such that it—rather than Sullivan himself—became the basis of other comedians'

---

* On *Clutch Cargo,* a cheaply produced syndicated cartoon series first aired in 1959, the characters' mouth movements were provided by the superimposed lips of the voice actors. *Late Night* uses a similar technique with photos of political figures and other celebrities.

impressions. "Jackie Mason," Jordan says, with a bitterness that has long out-lived Sullivan himself, "exaggerates the mannerisms that I made up."[27] Indeed, the Sullivan that lives on in popular memory bears a closer resemblance to Jordan's much-copied "big shew" version than to the original—even if it came by way of Jackie Mason, John Byner, or any of the other bazillion comics who "did" the stone-faced emcee. As with Picasso's Gertrude Stein, or Carvey's George H. W. Bush, Sullivan came to look like his portrait.

The same photocopy-of-a-photocopy process can be seen in late-night's semi-plagiaristic construction of political caricatures: if Letterman's Con-doleezza Rice is a technocratic neuter, Leno's and O'Brien's versions will likely follow suit. The proliferation of the comedy-industrial complex has exaggerated the already reductive process of turning a real person into a comic character. The danger is that *this* form of imitation may also, as in the case of Jordan's fanciful Sullivanisms—or Gore's "invention" of the Internet—reinforce a portrait of the original that is not only incomplete but misleading.

I Know a Shortcut

One would think that, with the all the exposure politicians get via twenty-four-hour news and C-SPAN, whatever liberties comedians take in depicting them ought to be readily apparent. But this is not always the case. If you compare Carvey's George H. W. Bush—entertaining as it was—with video of the genuine article, the level of abstraction in the portrait makes Picasso's Stein look like a Polaroid. How does an impressionist, or a comedian, get away with such distortions?

Well, as Picasso also liked to say, "Art is not truth. Art is a lie that makes us realize truth."[28] On some deeper-than-literal plane, comedy's distortions *are* "true": the late-night version of John Kerry, like that portrait of Stein, looks more like Kerry than Kerry himself. As noted in chapter three, audiences generally won't laugh at a characterization that contradicts their own per-ceptions. Exaggeration is allowed, but only in the right directions.

And as for simplification—the notion, for instance, that not only is Bush Sr. a wimpy guy who speaks in sentence fragments, but that's pretty much *all* he is—this is a function not just of how comedy works but also of how our minds work. Some social psychologists maintain that our brains are rather lazy, and that we therefore like to keep our perceptions on the simple side. A more charitable view holds that they are merely busy: what with everybody having three phone numbers and Junior's soccer practice and dental appointments and a million other things to keep track of, we can only devote so much brain space to current events and such. Whatever the reason, we tend to be *cognitive misers,* who dole out our mental energy sparingly.[29] If there's a shortcut to perceiving a person, or sorting out an issue, we are usually happy to take it.

This is why we have *Headline News* and *USA Today,* of course. But it's also one of the reasons we like jokes, political or otherwise. Freud initially thought that one of the pleasures of a joke was that, because it is a story that takes a sudden detour, it represents an unexpected savings in cognitive energy—"Oh, is that *it?* I was prepared to follow a whole narrative about that priest and rabbi—ah. . . ." Freud later abandoned this balance-book model of the mind, but he was right that we get a charge out of complexities being rendered suddenly simple, which is more or less comedy's principal MO.[30]

This is not to suggest that our minds operate in an entirely different way when enjoying comedy than when watching *Meet the Press.* The temptation to be a cognitive miser is present whether our brains are in recreation or work mode. We make snap judgments, leap to conclusions, and overgeneralize as a matter of course—some of us more than others, perhaps, though when it comes to lazy thinking, none of us is wholly innocent.

Psychologists have devised a number of theoretical models to describe the nature of the mental shortcuts we take while constructing our memories and perceptions. One of the most useful of these—which is to say, the most comprehensible for all of us nonpsychologists—is *schema* theory.[31] Schema theory proposes that we construct rudimentary mental diagrams made up of "associative clusters" in order to perceive, categorize, and remember people, places, and things. For example, a schema for "chef's salad" might include "lettuce," "ham," "cheese," and "delicious." These associations don't add up to a complete (What about the hardboiled egg? What kind of cheese?) or objective

(Delicious? Says you!) picture of reality, but in many cases, it's sufficient. Why devote more brain space than necessary to chef's salad?

One big problem with schematic thinking is the tendency to leap to conclusions. A schema-driven thinker may hear "ham" and "cheese" and immediately think, "Ah, chef's salad," when in fact what's being served is a sandwich, an omelet, or even a Hawaiian pizza.

More troubling is the ease with which a mistaken association can be incorporated into a particular schema and get stuck there, like one of Jordan's made-up Sullivanisms. Let's say that your local pizza place features a "Luau Special" with Canadian bacon instead of ham. Clearly, this would be a crime against geography, though it might still taste pretty good. But if you regularly order from this misguided pizzeria, you may come to consider its recipe "correct," and the Hawaiian pizzas made with ham (and a decent respect for the distance that separates Honolulu from Toronto) "wrong."

This is no big deal, if we're just talking about chef's salad and pizza. But we also use schematic thinking—and are prone to make the same mistakes—in perceiving, defining, and categorizing people. A stereotype is a species of schema: a simplified, categorical view of a racial, ethnic, or other group, built on overgeneralizations and distortions. Substitute some trait— cheap, lazy, shifty, or even such "positive" generalizations as "natural rhythm" or "good at math"—for the lettuce in the salad, or even the Canadian bacon on that weird-ass pizza, and you've got a cognitive shortcut that can lead to an outcome far worse than an argument with your waiter.

Stereotypes have, of course, played a prominent role in the history of American humor. The hard-drinking Irishman, the slow-witted black, and the penny-pinching Jew all took their turns on the vaudeville stage, the comics page, and the silver screen. Television flirted with ethnic humor in its "innocent" youth (*The Goldbergs, Amos 'n' Andy*), and has allowed it to return, at least on the "edges," in its postmodern decadence (*In Living Color, South Park, Mind of Mencia*), but that sort of thing has never gotten much of a hearing in the late-night mainstream. Not so much because late-night's topical approach is too "sophisticated" to stoop so low, but because it focuses more often on individuals than on groups.

This is not to say that late-night humor is free from group-defining stereotypes. Assumptions about political parties, for instance, are frequently invoked. Shortly after he took office, Vice President Dick Cheney (who has a history of heart trouble) was the subject of this Jay Leno joke:

> Dick Cheney's cardiologist said today, although his heart function is not normal—his heart is not normal, his health is excellent. What does that mean? See, for Republicans, the heart is considered a secondary organ. It's like your tonsils.[32]

A couple of years later, Leno told a similar joke about a less well known Republican, reinforcing the salience of "heartlessness" as a stereotypical, group-defining trait:

> The number two Republican in the Senate, Mitch McConnell, underwent heart surgery last week. He's doing fine. Nothing was actually wrong with his heart, it's just that whenever a Republican is elected to a leadership position, they have to have their heart bypassed.[33]

If the Republicans are typically depicted as lacking hearts, the Democrats are characterized as being, if anything, *too* devoted to that organ of *amour*—among others. The Dem's reputation as skirt-chasing hedonists is actually drawn from the antics of a relative handful of bad boys, including Gary Hart, Bill Clinton, and the Kennedys, but it provides a handy brush with which to tar the entire party:

> Senator Jeffords says the reason he's leaving the Republican party, he's just fed up with George Bush and the tax cut and he's also fed up with his environmental policy. But the big reason, he says the Democrats offered to let him get in on some of that hot intern action. (Letterman)[34]

Like all stereotypes and schemas, these party designations are sufficiently entrenched to withstand the assault of a good deal of contradictory evidence. When the news media learned, late in the 2000 presidential campaign, that Republican candidate George W. Bush had once been arrested on a DUI charge, Jay Leno remarked, "You've heard of Reagan Democrats? [Bush is] a

Ted Kennedy Republican." When, in the midst of Clinton's Monica problems, Republican representative Bob Livingston was forced to step down due to revelations of marital infidelity, Leno's joke was, "All this time, we thought he was a Gingrich Republican. Now it turns out he was a Clinton Democrat."[35]

State and regional stereotypes—liberal "Taxachusetts," flakey California, mobbed-up New Jersey—are also fair game in late-night. Bill Clinton and George W. Bush—though they have little in common personally or politically—are both southerners, which prompted stereotypical jokes like this one, from David Letterman:

> Did you see . . . President-elect Bush with President Clinton at the White House yesterday? The only ones missing were Granny and Ellie May at the cee-ment pond.[36]

Examining this particular joke, it is not immediately apparent whose ox is being gored—or whose possum is being fried, if you like. The joke obliterates the political differences between Clinton and Bush, so as to be equally offensive to both parties, yet it perpetuates stereotypical notions about southerners. Some stereotypes are more acceptable than others.

And some are richer and more complicated, as well. Though schemas oversimplify things, they are multifaceted enough to accommodate some variation. Clinton's lower-middle-class Arkansas origins lend a note of trailer-trash disdain to the jokes about his appetites for fast food and sex. Smigel's "Clutch Cargo" Clinton impression on *Conan* made the president appear to be a lost Duke brother, just a good ol' boy, having a good ol' time—"neeeeehah!" Bush's southern streak shows itself in his disdain for book learnin' and, when his record as Texas governor was still fresh in the public mind, his rootin'-tootin' enthusiasm for the death penalty. Clinton's hillbilly hedonism and Bush's string-'em-up vigilantism reflect different aspects of the southern stereotype. "It's uncanny how alike these two men are," Leno observed, during an extended bit comparing the two southerners. "Clinton: Lady killer. Bush: Executioner."[37]

Generalizations about things like party and region are rarely much more than a starting point for late-night characterizations. For the most part,

late-night deals in stereotypes of one—or "person schemas."[38] These indi-
vidually tailored—but still narrowly and rigidly defined—characterizations
lie somewhere between the sweeping generalizations of an ethnic or regional
stereotype and the unfathomable complexity of any real, human individual.

I RESEMBLE THAT REMARK (BUT ONLY SUPERFICIALLY)

Just as the southern stereotype can accommodate both "yahoo!" and "you in
a heap o' trouble, boy" tendencies, person schemas can have several "nodes"
of access. These are like the individual charms of a single bracelet—distinct,
one from the next, but linked. When he first appeared on the national stage,
"Executioner Bush" was often dangled before our eyes. Later, "Dimwit Bush"
and "Childish Bush" were more often on display. (Top Ten Questions
George W. Bush asked of President Clinton: No. 1: "Which one of these is the
Bat-phone?")[39] But a common strand of petulance connects them. Bush's
schema has several nodes, but like Clinton's appetites for french fries and
interns, they sort of "go together."

As a person schema develops, a few more charms might be added to the
chain, but nothing that clashes. In fact, once in place, person schemas are
remarkably resilient. Hillary Clinton could bake a dozen apple pies a day and
hug everybody in America, and she would still be depicted as insufficiently
feminine and "cold." As with those who cling to racial or ethnic stereotypes,
we hold on to our person schemas even when confronted with contradictory
data. The transcript of his CNN appearance confirms that Al Gore did not
say he had "invented the Internet," but nothing could dispel the notion that
he was a liar and a braggart. The revelation of John Kerry's college transcripts revealed that his grades were no better than Bush's, but it did nothing
to change public perceptions of Bush's inferior intellect.[40]

Comedians do their part to keep established characterizations in place, even
when events fail to cooperate. Here is a Leno joke, from the 2000 campaign:

[This was] kind of embarrassing—on a recent campaign rally, Al Gore's
daughter Kristin mistakenly referred to Seattle as the capital of

Washington. . . . Boy, Bush was all over this. He said, "Even I'm not that bad with geometry."[41]

Thus, a "real-life," but schema-inconsistent, slip by a member of "Team Gore" (since Kristin Gore was not sufficiently well known to rate a caricatured identity of her own, she gets put on her father's "smart" side of the divide by default) is used as the basis for a schema-*consistent* joke about Bush. It's the same tactic Leno employed in the "Ted Kennedy Republican" and "Bill Clinton Democrat" jokes. And the audience is eager to go along with it, since it restores the proper order of things: *Wait, I thought* Bush *was the dumb one. Ah, he* is *the dumb one—that's better.*

Though Kerry's "botched joke" could be dealt with in terms of his humorless dullness and meandering language, this "boomerang" technique could also be used to play off, and reinforce, Bush's schema:

> Senator John Kerry gave his opponents in the struggling Republican
> Party a much-needed distraction when he told a college audience on
> Monday that if you don't do well in school, you might get stuck in
> Iraq. Some people are taking that as a slam against our troops. Kerry
> says it was a botched joke about the president being dumb. It doesn't
> bode well when you try to make a joke about someone being dumb
> and you wind up looking even dumber. (Kimmel)[42]

Leno even found a way to use the occasion for a *Kerry = dull / Bush = dumb* twofer:

> John Kerry is now getting slammed by the Republicans because of a
> botched joke he did about President Bush and Iraq in a recent speech.
> Kerry was stunned about this. He said, "What? People are listening to
> my speeches?" President Bush demanded that Kerry apologize. Can
> you imagine that—Bush demanding an apology for someone
> stumbling over his words?[43]

One of the funniest examples of reinforcing a politician's person schema by working against it was a 1986 *Saturday Night Live* sketch featuring the late

Phil Hartman as then-President Ronald Reagan. The premise was that Reagan's genial disengagement—captured perfectly by Hartman—was just an act, put on to fool the press and the public. As soon as he was out of sight of the media, Reagan became a super-competent, hands-on commander, schooling his meek and compliant underlings in the fine points of arms deals and Swiss bank accounts, conducting telephone diplomacy in fluent German and Arabic, and quoting Montesquieu: "Power without knowledge is power lost!"[44]

The joke, of course, was that everyone "knew" Reagan wasn't really like that. Still, the "amiable dunce" that Hartman portrayed at the beginning of the sketch—the familiar Reagan caricature—was itself reductive. The brilliance of the sketch was that it overtly refuted that image, even as it ironically reinforced its "truth." Just as the Warner Bros. animators kept finding new ways for the Coyote to fail in his quest for the Road Runner, topical comedians keep finding new ways to tell us what we already "know" about politicians.

THE DAN QUAYLE EFFECT

Prior to his selection as George H. W. Bush's running mate in 1988, the public knew very little about J. Danforth Quayle. On paper, at least, it would have appeared that at that moment he was approaching the pinnacle of a thoroughly charmed life. In spite of his youth and inexperience, Quayle would soon be within a heartbeat of the world's most powerful office, thanks to his bland but boyish good looks, his family's wealth and influence, the usual political calculations (he added geographical and ideological balance to the ticket), and a healthy dose of—excuse the expression—dumb luck.

Quayle, however, was *unlucky* in one important way. His debut on the national stage happened to coincide with the period when late-night was entering the first spasms of what would be its post-Carson proliferation. Jay Leno had taken over as *The Tonight Show*'s "permanent" guest host in 1987 and would replace Johnny in May 1992. Arsenio Hall's late-night debut, on Fox's *Late Show*, also came in 1987. He would get his own syndicated, self-titled show in 1989, the same year Pat Sajak's late-night show debuted. Arsenio turned out to be a flash in the pan, and Sajak more of a fizzle, but the format was clearly proliferating. Cable saw the premiere of not one, but two channels devoted to round-the-clock humor, the Comedy Channel in 1989 and "Ha!" in 1990. (By 1991 the two would merge to form Comedy Central.)[45] The eighties' comedy club wave was cresting, and Quayle's fellow Hoosier David Letterman was in the midst of a transition from upstart to institution. (A 1988 *Rolling Stone* cover story dubbed him "the Anti-Quayle.")[46] For that matter, Johnny himself was still around for much of the campaign. With all of these comedians, writers, programs, and channels hungering for material, clamoring and craning like a nest full of baby birds, poor Quayle didn't stand a chance. He hit the satire industry like the Second Coming of Watergate.

Until Monica Lewinsky came along, Quayle was late-night's all-time champ (or chump). But did the sheer volume of Quayle jokes—which was at least partly a result of an accident of timing—produce a distorted view of the veep? Looking back, radio satirist Harry Shearer, host of *Le Show* and no fan of Quayle's politics, expressed a belief in what he called the "Dan Quayle effect": the ability of late-night comedians to define a target so definitively, and so irrevocably, that this alone could seal his political fate. "If you are ridiculed too often on those shows," Shearer asserted, " . . .it's a death warrant. It's why I thought Clinton was going to have to resign."[47]

But of course, Clinton didn't have to resign. And the "Dan Quayle effect," if it indeed existed, is impossible to measure. Sure, the comedians picked on him, but it wasn't as if Quayle didn't give them a lot of opportunities. His propensity for malapropisms remains unparalleled, even by George W. Bush. Most of Quayle's misstatements were just dumb, such as his famous mangling of the United Negro College Fund's slogan. (The original, "A mind is a terrible thing to waste," was rendered by Quayle as "What a waste it is to lose one's mind, or not to have a mind is being very wasteful. How true that is.") But some of them reached the absurd heights of Dadaist poetry, such as his assertion, in a nationally televised debate, that he would never approve "another Jimmy Carter grain embargo, Jimmy, Jimmy Carter, Jimmy Carter grain embargo, Jimmy Carter grain embargo." (It sounds better with the bongos.)[48]

So if a majority of Americans developed a low opinion of Quayle's intelligence, it would be difficult to say how much of this was attributable to comedy and how much to Quayle's own public statements and demeanor. The vicious cycle of comic characterization defies such attempts at unraveling: if the audience didn't already think he was dumb, the jokes wouldn't be funny—on the other hand, where did they get the idea he was that dumb?

Partly from late-night, to be sure—though they had plenty of help. There were several books devoted to making fun of the veep, including *The Unauthorized Autobiography of Dan Quayle,* a compendium of the vice president's gaffes stitched together with such embarrassing biographical details as his college GPA and the story of how family connections helped him avoid Vietnam. There was a magazine called the *Quayle Quarterly,* and even a "hot line" (1–900–USA–DANNY) featuring Quayle's latest verbal misadventures.[49] As with Watergate, some of the humor Quayle inspired was genuinely satirical, but most was opportunistic and easy—dumb-guy jokes dressed up as topical commentary.

These comic sorties undoubtedly caused Quayle considerable distress, but late-night TV, with its large audience and its habit of returning again and again to a winning premise (which Quayle certainly gave them), was particularly worrisome. "I don't begrudge any honest laughter they gave people watching TV at the end of a hard day, but when it came to my career they were totally destructive," the vice president wrote in his 1994 memoir. "Do you know how many favorable stories it takes to overcome one zinger by Johnny Carson?"[50]

Quayle was so reliably laughable that he made the monologues even when he hadn't made any news. "There's never been anybody like him," proclaimed Robert Lichter, of the Center for Media and Public Affairs. "Dan Quayle is a running joke. There doesn't have to be a news peg. He has been defined politically to fit the needs of late-night comedians—a person who is foolish, childlike and not up to the job." *Newsweek* noted that "cartoonists and comics have seven field days a week with his lightweight image," in a story with the pitying headline, "Will the Jokes Ever Stop?"[51]

Quayle's defenders were asking the same question. Other politicians—and even journalists—misspoke on occasion without being indelibly labeled as idiots, they pointed out. So incessant was the ridicule that many predicted a backlash. The *New Republic* mockingly offered a "Quayle Revisionism Award" to the first media outlet to reevaluate the vice president, an eventuality the editors expected to arise through journalistic restlessness, rather than any of Quayle's heretofore undiscovered merits: "Can journalists keep writing indefinitely that Dan Quayle is a moron, just because he is one? We doubt it."[52]

And yet the jokes kept coming. As far as the satire industry was concerned, there was no reason to reconsider Quayle unless the audience demanded it, which they did not. But does this mean the "Dan Quayle effect" was a genuine phenomenon? Did a disproportionate late-night assault really damage or shorten Quayle's political career?

It is impossible to say how far Quayle might have gone in politics if there had been fewer jokes, but VP is pretty good, and his boss was one of the few to go from that job to the top one without his predecessor's dying in office. As for their culpability in convincing the public of his less-than-Einsteinian intellect, maybe Quayle could sue Leno and Letterman, as the old punch line has it, for *definition* of character?

"The dream of the satirist, which is to have an effect on the thing you're making fun of, they are in fact doing," Shearer said of the late-night assault on Quayle.[53] But this is giving them too much credit. The mainstream late-night comics are not really satirists, and they dream only of laughs and ratings. *Rolling Stone* may have hoped for an "anti-Quayle," but Letterman had no agenda in attacking Quayle other than picking on a "dumb guy" and making his audience laugh.

In principle, though, the notion that a torrent of focused ridicule might substantially contribute to the ruination of a political career is not at all implausible. But for such a thing to be a crime, it must be slander, not mere exaggeration; defamation, not "definition."

One could argue, for instance, for the existence of an "Al Gore effect"— late-night contributed considerably to the perpetuation of the Internet misquote, and the "exaggerator" narrative that grew out of it. Howard Dean might also have a case. The endless replays of his famous "scream"—which only seemed "crazy" because the directional microphone he was holding failed to record the noise of the crowd—constituted about as clear-cut a case of a media hit-job as one could imagine, and late-night was again a major contributor.

Quayle was right, however, about the difficulty of overcoming a dismissive characterization once it's planted in the public mind. Person schemas, constructed and elaborately reinforced by a media apparatus which includes both news and comedy, are as difficult to wash away as an ink stain on a silk shirt. A 1996 *Simpsons* Halloween special illustrated this point with a story that had that year's presidential contenders, Bob Dole and Bill Clinton, replaced by space-alien look-alikes:

> "CLINTON": I am Clin-Ton. As overlord, all will kneel trembling before me and obey my brutal commands. End communication.
> MARGE (hearing the speech on the radio): Hmm, that's Slick Willie for you, always with the smooth talk.[54]

THE PERSONAL IS ANTI-POLITICAL

Political ambivalence is embedded in the American grain. But late-night reinforces and exploits our anti-political prejudices. Because of its focus on personalities—and the depth-defying, two-dimensional lens through which that focus is presented—it depicts an electoral circus in which all men are created equally ridiculous.

The apotheosis of the ad hominem approach to political comedy was the 2000 presidential election. Given the consequences of presidential policies, actions, and inaction in the years since, it is almost embarrassing to recall the extent to which that contest was understood as a referendum on "character." That the choice between George W. Bush and Al Gore—two men whose ideologies, philosophies of government, résumés, and positions on everything from taxes to the environment could hardly have stood in starker contrast—should have been depicted as a race between, as Marshall Sella put it, "the Stiff Guy" and "the Dumb Guy" is a measure of the inadequacy of this view.[55]

Late-night does not deserve all, or even most, of the blame for this twisted perspective. The overemphasis on "character" is, more importantly, a symptom

of our anti-political irrationality. The American system is built on deliberation, compromise, and checks and balances; but the American public wants
bold action, pure message, and heroic leaders. Or at least that's what some of
us *think* we want.

So in 2000, some of us listened to the noble Ralph Nader tell us that
"Gush and Bore" were interchangeable, and that if we wanted purity, we had
better vote for him.[56] Some of us listened to George W. Bush talk about how
his favorite political philosopher, Jesus Christ, had changed his "heart," and
that was good enough for us.[57] Some of us thought Al Gore was a good man,
too, though many who voted halfheartedly for him thought he lacked
charisma. Many of us, of course, didn't vote at all.

The fact that the election ended in a virtual tie was a kind of validation for
those who championed the anti-political view that it hardly mattered. Of
course, this was late-night's view by default. "Okay, so now here's the deal,"
David Letterman explained. "We have George W. Bush, is not president of
the United States. Al W. Gore, not president of the United States. What do
you say we just leave it that way?" Leno concurred. "See," he said, "neither of
these guys is electable. We've been saying that from the beginning."[58]

Conan O'Brien made the anti-political argument even more explicit.
"Our country is still a mess," he said. "We still have no president-elect, and
we're still—maybe we don't need one. We may not need one. We're doing
fine without one. It's possible—we can just govern ourselves, I think."[59] *Late
Night's* audience roared its approval.

Of course, the anti-democratic subtext of this sort of humor suggests that
we *can't* govern ourselves, but the intent is to say that the fault is not in ourselves but in our "stars"—that is, in the people who run for office. They just
aren't good enough characters. Couldn't we vote for somebody like Rick Blaine?

SHOTGUN!

It may seem silly to accuse comedians of shirking their "duty," but in a government ostensibly of and by the people, citizenship carries responsibility—
and that goes double for those with a bully pulpit. One who has a nightly

audience of millions and is, moreover, afforded the privilege of addressing matters concerning the country's foreign and domestic policies, its legislative present, and electoral future is obliged to take that role seriously, even if his primary role is to be funny.

Though in our system the voters are ostensibly in the driver's seat, members of the media ought to help us navigate. But instead of riding shotgun and keeping an eye out for potholes, reporters, pundits, and topical comedians are concerned only with getting our attention, like unruly children acting up in the backseat. The comedians, who could use their uniquely appealing forum and the concision of comedy to help clarify the political world for us, choose to oversimplify it in a way that is neither helpful nor responsible. By avoiding issues in favor of personalities, and by "balancing" these shallow criticisms between conservatives and liberals, late-night comics are playing it safe but endangering democracy.

The following chapters will consider some of the dead ends and blind alleys down which topical comedy is liable to steer us. Where does the equal-opportunity offender path lead, and why, beyond the reasons we have already explored, is it the road more taken? What hazards await comedians and audiences who attempt to take a genuinely satirical route? Why does so much of contemporary comedy that proclaims its "edginess" seem so safe? Let's pull over and look at the map.

CHAPTER 5

PAY NO ATTENTION TO THAT MAN IN FRONT OF THE CURTAIN

You know what they say. . . .

But who are "they," exactly? To ask is to imply a conspiracy: there must be some nefarious cabal working in the shadows to convince us that America is divided into red states and blue, soccer moms and NASCAR dads; that bell bottom-pants are cool again; that Will Ferrell is the new Charlie Chaplin. That's what "they" say—but who are these people?

In fact, there is no simple or single answer to the "they" question; no actual convention where the conventional wisdom is determined. "They" are a loose and shifting confederation of co-conspirators, many of them unwitting. That said, a certain amount of paranoia regarding "them" is justifiable. Some of the promulgators of popular myths do work in the shadows, with malice aforethought, their dirty deeds to perform: the people behind John Kerry's "mistress" and John McCain's "black baby."[1] But much of the shaping of our discourse takes place right under our noses and is not driven by any ideological agenda—no conscious one, anyway. A lot of what "everybody knows" sprouts more or less organically from the seeds sown (or the fertilizer spread) by the hundreds of reporters tasked with turning messy, disconnected facts into coherent "stories." That some of these stories quickly congeal into misleading memes is an unfortunate by-product of the way journalism is currently practiced, but that doesn't mean it's a master plan to manipulate public opinion.

There are, of course, people who openly aim to influence public opinion: that small class of "name" columnists and talking heads who wear their interpretive license on their sleeves. The more traditional members of this claque—gray eminences like David Broder, Clarence Page, and Thomas Friedman—offer opinion and analysis that is "serious," which is to say sober and sincere, if not necessarily correct. But another class of pundits, more recently come into prominence, aims to entertain readers and listeners as much as to sway or enlighten them. Maureen Dowd often seems more interested in demonstrating her cleverness than in making a point. And television talkers are even more incorrigible; get Chris Matthews, Margaret Carlson, and Andrew Sullivan around a desk, and they seem to mistake themselves for the Algonquin Round Table.

Further blurring the line between reportage and performance art are such polemical vaudevillians as Rush Limbaugh and Ann Coulter. In fact, for this subsection of the punditocracy, fuzzing that border is to some extent strategic: whenever they cross some line of propriety, these professional provocateurs are apt to seek shelter from criticism by claiming (or allowing their defenders to claim) that they are primarily entertainers, and therefore not to be held accountable when they go too far. One of the confusing aspects regarding the incident in which radio host Don Imus was fired for a racist joke was figuring out just exactly what Imus was. With a guest list that regularly featured big-name journalists and politicians of both parties, he was clearly no mere entertainer. Yet despite featuring a good deal of political discussion, his show was more *Morning Zoo* than *Meet the Press*. Though he apologized for the joke, he could not plausibly ask to be dismissed as just a joker. As *The Daily Show*'s Larry Wilmore observed, "You just can't say, 'So let's talk about what's happening to the economy this week, and up next, nappy-headed hos!' People get confused."[2]

Late-night comics certainly play some part in promoting conventional wisdom, but they are careful to separate themselves from "they." Rather than using the "I'm just an entertainer" ploy only when it is convenient, late-night hosts base their public legitimacy on this premise. In fact, the chief distinction between late-night comedians and celebrity pundits is the former's calculated humility. Coulter, Limbaugh, and even the camera-shy Dowd are larger-than-life personalities; their words, and the weight they carry with their respective audiences, are inseparable from their status as (self-appointed) oracles.

Late-night comics—at least those who host the higher-rated, "mainstream," network shows—present themselves as smaller-than-life. They are not only "just" entertainers, they are *mere* entertainers. Even as the boundary between news and entertainment fades into invisibility, the importance network television still places on maintaining this line is reasserted every night, when the local Eyewitness News team hands the airwaves over to Jay or Dave: This has been a look at the real world; we now return to the world of entertainment.

Television *entertainers* are not supposed to address politics, and for most of the medium's history, they haven't. Though there have been a handful of "relevant" sitcoms and dramas (*All in the Family*, *The West Wing*), and a few thwarted attempts at prime-time satire (*The Smothers Brothers Comedy Hour*, *That Was the Week That Was*), entertainment programs have largely steered clear of the P-word, even as most other standards of taste and decorum have fallen by the wayside. For TV, politics is the last taboo—except in late-night.

Then how do the late-night comedians get away with ridiculing presidents, taunting Democrats and Republicans, and mocking Congress on network television? You wouldn't hear *The King of Queens* calling President Bush a dummy. It's okay for Dr. House to be a chauvinist, a semi-racist, a drug addict, and an all-around misanthrope, but if he were revealed to be a Democrat (or a Republican), there'd be hell to pay.

Some of the reasons for late-night's political focus derive from the peculiarities of the genre. The late-night production schedule—five nights a week, all year round (minus the occasional vacation)—makes topicality not just a possibility but a practical necessity. Compared to the tightly scripted prime-time shows that precede them, individual episodes of late-night shows are ephemeral, spontaneous, and disposable. Individual sitcom episodes are relatively timeless and endlessly (and profitably) repeatable. While *I Love Lucy*'s candy conveyer belt is an evergreen classic, last night's headline-driven *Tonight Show* monologue is already out of date.

There has also traditionally been a sense that the late hour at which these shows air allows them to deal with more "adult" concerns. In the days before such raunchy offerings as *Two and a Half Men* became acceptable "Family Hour" fare, one had to stay up till Johnny Carson came on just to hear a good *double entendre* (perhaps featuring "my high school girlfriend, Gina Stachitoré").[3] Nowadays, sex jokes are primetime staples—but politics still has to wait till the kids have gone to bed.

But there is more to the late-night hosts' special dispensation to discuss politics than the expediencies of production or the lateness of the hour. Hosting a network late-night show is a career to which many have been called—Arsenio Hall, Joan Rivers, Joey Bishop, Merv Griffin, Sammy Davis Jr., Chevy Chase, Alan Thicke, Sinbad, Pat Sajak—but few have been chosen.[4] Those who have made a go of it over the long term have chalked up some impressive tenures: thirty years for Johnny Carson, twenty-five and counting for David Letterman, fifteen years so far for Jay Leno, and fourteen for relative newcomer Conan O'Brien. There must be something extraordinary about these guys.

Or perhaps it is something extra-ordinary—what really stands out about the successful mainstream hosts is how little stands out about them. Considering how famous they are, Letterman, Leno, and O'Brien seem, like Carson before them, surprisingly inconspicuous. All are white, male, and not "ethnic" in any noticeable way. They are comedians, of course, but not particularly "wacky" ones. And though they are celebrities, they are notably short on glitter: Johnny was perhaps a minor-league playboy, but Jay, Dave, and Conan rarely show up in the tabloids. Nor are you likely to see them touring refugee camps with Angelina Jolie or demonstrating alongside Martin Sheen or Sean Penn. They don't have causes, they don't court controversy, and in a culture that increasingly embraces the outrageous, they project a determined blandness.

Consider the fact that, in addition to the aforementioned also-rans, there is an even longer list of talented comedians who never came near getting their own late-night desks. Significantly, these include almost every overtly political comic you would care to name: Mort Sahl, Dick Gregory, Bill Hicks, Margaret Cho, Harry Shearer, Janeane Garofalo, Bill Maher (now back on cable after proving himself too controversial for network TV). The permission to talk politics—which network television otherwise reserves only for certified pundits—is inextricable from the question of the hosts' identity.

So what is it about Johnny, Dave, Jay, and Conan that lets them get away with it, night after night, year after year?

License to Kid

The basic principle of comic license is simple enough: opinions that might be too provocative if expressed in a straightforward manner are permissible when presented as jokes. George Bernard Shaw recognized this principle when he observed that Mark Twain "[had] to put things in such a way as to make people who would otherwise hang him believe he is joking." A comedian can get away with sedition, or even blasphemy, as long as it's funny sedition or blasphemy. This has been true since the days of the medieval jester, the only member of the royal court allowed to insult the king.[5]

The courtly fool represented no real threat to the king's dignity—nor, certainly, to his authority. The fool, in fact, was appointed by the king and kept on hand as a living accessory to power. The arrangement was not unlike what is supposed to happen at events like the Correspondents Dinner: a comedian is brought in not so much to mock the president, but to show everyone what a good sport he is. (Stephen Colbert can consider himself lucky to live in an era in which offending the head of state can't cost you your own.)

In a democratic system with commercial media, the license to mock the nation's leaders is bestowed by the public. Television viewers have granted the tiny elite of late-night hosts the jester's privilege. As in politics itself, however, the race is not always to the swift, and the field is far from wide open. Candidates competing for one of the coveted network-jester spots must pass muster not only with viewers, but with industry executives and sponsors, who—like the party bosses who used to pick candidates in smoke-filled rooms—have a good deal of say as to who is on the ballot, or rather schedule.

Like the forty-two presidents the United States has had to date, the successful mainstream hosts have all been white males.[6] For that matter, Conan O'Brien and JFK are the sole Roman Catholics on their respective lists.[*]

---

[*] Jimmy Kimmel was raised Catholic, but the jury's still out as to whether he can be called "successful."

And while the nation's editorial pages and prime-time TV's workplaces and neighborhoods have become a bit more integrated over the last few years (more so, perhaps, than real American workplaces and neighborhoods), late-night remains a white, male preserve.

But beyond these demographic similarities, the successful mainstream hosts share a more or less common temperament. For all their topical irreverence, these mild-mannered fellows could hardly be called iconoclasts, provocateurs, or disturbers of the peace. They're not out to make us rethink our political assumptions; they are content to play off of (and thereby reinforce) what we already "know." They don't intend to challenge us but to welcome us. They are not, after all, billed as satirists but as *hosts*.

STAND-UP AND STANDOFFISHNESS

They are also, at least in their shows' opening minutes, before the guests arrive, stand-up comics. And this presents another complication in understanding their role. Stand-ups, even if they don't address topical issues, are more like pundits than mere clowns, simply because of the way they address their audiences. David Marc has even referred to the "totalitarian" nature of stand-up address.[7] But center stage can be a site of vulnerability as well as power.

There are a lot of comedians you might find funny but wouldn't want to hang out with. Many seem to go out of their way to convince us of their misfit status: Rodney Dangerfield was a perennial loser, Sam Kinison a volatile misogynist; Larry the Cable Guy is an unsophisticated hick, Steven Wright a spaced-out weirdo. Generally speaking, this is by design. By convincing the audience that, compared to him, they are luckier, saner, smarter, or more "normal," the comedian gains their sympathy and trust. We need to laugh *at* these guys for a while before we are willing to laugh *with* them, at some common enemy—say, bad drivers, or hard-to-program remote controls, or the makers of Head On (apply directly to the forehead).

Lawrence Mintz, a University of Maryland professor and the director of the Art Gliner Center for Humor Studies, refers to these opposite poles of comic identity as "negative exemplar" and "comic spokesman."[8] An "outsider" comedian gains the right to speak for us because he's not quite one of us. Dangerfield or Kinison or Lenny Bruce could say out loud what we would only dare think, whether the subject was politics, race, religion, sex, or our violent fantasies involving those who precede us in the supermarket express lane despite having not twelve but thirteen items in their baskets. (Don't you hate those people?)

But the mix of negative exemplar and comic spokesman is not the same for every comedian. The late-night elites definitely emphasize the latter; they "speak for" the audience, without being especially weird. Carson, with his sartorial flashiness, Hollywood lifestyle, and multiple marriages, was just a little bit racier than the small-town Rotarian he otherwise resembled; O'Brien, despite his Ivy League education and stable family life, constantly mocks himself as a nitwit and nebbishy loser; Leno—an arrow so straight as to make the editor of the *National Enquirer* cry—leavens his nice-guy shtick with a hint of macho boorishness; and Letterman—probably the most ostentatiously maladjusted of the mainstream hosts—depicts himself as a cranky curmudgeon with a stunted personal life. Still, as far as "outsider" status is concerned, these guys are a far cry from Emo Phillips or Andrew Dice Clay. Though they skew just far enough from dead level to maintain a comic angle, they are neither "sick," bizarre, nor outrageous. The truths they deal in, though delicate for commercial television, avoid the deeper recesses of the collective id.

As a general rule there is a direct, proportional relationship between the outrageousness of the comedian's character, and the unspeakability of his message. Lenny Bruce was a wild guy who talked about some wild stuff. While it's true that the mainstream hosts talk about politics, their message is anti-politics—which perhaps should be unspeakable but isn't. The least controversial joke you can make about our system of government is that the system itself is a joke.

Not that stand-up comedy is ever completely safe. Because a comic is perceived to be his own auteur—the writer, director, and performer of his act—he is held responsible for what he says in the way a comic actor is not. "We can be confident that Norman Lear will punish Archie Bunker for his sins," writes David Marc, "[but] who will punish Don Rickles?"[9] Michael Richards was never to blame for the bizarre behavior of *Seinfeld*'s Cosmo Kramer, but he got himself in a lot of trouble for his angry use of the N-word on the stand-up stage.[10] Whoever he is, a stand-up comedian is understood to be speaking for himself.

Just as there is a continuum of outrageousness, though, there is a broad spectrum of self-revelation among comedians. We understand, for example, that the real Steven Wright probably isn't *that* weird. Biographical comics, like Ray Romano and Bill Cosby, derive much of their comedy from personal experience, though they stop short of Richard Pryor's open-soul surgery. Observational comics' acts are more abstract and impersonal. Jerry Seinfeld actually revealed more of "himself" playing the eponymous hero of his sitcom than in a long career of stand-up (though how closely TV's Seinfeld resembles the real Seinfeld is unclear). Ellen DeGeneres was able to avoid making an issue of her sexuality for a good portion of her career, because her comedy depended more upon how she saw the world than who she was.

This is true, in a way, of the late-night hosts, who despite their weekday familiarity and their lack of "character" artifice reveal very little of themselves. Conan O'Brien is "just" Conan O'Brien, but who *is* that, exactly? Like Ray Romano, he has a wife and kids, but you'd never know it from his monologues. Unlike Bill Cosby, David Letterman rarely talks about his childhood, though we can presume that he had one. Jay Leno wants us to think of him as our pal, yet he remains remote and closed off to us.

There is a temptation to call late-night's equal-opportunity offenders bland. But what they really are is *blank*—poker-faced, inscrutable. Unlike, say, Sam Kinison, you could imagine hanging out with them, but you couldn't get to know them—if, indeed, there is anything to know. Yet it is their very blankness which allows this unremarkable elite to talk about that most volatile of topics—politics—night after night, on network TV, without stirring up wrath or resistance.

Like presidential candidates, late-night comedians are expected to be both "of" the people and above them; ordinary but special. Yet the mainstream hosts, with their mild gestures of outsider aloofness, preempt the kind of examination of "character" to which we subject our politicians. The George W. Bush we know from late-night may be a cartoon, but we still know him better than we know his caricaturists.

THE EVOLUTION OF *HOSTO SAPIENS*

The connection between the late-nighters' identities and the nature of their comic license becomes clearer if we go back and trace the evolution, so to speak, of *Hosto sapiens*. We'll look at the lineage of network hosts from the pre-Carsonian through the Conanian periods, and consider a few mutants and subspecies along the way—some who thrived briefly in the late-night mainstream, and others who found a more hospitable environment with the emergence of cable narrowcasting.

The epitome of the mainstream host, past master of the topical yet anti-political monologue, and acknowledged prototype for all who have followed him is Johnny Carson. In terms of the ascent-of-man metaphor, it was Carson who first developed the simple tools later generations of hosts would adopt and employ: the ad hominem approach to the headlines, the ideological balancing act, the trivializing juxtaposition of Washington, D.C., and Hollywood, in which Condoleezza Rice might at any moment bump into Paris Hilton.

Carson was the very model of a modern late-night talk show host. Yet this specimen did not simply emerge, fully formed, from the primordial ooze. His *Tonight Show* predecessors, Steve Allen and Jack Paar, contributed much of Johnny's host-DNA. Carson was indebted to Allen for a few recurring bits (Carnac was just Allen's "Question Man" in a turban) and for the precedent of late-night as a forum for humor that was hipper and more "adult" than prime time.[11] Paar—a fellow midwesterner who even looked like a distant Carson cousin—introduced a political element, with timely and sometimes topical monologues. Paar was, like his successors, non-partisan, though he occasionally showed a disturbing tendency to take the subject of politics seriously. He interviewed Nixon, the Kennedys, and Fidel Castro. He even hosted one episode of *Tonight* "on location" from the Berlin Wall.[12]

Carson talked about current events from the beginning but eschewed Paar's risky and earnest adventures. It would be a disservice to his artistry to say that Carson managed to make topical jokes into something as harmless as other comedians' mother-in-law gags, but it's not far off the mark.

Facing the camera five nights a week, yet revealing little of himself, Carson was simultaneously television's most familiar and most enigmatic figure, an irony that struck everyone who tried to describe him. "Oddly," wrote *Time*'s Richard Zoglin, "Carson, one of the most intimate of comedians, has always been one of the most remote of public personalities." An acquaintance once famously described him as "sealed as tight as an egg." Carson himself was well aware of how he was perceived. When the city of Burbank named a municipal park after him, Carson quipped that "the [formerly] warm water in the drinking fountain will now be cool and aloof."[13]

The "King of Late-Night" was not very forthcoming about his personal life, and he held his political views particularly close to the vest. "Nobody knows what I am," Carson liked to boast, referring to his political affiliations.[14] He did drop a clue now and again, though. In an unusually candid interview in *Life* magazine in 1970, Carson explained that "in my living room, I would argue for liberalization of abortion laws, divorce laws, and there are times when I would like to express a view on the air. . . . But I'm on TV five nights a week. I've got nothing to gain by it and everything to lose."[15]

If he rarely let such feelings show, some observers were nevertheless prepared to read between the lines of Carson's public demeanor. Gore Vidal, an inveterate critic of the American status quo, once claimed, "Johnny treated me as a surrogate for him politically. Though we agreed on some points, he always took the opportunity to look bewildered at the radical things I had to say. He was delighted."[16]

It's hard to say whether views such as Vidal's were true insights into Carson's politics, or mere wishful projections. The blank screen of Johnny's personality undoubtedly let conservative viewers feel that he shared their views and values, as well. Carson understood the value of playing things on the coy side. He had debuted in show business as a magician ("the Great Carsoni"), and understood that there was power in a performer knowing more than his audience.[17]

But Carson's reserve was not entirely calculated; he also had a certain reticence bred into him. Born in Iowa and raised in Nebraska, Carson was often
said to epitomize the midwestern American. "If the heartland had a body
and a voice," *Newsweek* once claimed, "they'd have no choice but to name it
Johnny Carson."[18] Terms like "heartland," "middle America," and even
"Midwest" are often invoked by magazine editors, political consultants, network executives, admen and others whose only experience of the region
is changing planes at O'Hare to suggest a center that is not just geographic,
but also demographic, and political. Robert Balkin, editor of D.C.'s inside-
the-Beltway newsletter *The Hotline*, summed up Carson's politics as
"Midwestern and fairly mainstream," as if these were the same thing.[19] The
fact that he came from the center of the continental United States dovetailed
nicely with the notion. *Everything* about Carson was straight down the
middle, according to *Newsday*. "If Carson's sense of humor wasn't as hip as
Lenny Bruce's, it was a lot hipper than Bob Hope's. And through the years,
Carson's humor kept shifting, always finding a comfortable middle ground.
Even today, Carson's humor may not be as out there as David Letterman's,
but it's still a lot hipper than Jackie Mason's."[20]

The real Midwest is not, in fact, the golden mean of American society. Nor
is it a bucolic utopia, where common sense and common people rule. It is,
like any region, no single thing: it is urban, rural, innocent, corrupt, liberal,
conservative. And, far from Averageland, USA, it is a region that has seen
extremes of every kind, from the meteorological to the political. The "red
states" of 2000 and 2004 were hotbeds of populist radicalism in the 1890s.
Milwaukee had three Socialist mayors between 1910 and 1960.[21] And as far as
heartland "normalcy" and "decency" are concerned, let us not forget that
Jeffrey Dahmer and Ed Gein (the inspiration for *Psycho*) were from Wisconsin,
while Norman Rockwell was from Connecticut.

Deservedly or not, however, being from the Midwest means that one lacks
any regional "baggage." A midwesterner isn't dumb like a southerner, effete
like an easterner, combative like a New Yorker, or flaky like a Californian. He
doesn't even have an accent—which is why announcers, anchormen, and
game show hosts so often hale from the heartland. Stereotypes aside, though,

there is a set of attitudes and behaviors, and a way of looking at the world, that could, with some justice, be deemed "midwestern." What's more, these fit Carson to a tee. Folks from Carson country indeed tend toward the laconic, the reserved, and the skeptical. They are outwardly polite but secretly judgmental. Their humor is understated but sly and cutting.[22]

Carson the midwesterner has been compared, by several observers, to another regional character: the Yankee.[23] The stereotypical Yankee character emerged from the folklore of the early republic and went on to appear in innumerable anecdotes, comic sketches, and plays (including, notably, *Our American Cousin*, the play Lincoln was attending the night he was assassinated).[24] Constance Rourke offered this description of the Yankee in her classic 1931 study, *American Humor*: "Though he talked increasingly his monologues still never brimmed over into personal revelation. He was drawn with ample color and circumstance, yet he was not wholly a person. . . . A barrier seemed to lie between this legendary Yankee and any effort to reach his inner character. The effect was so consistent, so widespread, so variously repeated that the failure to see him closely must be reckoned not a failure at all but a concerted interest in another direction. . . . Over-assertive yet quiet, self-conscious."[25]

The comparisons between Rourke's Yankee and Carson are striking. The Yankee looked to be a bit of a hayseed, but his apparent naïveté masked a sharp, controlling intelligence—just as Carson's Nebraska innocence cloaked his shrewd comic insights. The Yankee hid his "inner character" and used his gift of gab to pursue "a concerted interest in another direction." Carson hid behind his midwestern impenetrability and used his gift to talk about the nation's politics without ever exposing his own. Like the rustic Yankee, a nice Nebraska boy can get away with things a city slicker never could.

HOOSIER HERMITOUS VERSUS JAW-VA MAN

The retirement of Johnny Carson and the division of his former fiefdom among his dueling heirs apparent—neither of whom has succeeded in recapturing his legendary dominance of the ratings or his iconic status—may strike some as evidence of *de*volution, rather than Darwinian progress. Evolution, though, is not a matter of ever-increasing refinement but one of environmental adaptation. And by the time Johnny said his last good night in 1992, the late-night environment had entered a period of drastic change.

Cable proliferation had shrunk the overall network audience, but the battle for Carson's crown introduced something late-night hadn't much seen during Johnny's thirty-year run—serious competition. Viewers now faced a choice between two successors, who exemplified different sides of Carson's legacy: Jay Leno made a more convincing claim for Carson's relentlessly topical comic anchorman role, while David Letterman better approximated Carson's McLuhanesque "cool."

Rolling Stone attributed Carson and Letterman's similar sensibilities to their common midwestern roots: "[Letterman] shares with Johnny Carson a certain irreducible farm-belt loneliness. Somewhere not too far behind him is one of those bleak outskirts-of-town intersections where the stoplight swings in a breeze that's made partly of arctic air. His jaggedly sarcastic grin and mock-angry stares speak of human distances, not connections."[26] Despite their similarities, though, Letterman's "mock-angry stares" indicated an anti-social edge that surpassed Carsonian aloofness. Whereas Johnny was detached, Dave was positively isolated; where Johnny came across as a loner, Dave depicted himself as a misfit. This is partly a generational difference: simply duplicating *Tonight*'s Hollywood-Vegas vibe would have seemed a bit dated and hokey to the college crowd who stayed up for Letterman.[27] But Dave's worn-on-his-sleeve alienation appears to be truly a part of his personality.

Letterman guards his off-screen privacy even more zealously than Carson did. Johnny was open enough to turn his multiple divorces into monologue fodder (though the punch lines centered on alimony rather than emotional distress). By comparison, Dave's reluctance to discuss personal matters seems almost pathological. Though he has occasionally mentioned son Harry since his birth in 2003, he has rarely uttered the name of the boy's mother—Regina Lasko, his girlfriend of many years—on the air.[28] If Carson was "sealed tight as an egg," Letterman is an egg surrounded by bubble wrap, placed in a vacuum tube, and left on Funk & Wagnall's porch since noon today.

Jay Leno is a different story. It's apparent from the moment he steps onstage. As the theme music bubbles to its climax, the lantern-jawed comic practically runs to greet his audience, who crowd the stage to exchange handshakes and high-fives with the *Tonight Show* host. The glad-handing Leno seems less like a political joker than a politician in his own right, pressing the flesh and greeting each well-wisher with a hearty "How ya' doin'?" Leno's production company is called Big Dog, and anyone watching him bound out onto the stage can see why. If he had a tail, it would be wagging.

Having grown up in Andover, Massachusetts, Leno is, geographically speaking, more a Yankee than midwesterners Carson and Letterman. But he's miles away from the cool, WASP-ish reserve of his predecessor, or the prickly detachment of his chief competitor. With his Italian surname, "ethnic" features, and urban energy, Leno was once described as resembling "the immigrant arrival—eager, aggressive, resourceful."[29] That may be a little much—if Carson and Letterman are plain as vanilla, Leno is, by comparison, no more exotic than French vanilla—but he is a somewhat "hotter" television presence than Johnny or Dave: louder, faster-talking, more ingratiating.

In *The Road to Mars,* a fascinating treatise on comedy buried within a so-so science fiction novel, *Monty Python*'s Eric Idle draws on the iconography of clown makeup to divide stand-up comedians into two categories, which he designates as "White Face" and "Red Nose." "The White Face," writes Idle, "is the controlling neurotic and the Red Nose is the rude, rough Pan. The White Face compels your respect; the Red Nose begs for it. The Red Nose smiles and nods and winks, and wants your love; the White Face rejects it. He never smiles; he is always deadly serious. Never more so than when doing comedy."[30]

While it would be a stretch to call any of the late-night hosts a "rude, rough Pan," Leno (along with late-night minor-leaguer Craig Ferguson) is at least a little pink around the nostrils. Carson, Letterman, and Conan O'Brien, on the other hand, are most definitively White Face (as Idle himself told O'Brien in an appearance promoting the book).[31]

That said, it would be a mistake to overemphasize the differences between Jay and Dave. Letterman has in fact acknowledged Leno as one of his major comedic influences. In turn, his frequent guest appearances on Letterman's NBC show were a big boost to Leno's career.

Once they became competitors, their differences were muted rather than sharpened. Carson's twin progeny adapted to the new late-night environment by becoming more like each other, and more like their mutual mentor. Leno's comedy incorporated some Lettermanesque touches, such as featuring members of the show's production crew in mini-sketches. When Letterman moved to CBS and the 11:30 time slot, the show got glitzier and the host more self-consciously ingratiating. The stage of the Ed Sullivan Theater was decked out in unabashed Broadway glamour, as opposed to the funky cheapness of the old *Late Night* studio. Gone were the sneakers and khakis; the New Dave wore expensive suits. Gone, too—or at least submerged—was the bored disdain Old Dave sometimes exhibited when interviewing guests. If he was going to compete in Johnny's time slot, he was going to do his best to emulate the master's good manners.

For his part, Leno adjusted his thermostat, dialing down the emotive, slightly combative tone that had previously characterized his comedy. His appearances on Letterman's old NBC show always kicked off with Dave asking, "What's your beef?"—to which Jay would respond with an amusingly cranky tirade. Leno's "beefs" usually focused on trivial annoyances—stupid commercials, annoying trends, idiotic movies—but they were *complaints,* delivered with an outraged edginess Letterman and his audience found highly entertaining.

But by the time Leno supplanted Letterman on the inside track to take over the *Tonight Show,* some critics and former fans couldn't help asking, "Where's the beef?" "The Leno who opens every *Tonight Show* is a shadow Leno, a beige Leno," wrote the *Los Angeles Times*'s Paul Brownfield. The new Jay seemed tame, domesticated—not like the mock-angry young comic "for whom words were like daggers." For his part, Leno admitted having purposely made his comedy "more bland," but insisted, "this is what I have to do to get the job."[32]

Getting the job entailed a change not only in the tone of Leno's comedy but also in its content. The old Leno may have used words like daggers, but his targets were rarely anything more formidable than fast-food slogans. Once he was in the running for the *Tonight Show* gig, however, he would be expected to tell a lot of jokes about national politics and world events.

Neither Letterman nor Leno became a topical comic due to any driving political passion. Letterman, in fact, had always professed to be bored by politics. In an early interview, he recalled a mid-1970s stint hosting a radio call-in show with little fondness: "The Nixon-Watergate nonsense was the perfect example of something about which I knew nothing and couldn't have cared less."[33] Letterman's political detachment, like his personal remoteness, goes beyond Carson's—past mere neutrality into outright alienation. Carson, for all his careful nonpartisanship, seemed to delight in talking about political events. Underneath his personal aloofness and his carefully maintained detachment, Carson always radiated that "concerted interest in another direction" Rourke ascribed to the Yankee, while Dave's political gags often seem merely obligatory.

Leno didn't betray any more political passion or interest than Letterman in his early career. Nevertheless, he rose to the challenge of co-writing and delivering a convincingly Carsonesque monologue the way he seemed to do everything else: through energy, professionalism, and sheer effort. Leno's first job was auto mechanic, and his blue-collar work ethic is legendary. Even with his current *Tonight Show* duties, he still does something on the order of 150 stand-up dates a year.[34†]

Though some found the end result of Leno's late-night makeover lacking in sincerity or soul, he succeeded pretty well in tailoring himself and his act to fit the Carson model. He not only told more political jokes than Letterman but, according to statistics compiled by *USA Today,* surpassed even Carson, averaging 9.6 topical jokes per monologue, compared to Johnny's 6.4.[35] At least a few observers, including the late political humorist Art Buchwald, claimed Leno's political jokes were also better and sharper than Carson's. But Tom Shales complained that Leno was telling *too many* political jokes, "and not particularly good political jokes, either. . . . Leno forgets that the monologue

---

[†] Leno claims never to have touched a cent of his *Tonight Show* salary, supporting himself, his wife, Mavis, and his car collection on his stand-up roadwork alone.

is not a lecture, it is a conversation." Worse, Shales implied that Leno was doing it all by the numbers. Hosting *Tonight*, wrote Shales, had turned the once-sharp comic into "RoboClown, a heartless joke-telling machine."[36]

Indeed, there is something mechanical about Leno's topical joking, in spite of the flashes of the old "oh, please!" aggression in his delivery. Meanwhile, Letterman's comedy and increasingly frequent "serious" interviews have, in recent years, begun to show unexpected hints of political passion.

Not that these fitful feelings add up to an ideology—Letterman's opinions seem consistent only in their crankiness. While he seemed to regard President Bill Clinton's adulterous escapades with a certain amount of revulsion, Letterman's feelings about George W. Bush have lately curdled into contempt. A running feature titled "Great Moments in Presidential Speeches" that debuted in 2006 exists only to replay Bush's most oafish sound bites. Letterman has shown little patience when interviewing right-wing blowhards Bill O'Reilly and Rush Limbaugh, but seems awfully impressed with macho conservatives like Rudy Giuliani and John McCain (who announced his 2008 presidential bid on *Late Show*).[37] He seems genuinely distressed by global warming, but co-owns a fleet of Indy cars, which probably pump out pretty impressive quantities of greenhouse gasses.

Though he has been called a liberal by conservatives (including O'Reilly), and a "non-voting Republican" by a former writer (a charge to which Letterman responded, on the air, "I'm not registered with any major political party. I'm not a Republican and I vote"), Letterman generally maintains late-night's traditional EOO neutrality.[38] The truth may be that Letterman—like a lot of Americans—has for so long sheathed himself in anti-political cynicism that now that he has begun to care, he doesn't know what to think. John Limon may have the best description of Letterman's unfocused political disaffection: "The conundrum that he seems to confront every day is how it is possible to think dangerously fast yet possess no ideas at all. His condition is the intellectual equivalent of priapism among mannequins. It seems to make him furious."[39]

Neither Leno nor Letterman could fill Carson's shoes, but each succeeded— with some effort and to some extent—in following in his footsteps. They learned from their common ancestor the value of detachment, so necessary for survival in television's treacherous topical-comedy jungle. They learned to use such simple tools as the focus on "character," the public denial of any personal motive behind one's professional fun-making, and the importance of maintaining a "balance" of mockery, doling out the punch lines equally to "both sides."

But if part of Leno and Letterman's adaptation to late-night hosting drew on Carson's precedents, they also responded to the upheavals in their contemporary media environment. The news media's increased focus on "the personal" further encouraged late-night's inherent ad hominem tendencies, as we have already seen. And things continued to get even more personal as the erosion of broadcast standards—fueled by competition with cable—met a timely presidential sex scandal, leading Leno and Letterman's into an R-rated arms race to see who could tell the most and grossest Monica jokes.

All of these factors combined to make Leno/Letterman Era late-night comedy even more profoundly anti-political than it had been in the Age of Carson. Perhaps this was inevitable—the result of ever-increasing public cynicism, coupled with the television networks' innate commercial caution (made even more desperate by the coming of cable). Still, neither Leno nor Letterman chose to distinguish himself by becoming *more* politically engaged, or adopting a tone that was genuinely provocative. Whatever generational "edge" or comedic innovation they brought to late-night, in political (or rather, anti-political) terms, the post-Johnny generation continued to play it safe.

Cono sapiens

"Johnny Carson is the model for all talk-show hosts," Conan O'Brien once told an interviewer. "You never knew his politics. He's a very intelligent man, but you just didn't know. And I think that's the job."[40]

O'Brien had the advantage of entering the late-night arena as an unknown. Before being tapped to take over *Late Night* from the CBS-bound Letterman, he had primarily been a writer—and had never been a stand-up comic. But thanks to the blueprint left by Carson, along with Leno's and Letterman's updates and minor modifications, O'Brien came to the job with a clear idea of what worked, what didn't, and what was expected of a network host. Conan is the first late-night comic whose preparation for the job consisted primarily of observing his predecessors and applying their hard-won lessons.

By the time of O'Brien's 1993 debut, the parameters and procedures of late-night hosting had become as well defined as those of any profession. So instead of serving his apprenticeship in comedy clubs (like Leno) or local radio and television (like Letterman), O'Brien followed the preparatory path common to most other professions: he got a college degree.

In fact, he graduated magna cum laude from Harvard, with a degree in American history. More relevant to O'Brien's future career, though, was the training he received as editor of the *Harvard Lampoon*—a post to which he was elected twice, a distinction he shares with only the renowned humorist Robert Benchley.[41] The Ivy League, and especially the *Lampoon*, have in fact been among professional comedy's main proving grounds (along with Chicago's Second City troupe) for the last couple of decades.[42] But although sitcom and late-night writers' rooms have long been hip-deep in Ivy Leaguers, Conan is Harvard's first network host.

O'Brien's graduate instructors were his late-night predecessors; and he takes something of value from each of them. In his jerky physicality, one can see echoes of Carson's twitchy energy. In his Irish Catholic, off-WASP whiteness, one sees Leno's slightly more urban and "ethnic" variation on Carson's midwesterner/Yankee. In his conceptually adventurous comedy, there are traces of Letterman's more absurdist approach.

Despite his impressive education, O'Brien's early reviews were famously (and unfairly) disparaging. The always acerbic (but often comedically tone-deaf) Tom Shales called O'Brien a "fidgety marionette" and *Late Night* "an hour of aimless dawdle masquerading as a TV program."[43] He actually got up to speed within a remarkably short period of time, considering his lack of on-camera and stand-up experience.

As a topical comedian, O'Brien's lack of a track record may have been an advantage. Letterman was compelled, by Carson's example, to deal comedically with a subject he has found alternatively boring and frustrating. Leno had to modulate his aggressive delivery. O'Brien came to the job with a clear understanding of the necessary balance of intellectual engagement and emotional detachment that had let Carson handle politics with interest but no obvious investment.

You might expect a Harvard history major to have some well-formed ideas about the course of American democracy, but O'Brien's comedy is, for the most part, as anti-politically neutral as that of the other network hosts. However, his show has introduced one innovation that, while protecting the host's neutrality, allows him to at least flirt with genuine satire. This is the aforementioned "Clutch Cargo" feature, in which Conan "interviews" such political celebrities as Bush, Gore, and Clinton, playing straight man to their wildly caricatured doppelgangers, usually voiced by Robert Smigel. At the very least, the "Clutch" pieces raise the comedy of character assassination to a higher level. It is one thing to verbally conjure the stiffness of Al Gore or the denseness of George W. Bush in a monologue joke, quite another to turn the candidates into living embodiments of these traits. "Clutch Cargo" puts flesh on the bones of such premises but also, arguably, connects "character" to political performance in a way that goes beyond easy ad hominem teasing:

> CONAN: Sir, let's talk about your new plan for the war in Iraq. You said you want to send in 21,500 more American troops. Tell us, how did you arrive at the number 21,500?
>
> "PRESIDENT BUSH": Well, it's very simple, Conan. I figured we needed six thousand troops; and then, just to be safe, I doubled it.[44]

Even when Smigel's "Clutch" characterizations threaten to shift the comedy out of anti-political neutral, Conan's cool detachment is never compromised. For all his intelligence and obvious talent, Conan O'Brien does not appear to be driven by anything but the desire to present an entertaining show. "My mantra," he told an interviewer, is "'Funny man, be funny.' . . . I don't hold an elected office and I don't take myself that seriously."[45] Like Carson, Letterman, and Leno before him, O'Brien is not a satirist—just a more refined version of the topical yet anti-political, familiar yet unknowable, late-night host.

THE LAUGH CEILING

As I write, the question being bandied about on TV news and magazine covers, is this: is the U.S. ready to elect a woman or an African American president? Perhaps we shall soon see. But if late-night's standards of mass "acceptability" are any indication, there may be trouble ahead for Hillary Clinton and Barack Obama.

Though I have referred to evolution rather than "intelligent design" (this *is* network television we're talking about, after all) in describing the development of the late-night mainstream, to switch metaphors just for a moment, it is striking to note the abundance of Adams and the lack of a single Eve in this comedic Eden. Forty-plus years since the publication of *The Feminine Mystique,* television talk is still as segregated by sex as it ever was. Female talk-show hosts do not joke about politics, nor do they even take to the air after sundown. Oprah is a phenomenon, Ellen is a treat, *The View* is—well, *The View,* but there are no female Carsons anywhere on the dial.

There have been a handful of attempts to break through late-night's glass ceiling. Joan Rivers parlayed a steady gig as Carson's guest host into her own, competing show. Many believe that this maneuver, which her erstwhile boss and (apparently) much of the viewing public saw as a betrayal, hurt her chances right out of the gate.[46] There was more than a bit of sexism behind the characterization of Rivers as the fickle *femme*; on the other hand, one hardly needs to be a misogynist to dislike Joan Rivers.

The only other notable effort to storm the late-night talk-jock locker room was undertaken by Stephanie Miller, who jumped into the post-Carson fray in 1995. Her comedy definitely showed a polemical edge, but *The Stephanie Miller Show* ended after a run of only four and a half months. After bumping around the Lifetime network for a while, Miller eventually found her niche as the host of a progressive—and genuinely satirical—syndicated talk radio show.[47]

The most successful woman in all of late-night television so far has been Tina Fey, who served as *SNL*'s head writer and co-anchor of "Weekend Update" from 2000 to 2006.[48] Fey was praised for "reviving" the show (*SNL* has, at this point, been reanimated more often than Frankenstein's monster and Rocky Balboa put together), and her appointment to head the writer's room did much to offset the franchise's sexist reputation.

But Fey was also criticized for soft-pedaling the show's political humor (which, as nostalgists always seem to forget, had always accounted for a fairly small percentage of *SNL*'s comedic content) in favor of catty attacks on celebrities. "Veterans of *SNL*, as well as longtime fans, wonder whether a show that once built skits around Chevy Chase's impression of Gerald Ford . . . can still be regarded as dangerous or inventive when it now takes aim at sitting ducks like Britney Spears," wrote Dave Itzkoff in the *New York Times*.[49] Fey's defenders pointed out that *SNL* was hardly unique in its ever-increasing focus on celebrity-bashing humor (so easy, even David Spade can do it!). Furthermore, the fact that women also comprise a minority of officeholders meant that there were few opportunities for the Fey era's popular female cast members, Amy Poehler, Rachel Dratch, and Maya Rudolph, to develop political impersonations.[50]

A fairer criticism of Fey's *SNL*—particularly her own performance on "Weekend Update"—concerns the tendency to deliver every joke in a self-conscious, insincere, too-cool-for-school manner. "Did you like that one?" Fey seemed to ask—and often literally *did* ask—after delivering a punch line. Whether this reflected feminine insecurity or yet another encroachment of postmodern meta-humor, it robbed some fairly good topical jokes of their sting. Worse, it shattered any sense of "Update" as a parody of a news program (though perhaps Lorne Michaels has decided to cede that territory to Comedy Central).

A more promising sign for the future of female political satirists is the example of *The Daily Show*'s Samantha Bee. While it's true that she is only the latest in a long line of the show's "token" female performers, she is also the first who has been allowed just as wide a range of topics, and as much screen time, as any of the show's male correspondents.[51] Whether this encouraging development should be credited to Bee's talent (she's a very funny performer) or to some belated enlightenment on the part of the show's producers ("If Lorne Michaels can learn that women are funny, so can we!") is unclear.

In any event, Bee is the first fake-newswoman (the smirking Fey, cutesy Amy Poehler, and "Get a load of these, Connie Chung!" Jane Curtin notwithstanding) for whom gender is as inconsequential as it has become for real newswomen—which is to say, not entirely, but progress is progress.

Though women make up half of the U.S. population and more than half of its voters, they have always represented a minority of stand-up comics. The well-marinated journalist/provocateur Christopher Hitchens raised a bit of a stink when he wrote in *Vanity Fair* that the few genuinely funny female comics tended to be "hefty or dykey or Jewish, or some combination of the three."[52] Conventional sexist wisdom suggests that stand-up is too "assertive" an idiom for most women to master, or even to want to pursue— the same cliché, it should be noted, that was routinely invoked by those who opposed female suffrage and women's participation in politics. It is nonsense, of course. Women's participation in stand-up has been steadily increasing for years, and the proportion of funny-to-unfunny is about the same as for male comics. On the political side, the House of Representatives has its first woman Speaker in Nancy Pelosi, and the first woman president might not be far behind. More female politicians will almost certainly mean more room for women in political comedy, and in the coming years we may see a female Leno, or even a Samantha Bee sitting in Jon Stewart's chair.

SOCIAL DARWINISM?

On television, as in national politics, to be black or female is to be *something*—and for a late-night host, this is a handicap. The rare privilege to come into millions of American living rooms to talk about matters political is given only to the cool, un-"ethnic," unaccented "everyman" (accent on the "man"—better yet, accent on "the Man"). The ideal mainstream host, it seems, must be not only unobjectionable (sure, Dick Gregory's funny, but how is he going to play in the rural South?) but unobtrusive enough to avoid getting in the way of the jokes. And for this he must be—literally—colorless.

If late-night is still waiting for its Sally Ride or Sandra Day O'Connor to bridge the gender gap, it also awaits a Jackie Robinson or Thurgood Marshall to broach the color line. For a short period in the early 1990s, Arsenio Hall appeared to be late-night's Great Black Hope. He was an unlikely host, differing from the Carson prototype in more than just pigmentation. Arsenio was "cool"—not in McLuhan's definition of the word but in the more common sense, meaning "hip." Unlike Carson, Paar, and Letterman, he was no midwestern hayseed; nor was he a benign goof like Conan or Leno. While his "blackness" was far from threatening—Arsenio was no Eldridge Cleaver, or even Snoop Dogg—he did bring a somewhat brasher, urban, after-hours "edge" to late-night. *The Arsenio Hall Show*'s more assertive sensibility was apparent before the host even began speaking. Whereas Carson burst through the *Tonight Show* curtain with a flurry of fidgety gestures, and Letterman loped toward center stage smirking, in suit coat and sneakers, Arsenio stood in silhouette, index fingers pressed together, head slightly bowed—a self-regarding pose that communicated "attitude" rather than self-conscious reserve.

This was something new in itself—and the novelty of *Arsenio*'s flashy style, along with a roster of younger, hipper guests, succeeded in attracting a new audience to late-night. The show, as Bill Carter noted, "truly had a different sensibility for late night: It wasn't a talk show as much as a big, fun party, geared expressly for the young party crowd. Arsenio didn't break the color barrier in late-night as much as he broke the hip barrier."[53] Of the many would-be challengers rival networks and syndicators trotted out to face Carson over the years, none made the TV establishment—including NBC—sit up and take notice like Hall. While Arsenio's viewership did not approach *The Tonight Show*'s in terms of total numbers, his show scored impressively in the 18-to-34-year-old demographic, the sweet spot of TV ratings in the post-network era. Hall's success with this group suggested that he understood the new playing field better than Carson's other challengers. What Rivers, Sajak, and the rest "all had in common is that they tried to out-Johnny Johnny," Hall told *Newsweek*. "I'm not going after Johnny's crowd. I'm going after Johnny's crowd's kids."[54]

Yet Hall knew his demographically targeted challenge to *The Tonight Show* could go only so far as long as Johnny remained on the scene. Despite their competitive relationship, Hall showed nothing but respect for late-night's gray eminence and the institution he had built. When Carson entered his final week before retirement, Hall put his own show on hiatus and urged his fans to tune in to *Tonight*.[55]

But Arsenio came out swinging against his new competitor (and erstwhile "friend"), Jay Leno. For the first time in thirty years, the late-night lead was up for grabs, and Hall intended to go for it, telling *Entertainment Weekly* that he was going to "kick Jay's ass."[56] It was an empty threat. In short order, the bulk of Hall's 18- to 34-year-olds deserted him for the new host of *Tonight* and for Letterman's promised new 11:30 show (which, not so incidentally, cost the syndicated *Arsenio* many of its client stations).[57] Only five years after his debut, Hall's late-night career was over.

Yet the writing was on the wall from the beginning: as Carter noted, "the hip crowd . . . never finds anything hip for the long term."[58] As far as breaking the color barrier, Hall's brief ascendancy was probably more a function of the fracturing of the mass audience than a sign of its multicultural enlightenment. In fact, there is little reason to believe that the comedy audience has gotten less segregated in the thirty years since Flip Wilson had a popular NBC variety show and *Good Times* and *The Jeffersons* were sitcom hits. This was the network era, after all, and to succeed, these shows had to appeal to black and white viewers. Compare this high tide of "crossover" comedy to the *Original Kings of Comedy* phenomenon, documented by Spike Lee's 2000 concert film. *Kings* was a long-running stand-up tour, featuring African American comics, which played to sold-out, all-Black arena crowds, and advertised only on "black" radio stations and in the Black Press.[‡] Vaudeville may be dead, but what used to be called the "chittlin' circuit" has quietly risen again.[59]

And it has risen on cable TV, as well. Arsenio might have had a longer run on BET or Comedy Central (which has aired Lee's film several times), but narrowcasting didn't become viable in time to save him. Still, the show never would have had as long a broadcast run as it did if it had attracted only

---

[‡] *Kings* inspired a slew of other comedy tours and (mainly non-theatrical) films aimed at various subsets of the population: *The Original Queens of Comedy, The Original Latin Kings of Comedy,* and Jeff Foxworthy's *Blue Collar Comedy Tour,* now a Comedy Central series.

African American viewers. Much of *Arsenio*'s young audience was in fact white, but we should not be too quick to read their short-lived infatuation with the show as evidence that America is ready to judge hosts not by the color of their skin but by the content of their comedy.[60] We cannot overlook the peculiarly American phenomenon of racial voyeurism—which also manifests itself in the popularity of hip-hop music and fashion among sub-urban, and even rural, white kids. For some portion of Arsenio's audience, watching this cool, "urban" performer from the comfort of a suburban living room (or one's parents' living room) was a safe way to hear some top hip-hop acts, check out the host's credibly stylish clothes, and pick up on the lat-est "ghetto-authentic" slang.

It may be unfair to Arsenio and his viewers to credit his brief success to exoticism and the novelty of "hip"—but there was, it must be said, little else to explain it. Hall was, at best, a mediocre comic, and his monologues were notably and consistently weak. His manner when interviewing guests was often unbearably obsequious, leading at least one critic to dub him "Merv Griffin's show-biz heir-apparent" (though, to be fair, none of the post-Carson network hosts is any great shakes as an interviewer, either).[61]

Was *Arsenio*'s ultimate failure a sign that the late-night mainstream was "not ready" for a black host? Is the fact that neither his show nor the Quincy Jones–produced, Sinbad-hosted *Vibe* had a broad enough base to stay on the air something that ought to make Barack Obama think twice about his pres-idential prospects?[62] Or was Hall's fall nothing more than the result of weak jokes and the short shelf-life of "hip"?

It's impossible to say for sure, just as there is no way of knowing whether the environment has changed since 1994, when *Arsenio* went off the air. Certainly there are more opportunities for African American comedians on television now than in most of the medium's history: *Kings* Steve Harvey, Bernie Mac, Cedric the Entertainer, and D. L. Hughley have all enjoyed at least a shot at prime-time success, and *BET ComicView* will apparently point its camera at anyone darker than Jerry Seinfeld who knows at least two jokes.[63]

Post-*Arsenio* television has seen some notable African American forays into satire, as well. Dave Chapelle enjoyed a short-lived but spectacular "crossover" success with his sketch-comedy *Chapelle's Show* on Comedy Central. Politics was on the table, but race was always the central focus—see, for example, his depiction of "Black Bush" trying to justify a preemptive strike against Saddam Hussein's Iraq: "This niggah very possibly has weapons of mass destruction. I can't sleep on that. . . . That's not how I roll. That shit's serious. Now, if you don't want to take my word for it, why don't you ax Tony Blair?"[64] The sketch throws the administration's arrogance and dishonesty into sharp relief by translating it into a black idiom. (The danger of this approach, as Chappelle would learn, is that it is not entirely clear who bears the brunt of the joke.)

The Chris Rock Show (1997–2000), featuring some topical material and one of the best stand-ups ever to take the mike, also deserves mention. But these successes are inseparable from the phenomenon of narrowcasting—Rock's show was on HBO—and the emergence of a video "chitlin' circuit" is not a sign that the "mainstream" television audience has broadened its collective mind.

The question remains: given that he could reliably bring the funny, would a network-size chunk of the viewing public accept a "black Leno" joking about politics in the approved, anti-political way, five nights a week? The backdrop of American history—even just our television history—inevitably means that an African American comic who addresses politics will be understood as representing a "black" perspective (or even *the* black perspective). As funny and talented as they are, not even Dave Chappelle and Chris Rock could transcend this situation.

Nor can *The Daily Show* escape the straitjacket of color—though they have found a way to satirize it, recruiting Larry Wilmore (a seasoned TV writer, producer, and occasional performer whose credits include *The Bernie Mac Show* and *The Office*) to be the show's "Senior Black Correspondent." The meta-joke is that Wilmore is only called upon to address "black" topics, like Madonna's African "adoption" and former senator George Allen's "macaca" moment.[65] The designation of a "Senior Black Correspondent" can be understood as making a subtle satirical point about television's tendency to treat any African American as representative of *all* African Americans (overheard at CNN: "The first black player in the NHL? Call Jesse Jackson for a comment!"). But it can also be seen as an admission of defeat—if not for comedy, then for the liberal view *The Daily Show* implicitly champions. Though things have apparently progressed to a point where Samantha Bee can function as a Correspondent Who Happens to Be Female, Wilmore can still only be a Black Correspondent.

In the minds of television's decision-makers, if not the viewing public, race is still too "something" to allow an African American comic to subordinate identity to material—an absolute necessity for a mainstream, antipolitical host. Still, if the role of equal-opportunity offender is not an equal-opportunity calling, genuine satirists—who are not obliged to be neutral and "blank"—can come in any color. At some point, Arsenio seemed to grasp this fact (or perhaps he was just grasping at straws), turning up the political heat as his ratings cooled down. "[George H. W.] Bush wants to be everything," Hall said in a 1992 monologue, "the education president, the environment president, the business president. I personally won't be happy until he's an ex-president."[66]

In late-night terms, this was a remarkably polemical joke—more of a declaration, in fact—and there were more where that came from. When a Bush spokesman went out of his way to say that although the president had not ruled out appearing on other late-night shows, he would definitely not be seeking equal time on Hall's, where his Democratic rival Bill Clinton had made a celebrated, sax-playing cameo, Hall responded with indignation and no little sarcasm:

> Excuse me, George Herbert, irregular heart-beating, read-my-lying-lipping, slipping in the polls, do-nothing, deficit-raising, make less money than Millie the White House dog last year, Quayle-loving, sushi-puking Bush. I don't remember inviting your ass to my show. I don't need you on my show. My ratings are higher than yours.[67]

This was a departure from Carsonesque reserve, to say the least. Aside from their unequal-opportunity offender partisanship, Hall's remarks here reflect an unmistakable first-person, editorial perspective: "*I personally* won't be happy,"

"*I* don't need you on *my* show." When the mainstreamers employ the personal pronoun, they are likely to be setting up a self-deprecating joke; current events jokes are delivered in a matter-of-fact, reportorial fashion: "President Bush today. . . ." "Did you see in the news that Bill Clinton. . . ." Johnny Carson not only didn't reveal his opinion, he rarely even hinted that he *had* an opinion.

Hall's bracing (though still not really funny) political passion was too little, too late. What's more, it was probably too "hot" for broadcast television. Viable TV satire would have to wait for the era of narrowcasting ushered in by *The Daily Show,* and African American TV satire would have to wait for Rock, Chapelle, and Wilmore. It also seems clear that America will have to wait, possibly for a long time, before we reach the point where the full privileges of late-night host—especially the right to joke about politics for a broad, "mainstream" audience—are within the grasp of comedians who don't share Johnny Carson's color or gender.

The Goy Next Door

Within the larger context of comedy history, perhaps the most surprising aspect of late-night's homogeneity is the fact that none of the successful mainstream hosts have been Jewish. When Carson began his *Tonight Show* tenure in 1962, his unmistakable *goyischeness* set him apart from the majority of leading stand-up comedians. Steve Allen, *Tonight's* original host (also not Jewish, though he was often assumed to be), estimated that 80 percent of the nationally known comics working at that time were Jewish.[68] Given this unscientific but plausible statistic, the fact that Carson, his late-night predecessors, and his mainstream heirs have all been *goyim* seems not just anomalous, but unfair— why not *The Tonight Show Starring Shecky Greene?* The role of late-night host is, after all, perhaps the pinnacle of the profession—the steadiest job in stand-up, with annual paychecks in the millions. The fact that no Jewish comedians received these plum positions, despite their prominence in the field, is a historical injustice on a par with Elvis getting the rock and roll kudos that more properly belonged to Chuck Berry and Little Richard, or Benny Goodman— rather than, say, Count Basie—being dubbed "King of Swing."

1. President Gerald Ford meets *Saturday Night Live*'s Chevy Chase and Lorne Michaels at the 1976 Radio and Television Correspondents Association Dinner, before the administration's co-optation strategy went awry. *Courtesy Gerald R. Ford Library*.

2. First Lady Laura Bush keeping the D.C./Hollywood connection open with an appearance on *The Tonight Show with Jay Leno*, April 26, 2005. White House photo by Krisanne Johnson. *Courtesy The White House Media Office*.

3. Stephen Colbert's opening act: President Bush and his doppelgänger, Steve Bridges, at the White House Correspondents Association Dinner in 2006. White House photo by Kimberlee Hewitt. *Courtesy The White House Media Office.*

4. No armchair patriot, David Letterman made a surprise visit to Iraq over Christmas 2004. Here he interviews U.S. Marine Cpl. Wesley McNallie of Marine Wing Support Squadron 373, at Camp Taqaddum. *U.S. Department of Defense Photo.*

5. Let the Eagle Soar: Stephen Colbert uses the guise of a conservative super-
patriot to sink his talons into his satirical targets. *Photo by Martin Crook.*
Courtesy Comedy Central.

6. Though he maintains the pretense of being an "equal-opportunity offender," *The Daily Show*'s Jon Stewart has carved out a niche for genuine satire—and intelligent conversation—in late-night. *Photo by Norman Jean Roy. Courtesy Comedy Central.*

7. *Daily Show* correspondent Samantha Bee proves that women can excel at political—not just "social"—satire. *Photo by Frank Ockenfels. Courtesy Comedy Central.*

8. Artemus Ward (Charles Farrar Browne), an "equal opportunity offender" of the Civil War era and one of President Abraham Lincoln's favorite humorists.

9. Petroleum V. Nasby (David Ross Locke), another Lincoln favorite, played Colbert to Artemus Ward's Leno. *Library of Congress.*

10. The master of the anti-political mainstream meets a future firebrand of satirical "authenticity": Johnny Carson and Bill Maher on *The Tonight Show* in 1985. *Photo by Ron Tom/NBCU Photo Bank. Copyright © NBC Universal, Inc.*

11. "Almost the only first-string American statesman who managed to combine high office with humor was Lincoln, and he was murdered finally," E. B. White observed in 1952. Television's growing dominance would turn humor into a political asset. *Photo by Anthony Berger, 1864. Library of Congress.*

12. John F. Kennedy, the first television president, and only the second funny one. Photo by Abbie Rowe. *Courtesy John F. Kennedy Presidential Library and Museum.*

13. Ronald Reagan, the third head on the comedic Mount Rushmore. *Library of Congress.*

14. Conan O'Brien visiting the U.S. Embassy in Helsinki. O'Brien was not constrained by a need to maintain "balance" when he lent his tongue-in-cheek support to Finland's look-alike presidential candidate Tarja Halonen. *U.S. State Department.*

15. Finland's president, Tarja Halonen. Conan's support may have helped her win reelection. *Photo by Roosewelt Pinheiro. Agencia Brasil.*

Certainly it would be unfair to blame the performers for this discrimination. In fact, just as Benny Goodman used his clout to break the color line in jazz, Johnny Carson welcomed such non-WASP comic performers as Mel Brooks (who appeared on Carson's first show), Jack Benny (his acknowledged role model and main influence), Steve Landesberg, David Steinberg, and many other Jewish comics, not to mention female comics like Rivers, and African American comics like Flip Wilson and Richard Pryor. As Frank Rich noted, the "exotic" guests Carson introduced to Middle America included "even the occasional recognizable homosexual, like Truman Capote."[69] In terms of reflecting American diversity, late-night was ahead of the television curve—except when it came to the man behind the desk.

The pattern has been so consistent, John Limon found Martin Scorsese's casting of Jerry Lewis as a Carsonesque host in 1982's *King of Comedy* utterly implausible. "Don't they understand that Jerry Lewis cannot under any circumstances be *The Tonight Show* host?" he writes. "Its star must be a pseudo-hick with attitude arriving in New York from the heartland; he hosts Jewishness there. . . . He cannot be a Jew himself."[70] It seems that American "kings"—of swing, of rock and roll, and of late-night—are always white, and usually WASPs (except for the Original Kings of Comedy!).

The presumed or actual anti-Semitism of the American public has apparently diminished somewhat since the days when stars like Bernie Schwartz and Betty Perske routinely changed their names to WASPy monikers like Tony Curtis and Lauren Bacall. But if you don't count Joey Bishop's meager two-year run at ABC, it was left for Jon Stewart to definitively break late-night's "Jew barrier." Even then, he proved only able to do so at the basic cable level—prior to landing *The Daily Show,* Stewart hosted a short-lived syndicated show and was considered for the 12:30 CBS slot, before being—pardon the expression—passed over.[71]

In spite of changing his name from Jonathan Stuart Leibowitz, Stewart is no "look Yiddish, act Briddish" assimilationist.[72] He often calls attention to his Jewishness for satirical purposes, as when *The Daily Show*'s correspondents tweak him with some vaguely anti-Semitic remark. Stewart also draws heavily on Jewish-comedic history, frequently slipping into a Woody Allen or Jerry Lewis cadence for effect.

As successful and unabashedly "Jewy" (to use his favored term) as Stewart may be, *The Daily Show* is still a fringe phenomenon, and the late-night mainstream remains a WASP bastion comparable to the no-Jews-allowed "restricted" country clubs that were still commonplace in America until fairly recent times. However this earlier injustice may have limited the PGA prospects of Jewish golfers, though, it hardly approaches the irony of late-night's de facto discrimination. American Jews have a historical, cultural claim on stand-up comedy. Jews' disproportionate success in comedy is similar to African Americans' disproportionate success in professional sports, and arises from some of the same factors: discrimination that barred access to more "legitimate" professions, and the comparatively meritocratic nature of sports and show biz (the Old Boy Network can't help you if you're not funny, or haven't got game).

And even these professions didn't exactly welcome minorities with open arms. With many stages and playing fields closed to them, both Jews and blacks found opportunities in "alternative" institutions and circuits (the Borscht Belt, the Negro Leagues) that paralleled the mainstream, even if they didn't offer the same rewards. Negro League great Cool Papa Bell was once heard to complain, "They used to say, 'If we find a good black player, we'll sign him.' They was lying."[73] One doubts that Jon Stewart regards his high-profile basic cable niche with the same frustration. Still, if even Jewishness—a biographical fact common to so many popular and familiar comedians—continues to constitute a handicap for those who would deign to discuss politics on late-night TV, what chance do other minorities have?

SATIRICAL MAN

What really sets Jon Stewart apart from the mainstream hosts, though, is not his religion, but his faith in the political process. Carson's interest in politics was keen, but mostly recreational. For Letterman and for Leno, dealing with pols and elections seems to be largely a matter of professional obligation. Jon Stewart actually *cares* about politics—which distinguishes him not only from the other late-night hosts, but from most American citizens. He's different enough from the anti-political evolutionary line to be considered a representative of a separate species: *Homo satiricus*.

As smart and as funny as *The Daily Show*'s scripted material usually is, Stewart's interviews with authors and newsmakers are sometimes even more engaging. Though he is constantly on the lookout for a laugh line, Stewart usually comes to these "serious" interviews well prepared (if his guest is an author, he's almost always read the book) and ready to argue, in a lighthearted yet intelligent and persistent manner. Since he is easily smarter than the vast majority of television journalists (if this strikes you as an exaggeration, you have never watched Paula Zahn, Glenn Beck, Rita Cosby, Nancy Grace, Soledad and/or Miles O'Brian, the network morning shows, or Fox News at any hour of the day), this is a real treat.

Though no polemicist, Stewart is identifiably liberal—the show's comedic tone suggests this, and his interviews seem to confirm it. However, he is by no means an ideologue or a partisan cheerleader. Stewart and the show's writers can be counted on, in fact, to follow the equal-opportunity offender credo most of the time, missing few opportunities to take liberal politicians and the Democratic Party to task. It seems likely—and Stewart has often said as much—that the disproportionate amount of *Daily Show* airtime devoted to Republican foibles is more a function of who is currently in power than a determined ideological agenda. (Perhaps we shall see, after 2008.)[74]

To the extent that one can trace the outlines of Stewart's politics from such clues, they are more centrist than anything else. Though he shows the usual EEO contempt for parties, he evinces an enduring faith in bipartisanship, which is either noble or naïve. Stewart seems prone to value "authenticity" over ideology. (Like Letterman, he has shown a tendency to gush over supposed "straight-talker" John McCain.) He gives no quarter to far-left icons like Hugo Chavez and Fidel Castro. And despite his barely contained outrage at the Bush administration, Stewart is dismissive of more vitriolic critics who regard the president and his minions as demonic (Cheney excepted). Only in the Fox-ified climate of the last few years could such moderate views be deemed "radical."

In his anchorman role, Stewart generally plays the voice of reason, while the show's correspondents toss barely exaggerated chunks of conventional wisdom up like skeet, inviting Stewart to shoot them down in the name of all that is good and sane. Like O'Brien in his "Clutch Cargo" interviews, Stewart takes the role of straight man in these segments, leaving the outrageousness to others.

In short, Stewart is no *Air America*–style stump speaker for his (moderately) liberal views. The distinction between an anti-political and a political orientation—the difference between Stewart's satire and Carson/Leno/ Letterman/O'Brien's pseudo-satire—comes down to a basic question of democratic faith. Wherever he falls on the left–right spectrum, Stewart's comedic feet are firmly planted on the premise that government is—at least potentially—more a positive good than a necessary evil, and that political participation, far from being futile, is a privilege and a patriotic duty. For Stewart, as for the EOO mainstream, all things political are fair game; the difference is that he does not therefore pretend that they are *only* a game. On election eve, 2004, Stewart urged his viewers to vote, "not because it's cool, because it's not"—adding, with obvious sincerity, "On a personal note, I am a comedian who makes fun of what I believe to be the absurdities of our government. *Make my life difficult. . . .* I'd like that. I'm *tired*."[75]

While Leno, Letterman, and O'Brien have fans, Stewart has admirers. It is not just his comedy—good as it is—that earns respect but the seriousness that comes through in his newsmaker interviews, his memorable smack-down of CNN's shout-fest *Crossfire* (when, in a testy guest appearance he asked the hosts to "stop hurting America"), and sincere moments like his plea to "make my life difficult." Though *The Daily Show* has a tiny audience compared to the mainstream shows, its impact is considerable—and its value, for the disaffected citizens who find it a source not only of entertainment but of hope, is incalculable.

STAND-UP CHAMELEONS

The racist philosophy of "social Darwinism" was used to justify discrimination against minorities well into the twentieth century. Late-night's evolutionary process was not deliberately racist and sexist, but given the networks' institutional caution and the "colorlessness" the role of mainstream host seems to require, it might as well have been.

If late-night's failure to accommodate women and minorities results only from such indirect discrimination, the networks' rejection of genuinely satirical political comedy is direct and deliberate. Television has not traditionally provided a friendly environment for Satirical Man. *The Daily Show* could not have emerged, much less thrived, in the era before narrowcasting provided a somewhat more conducive environment.

Even Stewart only takes satire so far. Like the mainstream hosts, Jon Stewart appears on television as "himself," and though he reveals more political passion than his mainstream peers (possibly because there is more there to reveal), it still behooves him to play things a little coy—even to make some rather deliberate gestures in the direction of "balance." By lobbing the occasional EOO joke, Stewart maintains his credibility as an impartial judge of political silliness. Were he to openly embrace an ideological agenda, Stewart would be in danger of becoming a Dennis Miller of the left—and no one wants to see that.

There is, however, another possible adaptation that might allow Satirical Man to make polemical points without lapsing into straightforward advocacy. In evolutionary terms, it's an age-old trick, successfully employed by the snowshoe hare, various snakes, and chameleons: camouflage.

Instead of cultivating mainstream blankness, the would-be satirist can avoid the commercial and comedic risks of talking politics by simply pretending to be someone else. By imposing an alternative, invented "self" between himself and his audience, the comedian can take a position without taking responsibility for it. Adopting a persona is the television equivalent of using a pen name, as abolitionist David Ross Locke did when writing as Confederate sympathizer Petroleum V. Nasby.

This is Stephen Colbert's method, and though, like Stewart's, his success is defined within the narrowcast boundaries of basic cable, it is nonetheless a significant breakthrough in televised political humor. Colbert's same-named alter ego has given him the freedom to carry satire as far as it has ever gone on American television, without lapsing into preachiness or scaring off sponsors.

"Stephen Colbert"—the persona, as distinct from the performer—is a self-righteous and self-regarding conservative pundit, modeled on such un-ironic bloviators as Joe Scarborough, Pat Buchanan, and "Papa Bear" Bill O'Reilly. Posing as an unreliable spokesman for the purposes of satire is an age-old technique—Jonathan Swift's "Modest Proposal" being the most famous literary example. But though "character comics"—comic performers who perform in the first person but not as their true selves, like Andy Kaufman and the "Wild and Crazy" Steve Martin—have had some success on television, they have not generally used their undercover status to comment on current events.**

Still, Colbert's approach does have at least one late-night predecessor. The closest Johnny Carson came to genuine political satire was when he put on a plaid hunting jacket and earflap-cap to play Floyd R. Turbo (or, as he always identified himself, "Floyd R. Turbo, American"). Turbo was introduced as an angry citizen who had stepped forward to deliver an "editorial rebuttal."†† Turbo's views were unfailingly reactionary: he was in favor of capital punishment and nuclear energy, opposed to gun control and women's rights.

Presenting such positions as the views of a "redneck ignoramus," as Johnny once described Turbo, would seem to constitute an unambiguous, if only implicit, argument in the opposite direction. Indeed, as Carson explained to *TV Guide*, "What you're doing is showing the stupidity of that particular view so that you can make your point comedically. If he's for handguns and wants everybody to arm themselves, it's obvious to anybody who's watching, the point we're trying to make." As if to confirm that they were reading him loud and clear, the left-liberal magazine *The Nation* reprinted Turbo's pro-nuke editorial under the appreciative headline "Johnny Carson Sets Us Straight."[76]

But these quasi-satirical forays didn't ruffle any feathers, or damage Carson's reputation for evenhandedness. Putting on the costume and the name (or, in

---

**The notable prime-time exception being Pat Paulsen, the deader-than-deadpan "presidential candidate" featured on *The Smothers Brothers Comedy Hour*.

†† Televised editorials (so labeled) and rebuttals are now a relic of the days of the FCC's "Fairness Doctrine," which stipulated that the stations broadcasting opinions had to allow equal time for those with opposing viewpoints. Fox News could not have existed before the Fairness Doctrine was repealed.

Colbert's case, merely the attitude) of a different person introduces a protective layer of ambiguity, which keeps the performer from being held responsible for what his character says. In fact, even those viewers who might have agreed with Turbo's right-wing views probably laughed at him. He was, after all, a funny character—Carson's best and most original.

Part of what made Turbo work was that, while he surely resembled some of the rural and small-town midwesterners Carson grew up around, he was Johnny's opposite in several obvious respects. Carson came from the sticks and conquered the city; Turbo comes to the city and is conquered—even in a TV studio, he remains a hick. Carson was, for a time, a trendsetter in men's fashion; Turbo always appeared in full Elmer Fudd hunting mufti, wearing his unhipness on his plaid flannel sleeve. Carson's relationship with the TV camera was almost uncannily symbiotic; Turbo is a comically inept television presence, with ill-timed gestures (after using the phrase "I, for one," Turbo would raise his index finger to indicate "one") and a collection of nervous tics that were as off-putting as Johnny's were endearing.

And if Turbo could be enjoyed on a non-political level, the character also worked on an anti-political level. Though his views, to those who disagreed with them, might have seemed silly, Turbo *himself* was silly for having the courage of his ill-considered convictions. Right or wrong, smart or dumb, Turbo was also a sincere ideologue—which, given many Americans' low regard for politics per se, could be considered the most laughable thing about him.

Colbert's character is less a cartoon than Turbo. "Stephen Colbert" wears nice suits, possesses an impressive vocabulary, and always knows which camera is on. In contrast to Floyd R. Turbo's unlikely moniker, "Stephen Colbert's" name is no sillier than that of the real person behind it—in fact, their names are the same. Colbert's "Colbert" is a subtle creation, and a role performed with impressive skill. Colbert deserves an Emmy, though it might require the invention of a new category: "Best Performance as Yourself, Only Not."

Unlike Turbo, though, "Stephen Colbert" could not have made it in the pre-narrowcasting era—the political message, despite the ironic filter, is too unambiguous for network pseudo-satire. Conservatives would find little reason to laugh at the sheer silliness of the character as they could with Turbo. With Colbert, there's no joke unless you get the subtext.

Even if it is only on cable, the Colbert persona provides its creator with the freedom to boldly go where no television comedian with a regular late-night gig has gone before. The greatest danger the real Stephen Colbert faces may not be the threat to his career arising from nervous advertisers or angry ex-viewers but the threat to his own sense of identity, arising from the success of his first-person Frankenstein act. "I think I need to start calling him Col-*bear,* and me Col-*bert,*" he mused in a *Time* magazine interview. "It's getting weird."[77]

Survival of the Fittest?

Stand-up comedy really is a struggle to survive. Even the trade jargon— "I killed," "I died"—reflects this. The tricky business of talking politics on television presents its own challenges; as the long list of late-night extinctions attests, it's a jungle out there. To succeed in the late-night mainstream, one must not only deliver the comedic goods but also connect with the audience with the proper balance of aloofness and intimacy. The comedian who can routinely handle such volatile subject matter must be a cool customer; yet, as a "host" and a nightly presence in millions of homes, he must also seem welcoming and familiar. Carson, Letterman, Leno, and O'Brien represent a rare breed—but compared to genuine satirists like Stewart, Colbert, and others yet to be considered, they are toothless and clawless.

CHAPTER 6

TRUTH VERSUS TRUTHINESS; OR, LOOKING FOR MR. SMITH

There's an old question about the proper role of elected representatives: should they be leaders, or followers of the popular will; the people's champions, or merely their surrogates? We might ask the same question about our topical comedians.[1] The extra-ordinary men of the network mainstream are clearly stand-ins for us regular schlubs. Johnny Carson made the kind of jokes *we* would make about the president, if we were clever enough; he asked Dean Martin and Elizabeth Taylor what *we* would ask them, if we had the chance (and weren't too star-struck to speak). Conan, Jay, and Dave, too, are pretty much like us—but with shows.

Bill Maher isn't like us. Neither is Dennis Miller. Nor is Al Franken, or the gang at Air America radio. They are the Champions—our fearless comedic crusaders. They tell us what they think, not what they think we want to hear. Compared to the invisible men of the mainstream, these polemical comics assert a strong, even combative, individual presence. They are the comedic equivalents of larger-than-life pundits like Rush Limbaugh and Bill O'Reilly and, like them, justify their role by insisting on their own authenticity. Though they still aim to be funny, we are to believe that they are giving it to us straight—telling us the capital-*T* Truth.

This is a perfectly plausible stance for a satirist to take. H. L. Mencken and Lenny Bruce set themselves up as bold defiers of the prevailing falsity. The problem in applying this critique to the workings of government is that comedy and politics have entirely different relationships to Truth. Truth is the essence of comedy; in politics, it is peripheral at best.

This is not intended as a glib or cynical observation—it's just that comedy and politics have very different goals. Comedy is cathartic; politics is practical. Comedy is about getting satisfaction; politics is about getting results. Comedy is straightforward; politics is, of necessity, anything but.

Moreover, comedy, as we have seen, proceeds from *agreement*. Jay Leno and his audience *agree* that George W. Bush is dumb. David Letterman and his audience *agree* that Bill Clinton is one horny dude. The dynamic is the same for polemicists like Miller and Franken, assuming each is preaching to his respective choir: successful topical jokes affirm what the teller and the listener already believe. Politics, on the other hand, proceeds from *disagreement*. If we all agreed on war, taxes, abortion, health care, monetary policy, stem cell research, and so on, there would be no need for politics. Comedy is a search for truth; politics is a search for solutions we can all live with.

Thus politics is inherently less satisfying than comedy. Which is why the easiest kind of topical comedy—the equal-opportunity offender stuff the mainstream hosts have offered us over the past four decades—is based on a rejection of politics. It's too frustrating, too endless, too *hard*. To their credit, polemical comics like Maher, Miller, and Franken have avoided this easy route, for one more challenging, and perhaps more worthwhile. The question is whether it is worth it. In comedy or in politics, is authenticity all it's cracked up to be?

Truth Porn

It's been said that if you scratch a cynic, you will find a disillusioned romantic, and this is true of the anti-political American public. Though we affect hard-bitten hopelessness, we long, almost pathetically, for a politics of authenticity. Show us a candidate who talks "straight," and we will vote for him. Give us a Mr. Smith, and we'll see that he goes to Washington. Stop giving us bull and give us *Bulworth*!

Would a more authentic politics really do us any good, though? Consider a recent statement on Iraq by erstwhile straight-talk poster boy John McCain, as reported in the *New York Observer*: "One of the things I would do if I were President would be to sit the Shiites and the Sunnis down and say, 'Stop the bullshit.'"[2]

What "bullshit" is that, senator? The thirteen centuries of sectarian division? Ethnic and tribal conflicts that date back even further? The legacies of colonialism and forty years of Ba'athist dictatorship? That bullshit? Imagine if Abraham Lincoln had possessed McCain's boldness of vision. He could have merely told the southern states, "Hey, let's cut this slavery bullshit." Slavery, *over*. Civil War avoided. Ken Burns unemployed.

An unwillingness to come to terms with the realities of the Iraq War has damaged McCain's reputation for telling it like it is. But it's worth asking whether straight talk is really the political virtue many of us suppose it to be. Movies like *Bulworth* (in which a drunk and suicidal senator goes on a truth-telling bender and wins the hearts of the voters and Halle Berry) and the more recent *Man of the Year* (in which the straight-talking candidate is, significantly, a Jon Stewart–style TV comedian) are nothing but Truth Porn—fantasies that exploit our naïve notions about the political efficacy of honesty. A real-life Bulworth, in the unlikely event he was elected, would be incapable of conducting diplomacy, or of compromising with anyone who disagreed with him (hmm . . . sound familiar?). At least the comedian hero of *Man of the Year* seems to realize, in the end, that an ability to "tell it like it is" does not constitute a positive program for governance. Now if only somebody would tell John McCain.

Though an ability to "cut the crap" is of questionable practical value for a politician, it is, for a comedian, a one-line job description. All comedians set themselves up as truth-tellers, regardless of their subject matter. Ray Romano tells us the truth about marriage and family life. Dave Chappelle tells us the truth about America's racial attitudes. Jeff Foxworthy tells us the truth about southern working-class whites. Even a weirdo like Steven Wright tells existential truths about the limits of language and logic: "You can't have everything," he tells us. "Where would you put it?"[3]

Topical comedians have their truths to tell, as well. But mainstream, anti-political truth is not the same as political, satirical truth—nor does television treat them the same. The truth Jay Leno, David Letterman, and Conan

O'Brien tell, joke after joke and night after night, is that all politicians are equally defective, that government is thoroughly incompetent and corrupt, and that any attempt to change these basic facts would be futile. This is a pretty depressing "truth," but it is commercially safe; moreover, the majority of Americans are inclined to agree with it, which makes the joke-writers' task an easy one.

The truths a satirist tells, on the other hand, are subjective and contentious. If you like what he has to say, you will stay tuned—if not, you might turn the channel or boycott his sponsors. Satirical truths can start arguments, because they are arguments in themselves—not merely reflections of some anti-political consensus. Which is why, when it reaches our television screens at all, genuine satire is only likely to do so through the narrowcast channels of the cable spectrum.

Pseudo-satire's truth reinforces anti-political apathy. Real satire speaks truth to power, and is therefore widely supposed to be a force to be reckoned with. Consider Mark Twain's faith in "the assault of laughter." Or look at George Orwell—who, like Twain, was far from a cockeyed optimist, but who boldly claimed that "every joke is a tiny revolution."[4]

Yet the evidence suggests that for all the chutzpah and commercial risk satirical truth-telling entails, it may not be worth it. Speaking truth to power doesn't guarantee power will listen. A lot of laughter has been hurled at the walls of the Establishment, but they still seem to be standing. Indeed, the assault of laughter, like a backfiring cannon, may prove more injurious to the comedian himself than to his target. What's more, an overdose of Truth may be downright fatal to humor itself.

IRONY FATIGUE

Generally speaking, comedians don't age well. People under a certain age may now have a hard time understanding what their elders ever saw in Robin Williams—and even their elders may not remember, while sitting through *Patch Adams, RV,* or, indeed, *Man of the Year.* The Bob Hope who continued to host lackluster TV specials into his late eighties was the faintest shadow of the razor-sharp pro who quipped his way down the *Road to Rio* and elsewhere with Bing Crosby and Dorothy Lamour decades before.

Satirists grow older, too, but they go beyond merely wearing out their welcome. Instead of just fading into unfunniness, they are apt to become bitter. As the late Kurt Vonnegut once put it, "For whatever reason, American humorists or satirists or whatever you wish to call them, those who choose to laugh rather than weep about demoralizing information, become intolerably unfunny pessimists if they live past a certain age."[5] Having passed their prime, satirists are likely to find themselves not just over the hill but in a pit of despair.

Will Kaufman has described this unique occupational affliction as "Irony Fatigue." The condition results from the struggle to maintain a light comic touch while at the same time trying to convey a serious message. "Comedians are committed to irony in its broadest sense," writes Kaufman, "keeping open their escape route through the creation of abiding confidence in the *possibility*, at the very least, that in the end they are saying one thing and meaning another—in a word, that they are *joking*."[6] After a while, this subterfuge takes its toll; the fundamental contradiction between earnest intent and frivolous means becomes too much to bear. Even as genial a humorist as Garrison Keillor has shown symptoms of IF, once admitting a desire to "quit writing humor and just write irritation for a while."[7]

Dr. Kaufman's Patient Zero is Samuel L. Clemens, better known to history as Mark Twain. Clemens, in fact, grew to despise "Mark Twain," the ironic persona to whom he owed his success, as "my hated *nom de plume*."[8] So frustrated did Clemens become with the limitations that came with being known as a humorist that he used the late novel *Pudd'nhead Wilson* as a kind of symbolic revenge against his alter ego.[9] The title character—plausibly a stand-in for the author—earns his nickname by telling an absurd joke that "gages" him in the eyes of the citizens of the frontier town in which he has just arrived. From that day forward, as far as the townsfolk are concerned, Wilson is nothing but a "pudd'nhead." The insulting nickname is a measure of the public's low regard for comedy, and their absolute intolerance for failed comedy, both of which Clemens had also been forced to endure in the course of his career. Only when Wilson learns to keep his witticisms to himself and proves himself a "serious" person is he able to shed the sobriquet "Pudd'nhead"—his own "hated *nom de plume.*"

Clemens may have wished he could do the same, but was never able to. His non-humorous novels, such as *Personal Recollections of Joan of Arc,* did not measure up to his great, humorous works. Toward the end of his life, he indeed became a bitter pessimist, though not an "intolerably unfunny" one. Late writings like *Letters from the Earth* and *The Mysterious Stranger* (both published posthumously) have their share of black humor, though they are perhaps more famous for their misanthropy.[10]

Lenny Bruce, whose seriousness of purpose eventually overtook his comedy to such an extent that he would insist, "I'm not a comedian," provides another clear-cut case of Irony Fatigue.[11] On at least one occasion, Bruce actually scolded his audience for clapping, because it threw off his rhythm. Lenny ended his tragically abbreviated career hounded by the police, banned from many of the venues he had once sold out, and preoccupied with his ongoing obscenity trial. During his final stand-up appearances, he indulged his monomania by reading from the trial transcripts while onstage.[12]

Bruce's contemporary and rival Mort Sahl, though not profiled in Kaufman's book, fits the Irony Fatigue diagnosis to a tee. Never was a comedian's career so obviously undone by his refusal to "just" be funny. Though he paved the way for *The Daily Show,* appearing as a commentator for NBC during the 1960 political conventions, Sahl was never able to gain a toehold in TV.[13] This failure was a source of frustration for Sahl, but it was as much the result of his own stubborn (perhaps the better word is "perverse") integrity as anything else. He just couldn't pass up an opportunity to say something provocative. It was a tendency he had always exhibited. In 1957 Sahl had appeared on singer Eddie Fisher's variety show. Introducing the comedian, Fisher indulgently asked, "Say something funny, Mort." Sahl leered at the camera and snarled, "John Foster Dulles."[14]

Sahl never made the acquaintance of Ike's shadowy secretary of state, but he did get to know John F. Kennedy and wrote a few jokes for his 1960 campaign.[15] But after the election, Sahl refused to grant the new president comedic immunity—a principled stand for which Sahl has always maintained he was made to pay. Through his manager, Sahl received word that the president considered him "disloyal." Ever the contrarian, Sahl responded by doing even more Kennedy jokes. "Then the work began to dry up."[16]

But his refusal to play the harmless funster didn't really get the better of Sahl until after Kennedy was assassinated. Whereas Lenny Bruce tested his audience's patience with court transcripts, Sahl read from the Warren Commission Report onstage, alienating club owners and further dimming whatever TV prospects might have remained for him.[17]

A more recent example—somewhat closer to home for our study of late-night comics—is Dave Chappelle. His peculiar odyssey presents an interesting variation on the struggle to balance the desire to amuse with the desire to make a point. *Chappelle's Show,* on cable's Comedy Central, had gained a devoted following with edgy and intermittently brilliant sketches revolving around issues of race in America. But in the midst of filming sketches for the show's third season, and promised a contract that would have paid him fifty million dollars, Chappelle abruptly left for South Africa.

Lying low at a friend's home in Durban, amid rumors that he had lost his mind or entered rehab, Chappelle decided he could no longer continue doing his show, fifty million bucks notwithstanding. The comedian had often expressed a concern that in the process of mocking racist stereotypes, he might also be inadvertently perpetuating them—"I want to make sure I'm dancing, not shuffling," he liked to say. As *Chappelle's Show* took on the momentum of a juggernaut, its host began to feel that he was no longer doing the right steps, or even calling the tune. "Everyone around me says, 'You're a genius! You're great! That's your voice!' But I'm not sure that they're right." Shortly after his return to the United States—and to stand-up, indicating that his disillusionment was not with comedy per se—a perfectly sane and sober Chappelle explained to CNN's Anderson Cooper how he had come to feel that some of the sketches he was filming for season three were "socially irresponsible," and that some portion of the television audience might be "laughing for the wrong reasons."[18]

Chappelle's problem was not Irony Fatigue as such; he was not beset by a frustrating desire to speak seriously. His dilemma stemmed, instead, from an

inability to control the ambiguities of means and message. Chappelle's aban-
donment of his hit show and his subsequent return to stand-up is a story not
of a clown who wishes to be a pundit but of a dancer determined to choreo-
graph his own movements.

TERMINALLY SERIOUS

As Chappelle's ongoing story demonstrates, Irony Fatigue doesn't have to
end in intolerably unfunny pessimism. A comedian might find a better balance between purpose and method—something Chappelle may indeed be
searching for right now. On the other hand, a comic troubled by maintaining the contradiction between lighthearted mockery and earnest outrage
might simply leave comedy behind in favor of political action. Dick Gregory
abandoned a successful stand-up career to become an activist for peace and
civil rights.[19] Janeane Garofalo, while keeping a hand in both stand-up and acting, undertook a tour of duty as a serious pundit during the run-up to the 2003
invasion of Iraq. She received good reviews for her stint co-hosting CNN's
Crossfire, opposite alleged non-comedian Tucker Carlson. But Garofalo was
conscious of the hazards of "crossing over" from entertainment to news, and
suspicious of the motives of those who invited her to do so. "They have actors
on so they can marginalize the [anti-war] movement," she told *Washington
Post* media reporter Howard Kurtz. "If you're an actor who's against the war,
you're suspect. You must have a weird angle or you just hate George Bush."[20]

Garofalo has since left Air America, and how she will balance her dual
roles as political pundit and comedian/actress in the future remains to be
seen. So far, the most dramatic example of eschewing funny business to work
on the serious side is provided by Garofalo's erstwhile Air America co-worker
Al Franken, who at this writing has left comedy to run for the U.S. Senate.

Franken worked as a writer and performer on *Saturday Night Live,* focusing productively, though by no means exclusively, on political sketches. After
unsuccessful forays into primetime television (*Lateline*) and movies (*Stuart
Saves His Family*), Franken settled into a new niche as an author of humorous but unabashedly polemical political books.

It is easy enough to chart Franken's growing seriousness through his successive published works. *Rush Limbaugh Is a Big Fat Idiot (and Other Observations)*, which appeared in 1996, was a scattershot, and occasionally scatological, satire of the ad hominem invective Limbaugh and other right-wing bullies had unleashed on the national discourse during the Clinton years.[21] *Lies and the Lying Liars Who Tell Them: A Fair and Balanced Look at the Right* (2003) was a focused and (thanks to a cadre of Harvard interns the author dubbed "Team Franken") thoroughly researched critique of the Fox News/Ann Coulter/Richard Mellon Scaife propaganda nexus.[22] *Lies* still aims for laughs more often than not (though the chapter on how Franken's friend and political hero Senator Paul Wellstone's funeral was spun by media conservatives seethes with anger), but the book amounts to a sustained rhetorical assault on a well-defined target, and is quite effective on that level.

But by the time Franken completed 2005's *The Truth, with Jokes*, it was clear the author's sense of mission had transcended the desire to make his readers laugh. The book is heavy on the truth, light on the jokes. "I present THE TRUTH not just to shock you . . . not just to set the record straight— but to rouse you, to prepare you for battles ahead," Franken's introduction portentously announces. "This book is both sword and shield—with jokes."[23]

At this point, it's too soon to say whether Franken's sense of humor will win him votes or whether, conversely, any of his past comedic provocations will come back to haunt him. Considering the fact that Dennis Miller has been mentioned as a possible candidate for the Senate from California, though, one can only hope Franken isn't starting a trend.

Get "Real"

Another earnest satirist, Bill Maher, has made it clear that he will never run for office: "Can you imagine trying to win office in this country on a platform of religion is bad, marijuana is good, and babies are disgusting?" he told CNN. "I mean, those are some of my beliefs. You know, I wouldn't get three percent of the vote."[24]

It's not that he's not interested—but Maher simply considers himself too "real" to be a politician. Consider the name of his HBO show: *Real Time with Bill Maher*. Obviously, this bit of wordplay not only alludes to the fact that the show is cablecast live (that is, in "real time") but is also meant to evoke the host's self-appointed role as a crusader against "bullshit." Like its predecessor, *Politically Incorrect* (another title that promises to do away with niceties and get to the bottom of things), Maher's HBO program is packaged explicitly as a forum for unpopular, even dangerous, truths. The two titles— which refer to two shows that for all intents and purposes are the same— both announce Maher's TV salon as an island of candor amid a sea of spin. Print and Internet ads for the show's fifth season depict the host hooked up to a lie detector.[25]

Maher is a smart and capable comedian, but he often seems to expend more energy wagging his finger than flexing his funny bone. In fact, Maher has found a way around the Irony Fatigue–producing need to balance seriousness and jokiness, by simply availing himself of the opportunity to shift into outright pontificating whenever he chooses. There is something bracing about Maher's refusal to laugh *everything* off, though his self-righteousness can become wearying after a while.

The format employed for both *Real Time* and *Politically Incorrect* (sort of *The McLaughlin Group* with an intentionally funny host) has elicited a number of controversial remarks over the years, but most of the discussion is disappointingly banal. This results largely from the practice of including showbiz celebrities among the panelists—one of the unintended lessons of Maher's shows is that a great many of the stars of stage, screen, and song are really, really stupid. Maher also tends to take too firm a hand at the wheel, cranking up the sanctimony and tapping the audience's applause reflex to dismiss disagreements with some earnest, angry point.

Maher's Achilles' heel, though—one he shares with the fans of *Bulworth* and of John McCain—is his tendency to celebrate mere outspokenness as "bold," and therefore worthy. Take, for example, his inexplicable admiration for right-wing harpy Ann Coulter: "We are kindred spirits in certain ways," says Maher. "She is not afraid to say something that will make people boo, and we need more of that. . . . I certainly don't agree with everything she is, but I admire that."[26] Everything Coulter is, however, is a mean-spirited and irresponsible propagandist posing as a bold teller of "truth." Maher ought to be smart enough to realize that just because people boo you, it doesn't mean you should be listened to. Coulter is notorious for the deceptions and inaccuracies of her books, and the venomous intolerance of her public statements, such as her cruel slur of 9/11 widows. "These broads are millionaires lionized on TV and in articles about them reveling in their status as celebrities," Coulter said. "I've never seen people enjoying their husband's death so much."[27] Blunt, yes; boo-able, definitely—but hardly admirable.

Maher's own views are ideologically eclectic and rarely uninformed. And to his credit, his interest in politics seems sincere, not obligatory like Leno's and Letterman's. He created his own niche with *Politically Incorrect*—a show devised to focus on current events as a matter of course, not convenience. He is sometimes self-righteous, but often insightful, and frequently very funny. But his weakness for blunt bullies like Coulter is a sign of a satirical affliction that may be even more pernicious and widespread than Irony Fatigue.

CATCHER IN THE RYE-TIS

"I dropped out of high school," Chris Rock once told an interviewer, "and I'm not as smart as people think I am. A lot of times people come up to me and they start talking really smart, and I'm like, 'Dude, I don't know what the f*** you're talking about.' I'm an intellectual magnet. That happens a lot. I have to go, 'Hey, just jokes! That's all I know—jokes.' "[28]

Stand-up comedy demands a rare kind of intelligence: one must have the ability to see, and exploit, truths others only dimly perceive beneath everyday speech and appearances. But as Rock realizes, this is also a narrow and limited kind of insight. Just because the comedian's role gives him a license to *tell* the truth doesn't mean that he has any special purchase on what the truth *is*. Although he presents himself as a professional know-it-all, that doesn't mean he actually knows anything—though as Rock suggests, it may convince others that he does.

The kind of truth-telling comedians specialize in proceeds from contrarianism: an unwillingness to partake of popular delusions. The child who pointed out that the emperor had no clothes in Hans Christian Andersen's fairy tale was merely calling attention to a truth that others should have recognized, had they not trained themselves to ignore it. His insight was really only a "politically incorrect" expression of childish innocence. Comedians often affect such naïveté in order to get to some underlying "truth"—the boyish Johnny Carson was a master of this.

By contrast, Mort Sahl's career-damaging hubris was not so much childish as it was adolescent. Not content to uncover truths buried in his audience's subconscious, he aimed to educate—to bring them *his* truth—thus turning his performance into a lecture. Sahl and other comedians who lack Rock's humble self-awareness suffer from what could be called Holden Caulfield's Syndrome. In their messianic zeal, these comedic crusaders more closely resemble the teenage protagonist of J. D. Salinger's *Catcher in the Rye* than Hans Christian Andersen's ingenuous hero.[29] Like the fictional Holden Caulfield, self-serious satirists like Sahl, Bruce, Maher, and the late Bill Hicks believe themselves to be surrounded by "phonies." Some, in turn, believe themselves to be especially, nobly genuine.

Dennis Miller's got Caulfield's Syndrome so bad, he named his son Holden.[30] He combines the adolescent hubris of Salinger's hero with breathtaking intellectual arrogance, conducting himself as if he had spent his apprenticeship working for the Brookings Institution rather than *Saturday Night Live*.

Regardless of whether his ostentatious vocabulary and arcane cultural references have very deep foundations, Miller has certainly gotten a lot of mileage out of presenting himself as a thinking person's comedian. After six years behind *SNL*'s "Weekend Update" desk and a short-lived syndicated talk show, he went on to host HBO's award-winning *Dennis Miller Live*. (A top-flight writing staff, including future *Colbert Report* head writer Rich Dahm, helped.)[31] His career took a detour when he was recruited to join the *Monday Night Football* crew, where he was a decidedly odd fit. As James Wolcott put it, football fans "failed to ascertain what the Council of Trent had to do with an incomplete pass."[32] At the end of the season, Miller was dumped like a coach with a 0–16 record.

But Miller was about to find a new career niche. More important, he was about to find his very own Bulworth. Once a nominal left-libertarian, Miller veered to the right after 9/11. "I'm shocked," he said, "it didn't change everybody as much as it changed me."[33] By the time George W. Bush was leading the country into preemptive war with Iraq, Miller had become an unabashed cheerleader for the president and his cut-the-crap, dead-or-alive foreign policy. "Somebody's got to say something good in this community [i.e., Hollywood] about this man," Miller told Jay Leno. "And you know something, if you're watching tonight, President Bush . . . I just want to say, I think you're doing a hell of a job and I'm proud that you're my president. I want to thank you and wish you godspeed because you got a tough deal of the cards. I think there are a lot more people out here on your side than you would think."[34]

This undeniably impressive display of on-air sucking up got Miller a ride on Air Force One when the president next visited California. "I spent an amazing couple of hours with Dennis Miller," the president said of their cozy flight. "He keeps you on your toes."[35]

Miller was impressed, too—or perhaps the better word is "smitten." Bush struck Miller, the self-styled cynic, as particularly genuine—a trait the comedian was bound to appreciate, since, like his son's fictional namesake, Miller can conceive of no greater sin than being a phony. Al Gore, says Miller, is "a bad emissary for that global warming issue. Because I've always thought of him as such an inauthentic man, I translate some of that feeling to the cause" (never mind the science).[36] On the other hand, there is apparently no greater virtue than Bush's plain-talkin', squinty-eyed bluntness (never mind the failure to find Saddam's WMDs—facts are nothing compared to personal "authenticity"). "I . . . like it when President Bush gets P.O.'d and starts dropping the 'g's at the end of his verbs," Miller once gushed. "We're not 'hunting' anybody, we're huntin' 'em."[37]

In the wake of his political conversion, Miller landed a new show on CNBC. Incredibly, he introduced his new venture by announcing that he would be giving Bush "a pass," explaining, "I take care of my friends."[38] In a world full of phonies, regular guys like Miller and Bush have to stick together.

In fact, behind the scenes, there was something particularly inauthentic about *Dennis Miller*. The show's consulting producer was one Mike Murphy, a Republican campaign operative who had worked for the president's brother, Florida governor Jeb Bush, California governor Arnold Schwarzenegger, and Senator John McCain—the latter two of whom were also, coincidentally, Miller's guests on the show's debut episode. And while Miller fawned over his producer's former clients and other conservative guests, he treated liberals with undisguised disdain. When the *Nation's* Eric Alterman appeared to debate the Iraq war, Miller pretended to fall asleep from boredom and harangued Alterman with an impatient, "Oh, just finish the fucking segment." Time and again, the allegedly astute Miller came across as ill-prepared, ill-informed, and arrogant. He was also almost unwatched. By the time it was canceled, *Dennis Miller* was averaging just over one hundred thousand viewers.[39]

Clearly, there was only one place to go: Fox News. Miller had in fact done a few commentaries for *Hannity and Colmes* in 2003, before landing the CNBC gig, and the Murdoch empire welcomed him back with open arms. Miller has since contributed to both *H&C* and *The O'Reilly Factor,* whose host (another pretend-populist champion of "authenticity") occasionally grants the comedian a few minutes of "Miller Time."[40]

If David Letterman has, as John Limon claims, intelligence but no ideas, Miller has intelligence and the ideas of Roger Ailes. His embrace of Bush-can-do-no-wrong conservatism (while claiming, like O'Reilly, to be an "independent") may be sincere, but in his FOX commentaries, Miller seems to be reading from the same list of talking points as the network's other personalities, with a few pop culture references thrown in.

Miller is as out of his depth as a pundit as Mort Sahl was as a detective. Like Holden Caulfield, he is not as smart as he thinks he is, but is too full of himself to notice. CNBC and Fox News may be the only venues in America where Miller could be regarded as the resident intellectual. His April 2004 interview with *Democracy Now's* Amy Goodman showed that Miller's critical thinking skills were somewhat less impressive than his knowledge of the Rat

Pack. When Goodman pointed out that no link had been proven between Iraq and the 9/11 attacks, Miller responded, "It amazes me when people always think that there's no link between Al Qaeda and the secular state of Iraq. To think that they both think we're Satan tells me that they might have carpooled somewhere along the way." To this well-considered rationale, Miller added that while Goodman might be a journalist, "I'm a pragmatist, and I don't put an egg timer on finding evidence."[41] Well, it certainly would be far from pragmatic to use an egg timer.

Because he has been adopted as a comedy mascot by the likes of Murphy and Ailes, and because he has honed a method of *sounding* smart that seems to have fooled even himself, Miller has been able to stretch his "thinking man's comic" shtick into its third decade. But a specious argument decked out with references to King Leopold II of Belgium, Necco Wafers, and *The Maltese Falcon* is still specious.

Any comedian with an identifiable style risks losing his punch over the years, and Miller has certainly been on the scene long enough for people to forget, as they did with Williams and Hope, that he was *ever* funny. But Miller's Caulfieldism—his apparent belief that "authenticity" is a cure for every political ill—is a more serious affliction than his intellectual pretension or his overfamiliarity. What's more, it points to a pathology that afflicts the American voting public at large—a delusion that we ought to choose our leaders based on which candidate talks the most like Gary Cooper or is the one with whom they would most like to split a pitcher of PBR.

GREAT PUMPKIN POLITICS

Authenticity in politics is a lot like sincerity in acting—as George Burns was supposed to have said, "If you can fake that, you've got it made."[42] Candidates flipping pancakes in New Hampshire diners and posing on John Deere tractors in Iowa are sometimes reminiscent of Linus desperately hoping to impress the Great Pumpkin with the sincerity of his pumpkin patch.

But if our politicians spend too much time and effort on convincing us that they are "for real," it's only because we seem to demand it. Certainly a lot of journalists overvalue "authenticity." So do comedians, but they have a better excuse. Since comedy is all about exposing hidden or unremarked-upon truths, it stands to reason that they might be impressed by that rare politician who does not appear to be putting on an act.

Professional cynics though they may be, most late-night comics are prone to swoon when confronted with a straight-talking political "maverick." David Letterman and Jon Stewart have both shown a weakness for alleged enemy of spin John McCain. (Even in the midst of a contentious interview focusing on the Iraq War, Stewart went out of his way to tell McCain, "You know I love you and respect your service and would never question any of that.") Miller loves g-droppin' Bush, and Maher is a fan of Ralph "I only have the one suit" Nader. "How many Ralph Nader jokes do you hear?" Jay Leno, another admirer, once asked. "You don't. Here's a guy, he comes out and tells it like it is. My job's over!"[43]

"Straight shooters" get a pass from comedians, because they appear to have no hidden agendas to expose. But how genuine are these truth-tellers, really? Are comedians too eager to project their crusading sense of themselves onto politicians who make a show of eschewing politics as usual?

Tough talk isn't necessarily true talk, but to the straight-talk fetishist, a brash, bold-faced lie is the most seductive kind. On closer inspection, most of these icons of candor turn out to be as calculated as Bill Clinton in all his I-didn't-inhale, depends-on-what-"is"-is, prevaricating glory. Bush didn't learn to drop his g's in his native Connecticut, nor at Andover and Yale. He acquired his Texas twang (ever notice Brother Jeb doesn't have one?) as an adult, and his "ranch" less than a year before he began running for president. Before John McCain boarded the Straight Talk Express and championed campaign finance reform, he was best known nationally as one of the "Keating Five"— a crooked cabal of U.S. senators implicated in a money-for-favors scandal.[44]

Nader may be the biggest phony of them all: a multimillionaire who has parlayed the money he makes denouncing corporate greed into an impressive stock portfolio. (His mandated 2000 financial disclosure showed him to have a net worth of about $3.8 million.)[45] Despite this fortune, Nader costumes himself in a shabby, ill-fitting suit and Army surplus shoes. According to biographer David Sanford, Nader for years maintained a tiny Washington, D.C., apartment as his "official" residence while actually living in a large, comfortable house deeded in his brother's name.[46] And lest we forget, during the 2000 campaign this "straight shooter" repeatedly claimed that there was "no difference" between George W. Bush and Al Gore—which, assuming Nader learned the first thing about the power of the executive branch in all his years working in the capital, was the single most disingenuous statement of the entire presidential campaign (which is saying something).[47]

Still, for a number of people fed up with the all-too-obvious pandering of a John Kerry or the earth-toned image-mongering of an Al Gore, a convincing *portrayal* of authenticity may seem as good as the real thing. But would a country run on the *Bulworth* tell-it-like-it-is principle even work? There's a reason the most genuinely "authentic" politicians are figures of fiction. In real life, and especially in real politics, a propensity for bluntly speaking one's mind is of limited utility. An effective politician needs a certain amount of guile. If Frank Capra's Mr. Smith showed up in our world, he would seem to be too good to be true; but if elected, he would soon prove too true to be good.

This is not to suggest that dishonesty is a political virtue, exactly; just to reiterate that the role of truth in politics is complicated. Lincoln's Emancipation Proclamation was a fine piece of rhetorical sleight-of-hand, "freeing" slaves in the parts of the country that didn't recognize his authority to do so and leaving border-state slavery alone.[48] FDR's lend-lease plan to aid Great Britain's war effort prior to Pearl Harbor skillfully got around America's official neutrality, and Britain's inability to pay, like a limbo dancer going under a turnstile.[49] Yet these calculated and carefully calibrated acts were examples of true—and truly moral—leadership.

Even political lies that aim no higher than covering one's behind are less simple than they seem. The reason politicians' language has to be carefully parsed is not because they recklessly lie, but because they are careful to avoid outright lies. Even Bill Clinton's whopper about not having had "sexual relations" with "that woman" could be considered technically true, if one was inclined to accept Clinton's idiosyncratically specific (to put it charitably) definition of "sexual relations."[50]

Honest debate and honest disagreement are vital to a meaningful politics. But dishonest, or at least deceptive, rhetoric is a part of politics, too. Anecdotal evidence, unrepresentative examples, straw-man arguments, faulty statistics, and evasive language are all tricks of the trade. Sorting all of this out is more complicated than separating the "authentic" from the "phony." How, then, might satire deal with these complicated matters of truth and deception, while avoiding both Salingeresque naïveté and the exhausting, "just kidding/ not really" charade that can only lead to Irony Fatigue?

What the (Honorary) Doctor Ordered*

Once again, the alter-ego method exemplified by Stephen Colbert provides, if not a cure for these political and comedic ailments, then at least a more viable alternative to Maher-Miller bombast and Leno-Letterman surrender. When Colbert makes grandiose claims about being a messenger of the Truth, he is only pretending to do what Miller purports to do in earnest. We'll get some truth from Colbert, all right, but it will come out as a counterpoint to, rather than the substance of, his pontificating.

It so happens that there is a good deal of alter-ego comedy on the current scene—perhaps because the limits of stand-up preachifying are becoming apparent to a growing number of performers who are less prepared to set themselves up as oracles. Sarah Silverman plays a same-named character (on her same-named program) who is as wrong about race, sexuality, and any situation requiring the merest sensitivity as Colbert is about politics. Unfortunately, once the novelty has worn off, Silverman's cheerful sociopathy and gratuitously scatological humor are much poo-poo about nothing.

Sacha Baron Cohen's faux-naïve characters, which include hip-hop wannabe Ali G. and Kazakhstani journalist Borat Sagdiyev, use calculated

---

* Since receiving an honorary doctorate of fine arts from Knox College in Illinois, "Dr. Stephen Colbert, DFA" has been listed as an executive producer of *The Colbert Report*. This is not only a joke on the character's towering ego but a reference to Bill Cosby, who insisted *The Cosby Show* credit him not only as the show's star, co-creator, composer of the theme song, and co-producer, but also as "executive consultant Dr. William H. Cosby Jr., Ed.D."

outrageousness to evoke genuinely outrageous responses from ordinary people. But Cohen's comedy is a sort of stunt. Consider a couple of much-remarked upon "revelatory" moments from Cohen's film, *Borat: Cultural Learnings of America for Make Benefit Glorious Nation of Kazakhstan*. Should anyone really be surprised to hear drunken fraternity brothers making racist and sexist remarks? Or that rodeo patrons would boo a man who mocks the national anthem? (Surely the folks Cohen serenades with the lyrics "Kazakhstan greatest country in the world/All other countries are run by little girls/Kazakhstan number one exporter of potassium/Other countries have inferior potassium" realized, at that point, that they were being had?)

The concurrent popularity of other role-playing satirists only makes Colbert's achievement look more impressive by comparison. Like Cohen, he interacts with real people while in character—but most of the authors, celebrities, and congressmen Colbert interviews presumably know what they're up against, and Colbert gets the better of them anyway. Consider, for instance, the Bugs Bunny–style rhetorical trickery Colbert used to get Dinesh D'Souza, author of *The Cultural Left and Its Responsibility for 9/11*, to proclaim his "agreement" with al-Qaeda's view of America:

> COLBERT: I agree with you. There are some good ideas these guys [the terrorists] have. This is what you're saying, that there are some parts of our culture that are corrosive, and you agree with some of the things that they're saying.
>
> D'SOUZA: I'm saying that . . .
>
> COLBERT: No, you have the courage to say that, right? That you agree with some of the things these radical extremists are against in America.
>
> D'SOUZA: I'm more concerned . . .
>
> COLBERT: Do you agree with that statement? Just, do you agree with that statement?
>
> D'SOUZA: I agree with it.[51]

The Colbert Report also generally avoids the easy laughs upon which so much supposedly edgy comedy—including Silverman's and Cohen's—now depends. Sexual and scatological humor might get your film an R rating, but it is also inherently democratic, and somewhat "safe" for that. It reduces its targets, its perpetrators, and those who laugh at it to their common, gross physicality and implies a kind of outhouse egalitarianism. Borat, the frat boys, the rodeo crowd, Americans, Kazakhstanis: we are all implicated in the racism, jingoism, and sexism we see—all up to our eyebrows, as it were, in the common muck of messy humanity. There is a place for this kind of comedy (right now, it seems to be everyplace), but it is also in some sense a cop-out, comparable to the late-night mainstream's equal-opportunity political offense. Offend everybody in general, and you offend nobody in particular.

Colbert's comedy doesn't target our common humanity. His victims are specific politicians and specific policies. Nor does Colbert present an argument pitting Truth against deceit, of the kind that Sahl, Maher, Miller, and Stephen Colbert—the character—purport to fight. His comedy is not an aren't-people-funny tableau, nor a hear-my-truth moralistic screed, but something rarer and more valuable. *The Colbert Report,* at its best, is a meticulous rhetorical critique. Colbert is less concerned with telling the truth than with examining how our *ideas* of truth are used to manipulate us. His subject is not some abstract, capital-*T* Truth but *truthiness*—the slippery, manipulative ground of contemporary discourse that cannot be navigated on the two-dimensional axes of "true" and "untrue."

Colbert defined the word, on his debut program, as something you feel in your gut rather than think in your head. In a larger sense, though, truthiness is the ongoing, twenty-four-hour cablecast performance in which "authenticity" has been redefined as a new and more effective form of deceit, complete with its own prescribed phrases and gestures. "It used to be, everyone was entitled to their own opinion, but not their own facts," Colbert said, in a rare out-of-character interview. "But that's not the case anymore. Facts matter not at all. Perception is everything. It's certainty. . . . I really feel a dichotomy in the American populace. What is important? What you want to be true, or what is true?"[52]

Truthiness, as *New York Times* columnist Frank Rich has observed, is not just a clever conceit but the defining concept of our age. To take only the most drastic example, "it's the truthiness of all those imminent mushroom clouds that sold the invasion of Iraq."[53] In an age of sophisticated spin, it is not enough for comedy to "balance" the disingenuousness of one side with that of the other, as the mainstream late-night shows incessantly do. Nor is it sufficient to "cut through the bullshit" to whatever reality the authenticity fetishists think lies beneath. It's easy work to smash a few icons; what Colbert is up to is more like peeling an onion.

Speaking truth to power sounds like a noble calling; but Americans do not live in a society in which simple truth-telling is in itself a revolutionary act. Our problem, in this age of chatter and spin, is not a shortage of truth but an overabundance of *competing* "truths" and truth-tellers, all clamoring to be believed. With so many pundits and think-tank experts pressing their points—not to mention a passel of Holden Caulfield know-it-alls and Hans Christian Andersen naïfs shouting to be heard above the din—"truth" is much less of a meaningful concept than we would like to think. Even a "true" truth is unlikely to make much of a dent when it is merely hurled in the general direction of power. The difference between mere truth-telling and the contemplation of truthiness lies in the distinction between merely pointing out the fact that the emperor wears no clothes and leading us to understand how we could have been led to ignore his nudity in the first place.

CHAPTER 7

FOR WHOM THE BELL DINGS

As we have seen, it is difficult to do comedy that is both politically engaged and genuinely funny, without alienating viewers and sponsors, or falling prey to Irony Fatigue or Holden Caulfield's Syndrome. But if genuine satire is a challenge few take on, and fewer master, it requires little finesse, creativity, or bravery to do comedy that is considered "edgy." If, as the saying goes, all you need to write a country song is "three chords and the truth," all you need to be "edgy" is four letters and some bodily fluids.[1]

If all the contemporary comedy that claims to be on the "edge" really was, the periphery of the comedy universe would be crowded with loudmouthed stand-ups, radio's various *Morning Zoo* crews, and the creators of childish cartoons (not really for kids) and gross-out beer commercials, while the vast, un-edgy center would be unoccupied but for Yakov Smirnoff, and possibly the Muppets. Although some of today's self-styled "politically incorrect" comedy at least dabbles in social satire—see Silverman's playfully ironic bigotry, or *South Park*'s mockery of liberal pieties—most of it is as politically inert and equal-opportunity offensive as the comedy of the late-night mainstream. But the new, ostentatiously offensive shock comedy has nonetheless garnered an impressive number of fans, and no small amount of critical acclaim. Moreover, it has shown late-night's more traditional comics a way to appear hipper and sharper, without compromising their carefully maintained, anti-political neutrality. This should not be surprising. Going too far is easy; it's going in a politically meaningful direction that takes courage.

LOUDER AND DIRTIER (BUT NOT FUNNIER)

When the producers of pop culture talk about "pushing the envelope," we would do well to remember that it is the fat check *inside* the envelope that's really doing the pushing. The oldest tenet of capitalism is that sex sells, and sleaze sells even better. From the moment it debuted as a commercial medium, then, it was only a matter of time before television started pandering to consumers' basest and most basic instincts.

Some of the pioneers saw it coming. *The Tonight Show*'s original host, Steve Allen, kept a bell—of the hotel-counter, "ring for service" variety—on his desk. Whenever a guest said something risqué, Allen hit the bell. The jingling bell seemed to underline the double entendre, but Allen always claimed it was intended as a warning. Allen's bell was like a judge's gavel, and he sounded it to restore order.

It didn't work. There is no denying that TV has gotten dirtier since Allen's day. Of George Carlin's "Seven Words You Can't Say on Television" (a routine he debuted in 1972, long after Allen packed up his bell), those that remain to be incorporated into the primetime vernacular are readily available to any viewer of professional sports with the most rudimentary lip-reading skills.[2] Lurid tele-freak shows like NBC's *Fear Factor* and MTV's *Jackass* feature bug-eating, "poo-diving," and a host of other, equally unwholesome spectacles. At every hour of the programming day, and in every genre and format—soaps, dramas, infotainment, game shows, and especially sitcoms—a smog of smirky but rather joyless lasciviousness permeates the airwaves. Needless to say, if Allen were still manning his late-night desk, that bell would never stop ringing.

Not that you'd be able to hear it over the din. Television has gotten not only lewder but louder. There are more applause cues, more whistling, and a near constant refrain of "woo!" from the studio audience. On the network late-night shows, even the house bands are louder and more obtrusive than Doc Severinsen's NBC Orchestra ever was, interrupting the monologues with stingers and musical moans (*whut-whaa* . . .). Contemporary television keeps up a jackhammer assault of sensationalism, where the noise and provocation rarely cease.

I will leave it to Focus on the Family and other self-appointed guardians of public decency to fret about how television's raunchiness might be affecting our moral fiber, and leave what the noise does to our nerves to the makers of Excedrin. What concerns us here is what effect the decline of standards and the "woo"-ing of the audience might be having on comedy in general, and political comedy in particular. When did "edginess" become a worthy end in itself? Is it "political" to joke about a president's penis rather than his policies? And if laughing at social conventions is supposed to be "liberating," why does the current barrage of poop jokes, "politically incorrect" mockery of the handicapped, and the "ironic" revival of racial stereotyping seem so oppressive—and (despite the deafening roars of approval) so unfunny?

THE RISQUÉ VERSUS THE RISKY

Johnny Carson used to play an old black-and-white clip every year on his Anniversary Show, featuring Ed Ames (who played Mingo the Indian scout on *Daniel Boone*) throwing a tomahawk at the outline of a cowboy painted on a sheet of plywood. The hatchet flew through the air and, after a single revolution, landed with a *thwok* in the cowboy's crotch. The studio audience laughed hysterically as Carson patiently waited to deliver the perfect capper, "Welcome to *Frontier Bris*."[3]

Watching the clip today, one can still appreciate Carson's skillful exploitation of Ames's aim, but the audience's laughter seems out of proportion. These days, trauma to the groin is a staple of television comedy. When Mike Judge, in his satirical look at America in the year 2505, *Idiocracy*, predicts that television's biggest future hit will be a show entitled *Ow, My Balls!* this prophecy is depressingly easy to believe. But in 1965, the *Tonight Show* crowd went wild, because they knew that there were certain parts of the body that were not even to be alluded to in polite company—and certainly not on television.

Comedy cannot exist without a certain amount of repression. Indeed, in *Jokes and Their Relation to the Unconscious*, Freud argued that social sanctions against open expressions of lust and aggression were the whole reason people needed jokes.[4] It would not be worth reinstating the moral codes of

Freud's Victorian era—or even those of 1965—just because it might make for better comedy, but a society that has no taboos left offers nothing for humor to challenge. We have hardly reached this point, but there has been a significant shift in what is permissible and what is off-limits. There are still taboos that satirists might productively attack, but most contemporary comedy is too busy taking advantage of already fallen standards to shoot at dead horses, or fish in a barrel. Sex, scat, and celebrities provide the basis for more and more contemporary comedy, while actual satire is only a little less rare than it has always been.

What's discouraging about this state of affairs is that "shock" comedy is so frequently mischaracterized as bold or progressive, when it is, for the most part, both safe and reactionary. The works of Trey Parker and Matt Stone are praised as ingenious satire, and *The Sarah Silverman Program* is lauded (in the pages of the *New Yorker*, no less) as "the meanest sitcom in years—and one of the funniest."[5]

Yet most of the "edgy" comedy sold and celebrated as such is as nihilistically "neutral" in its way as the equal-opportunity offender political comedy of the late-night mainstream. If the subtext of Jay Leno's topical punch lines is "all politics is a joke," the subtext of *South Park*, *Family Guy*, and *The Sarah Silverman Program* is "nothing is sacred." Well, if nothing is sacred, nothing is at stake.

What are the actual targets of such self-consciously offensive comedy? The *New Yorker*'s Tad Friend praises *Sarah Silverman* for its parodic "allusions to sitcoms of yore," which come "swaddled in air quotes."[6] Does Friend truly find this "edgy," or worthwhile? Are there any sitcom clichés that haven't already been thoroughly deconstructed by *It's Garry Shandling's Show*, *The Simpsons*, and not one, but two *Brady Bunch* movies? Silverman's innovation, apparently, is to pound the rubble of these already bombed-out targets with a few extra megatons of poop references and jokes about AIDS.[7]

"Now, comic 'edge' is defined not by irony or subversion, but explicitness," complains journalist Andrew Corsello. The comedy of Silverman, the Farrelly Brothers, Parker and Stone—indeed, everything aired on Comedy Central during the twenty hours each day not devoted to showing *The Daily*

Show and *Colbert*—while celebrated as "edgy," is mostly just exploitative: *Fear Factor* played for laughs. Its very ubiquity—even kids' movies are now considered incomplete without a few fart jokes—proves that this type of comedy is not, in fact, a "challenge" to mainstream standards. It *is* the mainstream. "Tastelessness," as Mark Crispin Miller has observed, "is the new orthodoxy."[8]

The expansion of its vocabulary to contain certain four-letter words, and the permission to explore bodily functions in detail, have not made television a more effective medium for speaking truth to power. Despite the welcome addition of more satirical voices like Stewart, Colbert, and Maher on the cablecast margins, late-night's topical comedy, while it has gotten a lot dirtier since the days when Ed Ames's tomahawk brought down the house, has stuck to a safe—or even subtly reactionary—course in terms of its political critique. In fact, late-night's expanded license to joke about politicians' sex lives and to attack them on the level of gross physicality has only encouraged pseudo-satire's shallowest ad hominem tendencies.

BARKING, BUT NO BITE

One night in early 2007, Jon Stewart responded to an over-enthusiastic ovation from *The Daily Show*'s studio audience by ad-libbing, "Welcome to the *Arsenio Hall Show*." Indeed, Hall's most lasting contribution to late-night was probably the encouragement of a frenzied response from the people in the seats, in which cheering, applauding, and even barking came to be valued as much as actual laughter. This shift signaled not only the heating up of late-night's traditionally "cool" presentational style but also a change in the shows' comedy content.

As anyone who has ever been subjected to a bad joke told by the boss surely knows, a laugh is a difficult thing to fake. The fact that laughter is a reflex is precisely what makes comedy so hard. Johnny Carson was a master of wringing laughs out of jokes that didn't work. Occasionally, when a punch line was greeted by deafening silence, Doc would strike up a few bars of "Tea for Two," and Johnny would launch into a sheepishly desperate soft-shoe. Soon the audience was laughing in spite of the jokes rather than because of them. Carson was funnier bombing than many comics are when they succeed.

Of the current crop of network hosts, though, only Conan O'Brien has the audacity to try this—in fact, he's a pretty funny flopper. But Leno and Letterman, taking their cue from Arsenio rather than Johnny, have found a fail-safe method consisting of two simple rules: 1) applause, groans, or a "woo!" is as good as a laugh, and 2) there's no need for the band to have "Tea for Two" at the ready if they preemptively fill every silence with a stinger or a rimshot.

It wouldn't be fair to blame this all on Hall—who, in spite of the hyped-up ovation he received at the top of every show, still faced the proverbial crickets whenever a punch line failed, which was fairly often. All he did was bring a plague that had already infested prime-time programming to late-night.

In fact, *Arsenio*'s "dawg pound" merely represented a revival of the audience aesthetic common until the mid-nineteenth century, when theatrical subtlety was routinely sacrificed to satisfy the demands of the "gallery gods" who whooped it up from the cheap seats.[9] The "studio audience" is itself a legacy of radio, where it was found that the presence of live, laughing spectators helped stage-trained comics time their jokes.[10] Just as important, it gave the folks listening at home company to laugh with, and cues on when to do it. The practice carried over into early television, but the advent of the filmed (as opposed to live) television sitcom brought another refinement: the invention of "canned laughter." Unlike the 1950s classics *I Love Lucy* and *The Honeymooners*, most 1960s sitcoms dispensed with live audiences in favor of laugh tracks.

In the early 1970s, though, the live audience came back with a vengeance, and a great deal of cheering, hooting, and overeager applause. The chief culprit in encouraging this new form of pandering to the gallery gods was producer Norman Lear, whose "relevant" sitcoms, like *All in the Family, The Jeffersons*, and *Maude*, featured both boldly topical themes and obnoxiously vociferous studio crowds.

Lear deserves credit for taking on controversial issues in a manner that was both genuinely bold and frequently quite entertaining. But the reliance on boisterous and well-miked studio audiences often blurred the distinction between pushing the envelope and merely pushing buttons. Why labor for a laugh when a collective gasp or an "I can't believe she just said that" howl is just as good, and more easily gotten? Why write jokes for Maude when she can get as big a reaction just by saying something "outrageous"?

Lesser lights than Lear have learned this lesson well. The Fox network (briefly the home of Arsenio Hall before Paramount snatched him away for syndication) built its franchise on two shows that could be said to represent the two sides of Lear's legacy. *The Simpsons* (1989–present), an animated show, took on contemporary culture with some of the most sophisticated writing ever to appear on television—and did so without a laugh track. *Married . . . with Children* (1987–1997), on the other hand, was perhaps the most aggressively lowbrow sitcom ever produced, relying heavily on shock and gross-out humor—all underscored by the noisy approval of a studio audience that would not have sounded out of place at a pro wrestling match or the Roman Colosseum. Both were hugely successful, but even the most dimwitted television executive could see which hit show would be easier to duplicate.

Meanwhile, daytime television was pursuing its own version of the louder-and-lewder aesthetic, with a spate of talk shows (including the justly infamous *Jerry Springer*) so unabashedly noisy and exploitative they might have made Rome's lions and gladiators nauseous. These so-called tabloid shows peaked a few years ago, but the various parts of their legacy live on at all hours of the broadcast day, and in all genres of programming, not excluding "news." (All *Dateline NBC*'s "To Catch a Predator" lacks is a live audience, and Jerry Springer himself.)

With prime time and daytime upping the ante on crudity and crowd noise, it was only a matter of time before late-night joined in. *Arsenio*'s pep-rally vibe set things off, but the ratings war between Jay and Dave turned it into something like an arms race. Letterman's move from NBC to CBS, and from *Late Night*'s tiny Rockefeller Center studio to the 461-seat Ed Sullivan Theater, presented an opportunity for him to capitalize on the new rowdy-crowd paradigm. Gone was the experimental, "what the hell" looseness that had made the NBC show such adventurous fun. *Late Show* was going head-to-head with *The Tonight Show*, and the competition seemed to feed a bigger-is-better mentality. Everything about Letterman's CBS show was super-sized—not only the venue but the band, the sets, the guest list, and even the tone of Dave's monologue. Often, his jokes are little more than ritual incantations of conventional comedic wisdom that receive more applause than laughter.

Letterman sometimes seems to recognize that something was lost in his move to the 11:30 time slot. Early in his CBS tenure he often seemed annoyed at the way the Sullivan Theater crowd continually cheered and clapped in time to the music. More than once he has remarked that his NBC show was "much better" than the extravaganza he now hosts—this always gets a laugh, but Letterman doesn't really appear to be joking.

The current tenant of Dave's old *Late Night* digs seems aware that, in comedy, bigger is not necessarily better. "There's this phenomenon now in America of just, 'Yeah, woo!'" Conan O'Brien told an interviewer in 2002. "It's a phenomenon that depresses me. I think it's partly daytime talk shows like Jerry Springer and stuff. It's encouraged on so many shows. 'Woo!' It's kind of not why I got into comedy. If I wanted that, I'd have become a jai-alai player or something." O'Brien would prefer to follow in Johnny Carson's tap-dancing footsteps. "I like an audience that's listening and then laughing or not," he says. "If they listen and then don't laugh, I can usually have fun with the fact that they didn't laugh. . . . I think people like to see me work my way out of a situation."[11] One dares to hope O'Brien will remember this when he takes over *The Tonight Show* in 2009.

Stewart, too, sometimes seems taken aback by the boisterousness of his studio audience, often undercutting their loud enthusiasm with a remark like his allusion to *Arsenio,* and occasionally shushing them when their partisan cheering infringes on his ability to interview conservative guests. Colbert simply works the by-now-expected over-the-top audience responses into his insatiable egotist act. Occasionally, though, he has to finesse the crowd's demonstrative spontaneity to maintain the illusion that he is their conservative hero, as when he told an audience that cheered a guest's criticism of President Bush, "I'm going to assume those are 'woos' of disapproval."

There is some reason to believe the overbearing studio audience has begun to turn off their couch-bound compatriots watching from home.

"One-camera" sitcoms like *My Name Is Earl* and *30 Rock* have demonstrated that a comedy can survive and even thrive without a live audience or a laugh track. This isn't really an option for late-night, however, since stand-up without a responding crowd is as incomprehensible as the proverbial sound of one hand clapping. (A little "sweetening" could turn that into the sound of nine hands clapping, but still.)

Lost amid all the clapping, cheering, and shouts of "woo!" (or even, as in *Arsenio*'s heyday, "woof!") is the old, insinuating intimacy between late-night host and night-owl viewer, so often cited as key to Carson's long-lived appeal. This represents a major stylistic shift: Marshall McLuhan's notion that television favored "cool" personalities who offset the medium's inherent invasiveness may be obsolete.[12] Carson, of course, was the cool presence par excellence—so subtly ingratiating that he was welcomed even into the nation's bedrooms. But spurred on by the example of Arsenio, Johnny's successors have turned up the heat, along with the microphones positioned to pick up the audiences' response. Whether this has made them less welcome visitors in viewers' bedrooms is a matter of conjecture. It is clear, however, that late-night's turn to a noisier, more sensationalistic approach set the stage for the way late-night comics would deal with the president's own bedroom behavior, when the opportunity arose.

THE GOLD RUSH

When the news that President Bill Clinton had carried on an affair with White House intern Monica Lewinsky came to light in 1998, it hit late-night like the news that gold had been discovered at Sutter's Mill, California, 150 years earlier. But assayed by the standards of satire, most of the jokes late-night mined from Monicagate were nothing but fool's gold. Though they inspired a lot of roaring, hooting, and groaning on the part of studio audiences, they yielded only a little laughter.

On a purely quantitative basis, the Lewinsky scandal would appear to be the best thing that ever happened to late-night comedy. According to the Center for Media and Public Affairs, President Bill Clinton was far and away the top target of late-night political jokes in the years 1992 to 2002. Out of Leno's 18,802 political jokes during that period, 3,722 were about Clinton, or roughly one in five.[13] (Letterman told far fewer political jokes overall, but the proportion of his jokes that targeted Clinton was about the same.) Granted, Clinton was president for eight of those ten years, and not all Clinton jokes concerned the sex scandal. But even after the bizarre election of 2000 and the terrorist attacks a year later, Clinton's sex life was *still* the comedians' favorite topic. In the first four months of 2002, Leno, Letterman, and O'Brien told a combined eighty Clinton jokes, compared to only forty-eight that mocked incumbent president George W. Bush, and a paltry thirty that targeted 9/11 mastermind Osama bin Laden.[14] Letterman, with typical deconstructive flair, even began reusing *old* Monicagate jokes, introducing them as "Clinton Classics": "This is a Clinton Classic joke. We originally told this joke February 4, 1999. The Republicans want Monica Lewinsky to testify in front of the Senate so they will have the opportunity to look her right in the eye. Well, hell, even Clinton hasn't done that."[15]

There is no denying that, for better or worse, Monica was a big story. But the fact that the jokes keep coming years after Clinton left office suggests that the late-night comedians' disproportionate response reflects something beyond their usual tendency to parallel the news media's priorities.

Obviously, the story's inherent prurience gave comedians plenty to work with—if "work" isn't too strong a word for writing cheap-shot jokes about the president's "naughty bits." But Monicagate didn't just provide late-night with a mother lode of material, it addressed a problem that had been plaguing the network shows for some time. Television performers and producers had been chipping away at censorship for years, but when cable came along (especially "premium" channels like HBO, home of the uncensored comedy concert), it took to the old standards and practices with a jackhammer. Suddenly, network comics were working at a disadvantage; they just couldn't keep up with the rising tide of "blue." Then one day the president of the United States—as if through an act of divine (or profane) intervention—presented them with the gift of Monica. For the nets, it was the perfect excuse to get as dirty as they wanted, which is to say as dirty as cable (almost), where for years comedians had been getting away with the kind of stuff that used to get Lenny Bruce arrested. It was a chance to capitalize on the public's (and especially the 18-to-34 demographic's) appetite for "edge," without violating their anti-political, personality-based SOP.

When Johnny Carson debuted as *The Tonight Show*'s host in 1962, the Oval Office was occupied by one of the champion philanderers of all time, but as monologue fodder, President John F. Kennedy's extramarital liaisons were strictly off-limits. Even if the prevailing network standards had allowed such jokes, they would not have worked, given public ignorance of that side of the president's private life. A longstanding, if unspoken, gentlemen's agreement between political leaders and the press kept such seamy details strictly off the record.

Since then, concurrent revolutions in both social attitudes and our notions about the rights and duties of the press have rendered such discretion passé. Whether the contemporary no-holds-barred approach to politicians' private lives has been good for either journalism or government is perhaps debatable. But for comedy, which depends on a rather delicate balance between what is known and what may be spoken, the new frankness with which every aspect of our political leaders' private lives and persons is treated is decidedly problematic.

Though Carson was, in fact, renowned for his deft use of innuendo and double entendres, working "clean" was a point of pride for him. Kenneth Tynan's *New Yorker* profile quotes him complaining about "lavatory-minded" British comedians, whom he found "unfunny, infantile, and obsessed with toilet jokes"—an attitude Tynan found prudish and typically American (adding that he considered it "depressing" to consider that "if Rabelais* were alive today he would not be invited to appear on the *Tonight Show*").[16] Carson's 11:30 successors had followed a similar code of conduct throughout their early careers. Jay Leno, whose Lewinsky jokes would be among the crudest and cruelest, had spent the years prior to his *Tonight Show* ascendancy

---

* François Rabelais (c. 1494–1553), French novelist known for his bawdy, scatological humor in such works as *Gargantua and Pantagruel*.

building a reputation as a "nice guy" comic who never stooped to conquer an audience. "Leno doesn't do battle-of-the-sexes jokes, or gay jokes, or breast-implant jokes, he says, because they offend too many listeners. (In a foul-mouthed age, he's also incredibly clean)," wrote an admiring journalist in 1992.[17] Prior to the Lewinsky affair, David Letterman seemed almost to squirm when circumstances compelled him to tell an off-color joke. Often, he would follow up his more egregious punch lines with a shamefaced disclaimer: "Yes, ladies and gentlemen, it's my proudest moment."

But when Monica came along, Leno and Letterman seemed to have little trouble putting aside their professional principles or their innate prudery. In fact, they took to the subject and all its sordid details with unabashed eagerness, as the CMPA's figures and the most cursory sampling of their material suggest. Brent Bozell III of the arch-conservative Media Research Center joked that if there were, as Hillary Clinton famously suggested, a "vast, right-wing conspiracy" behind the ceaseless focus on her husband's sex life, Leno must be its leader.[18]

Leno would, of course, deny that any of his 3,722 Clinton jokes reflected any partisan bias on his part. Yet most of these jokes definitely skewed "conservative," not because they targeted Clinton but because of the view of sexuality—particularly female sexuality—that they invoked. If, by becoming more straightforwardly offensive, late-night humor has abandoned the Yankee reserve Carson epitomized, it has revealed an ironic affinity for the values of another stalwart archetype of Olde New England: the Puritan. For all their licentiousness, most of the Bill & Monica jokes are not titillating in the least. The "liberalized" sexual discourse let the comedians discuss all the dirty details even while they preached a message of moral judgment and condemnation as old-fashioned as Plimouth Plantation—a Cotton Mather sermon with "laffs."

No Sex, Please—We're American

Considering the sheer quantity of Lewinsky jokes, it will be helpful to sort them out by type. Though the distinctions blur a bit around the edges, the jokes seem to roughly fall into four categories. First, and least common, are the jokes that have some actual relevance to Clinton's official role:

> Monica Lewinsky's interview with Barbara Walters is this week. Monica Lewinsky's book comes out this week. And Monica Lewinsky's British TV interview airs this week. And today, President Clinton announced he's bombing every country in the world (Leno).[19]

This qualifies as genuine political satire, a rarity among Monicagate jokes and mainstream late-night jokes in general. It contains no explicit sexual details, yet it is an "exposing" joke, in that it purports to reveal the psychological motive (sexual shame) behind the president's actions. Arguably, this joke (and its handful of categorical cousins) represents late-night's typical approach at its best, demonstrating a connection between the personal and the political that is truly consequential. The only problem with this joke— and it's no small thing—is that it is based on a cynical (and widely discredited) interpretation of the coincidental timing of the President's grand jury testimony and airstrikes he ordered on Sudan and Afghanistan.[20]

The second category of jokes rely on hyperbolic descriptions of Clinton's supposed sexual insatiability:

> Did you all watch the president's speech last night? Regardless of what you think, I thought he did a great job—very inspiring, very uplifting. You know what I thought was the best part? That he remained faithful to Hillary through the whole thing. That was seventy-two minutes. And not once, not once, did he stray. (Leno)[21]

This is nothing more than a variation on the one-dimensional exaggeration of a trait upon which late-night political humor typically relies. The *Clinton* = *horndog* formula used here is just a racier equivalent of such schematic "character" premises as *Bob Dole* = *old* and *Dan Quayle* = *dumb*. These aim lower than the category one jokes, but can be said to have political value, in a democratic, "leveling" sense. Drawing our attention to the leader of the free world's libido reminds us that he is not just a powerful man but also a fallible (perhaps exceptionally fallible) human being. Bill Clinton, these jokes point out, takes his pants off one leg at a time, just like you and me—though probably more often.

The third category consists of evocative—okay, gross—allusions to specific sex acts:

> And this Thursday, Monica Lewinsky's book officially goes on sale. Well, I guess she goes into all the details of her sexual encounters with President Clinton. Don't assume this is a kiss and tell book. This is more like a kneel and duck book. (Leno—see also the "look her in the eye" Letterman example cited above)[22]

These jokes can be considered satirical only insofar as they address some cultural "uptightness" about sex and the body, and political only insofar as the presence of one type of repression (sexual) might indicate the presence of the other (political). This is an extremely dubious proposition: societies with strict sexual mores can in fact be radically egalitarian (for example, the Amish), while dictatorships can be licentious (as in Caligula's Rome, or *Brave New World*'s eroticized dystopia).[23] In any case, the reaction to most of the category three jokes—heavier on groans than laughter—suggests that they do not so much challenge repressive attitudes as exploit them.

The fourth category of Monicagate jokes—and by far the most common—depends upon a derogatory assessment of the physical attributes of Monica Lewinsky and other women with whom Clinton was linked:

> I've always been on Monica's side. And she's lost thirty pounds, which is nice, so that means that now finally she can walk through New York City with a yellow dress and not get hailed. (Letterman)[24]

This type of joke was a particular specialty for the once proudly "clean" Jay Leno:

> Today President Clinton visited—oh, here, I've been there, the Harley Davidson factory in York, Pennsylvania. Did you see him on the news? Did you see him on the news sitting on the bike? Huh? You know, it's not the first time Clinton's been on a hog.

With Halloween right around the corner, Paula Jones is naked in
the December issue of *Penthouse* magazine [scattered groans]. If
you have not seen this issue, just picture Yasser Arafat with
breasts.

Clinton is going to Arkansas Sunday to campaign for Gore. In fact, I
understand Arkansas state troopers started already started rounding
up really ugly women.[25]

All of these jokes at least indirectly concern the president, but it's a stretch
to call any of them "political." Inasmuch as the president is even the target of
these jokes, all they criticize about him is his taste in sexual partners. Clinton
can't possibly be worthy of his office, these jokes imply; not because of per-
jury, or even adultery, but because he digs fat chicks.

The crudity and cruelty of the category three and four jokes aside, most
of them don't even work as *jokes*. They elicit groans, hooting, sometimes
applause, but little if any laughter. Given that they are, for the most part, neither politically relevant nor funny, what accounts for their prevalence?

Despite the protestations of Special Prosecutor Kenneth Starr, his political allies, and the more obsessive media crusaders that the Lewinsky investigation was "not about the sex," it was obvious even to some Clinton-haters
that it was about almost nothing else. Kenneth Anderson, a conservative who
favored Clinton's removal, complained, "Despite the surface rhetoric of per-
jury and the rule of law, the trial is about adultery and sin."[26] The common
allusion to a witch-hunt, trotted out during every political inquest, was never
more apt: Starr needed only the tall black hat and the buckle shoes.

The late-night comics may not have shared Starr's sense of moral superior-
ity, but their jokes tapped into a deep vein of American prudishness. The
groans, hoots, and applause that greeted these jokes did not mean that they had
failed; where ordinarily an audience's laughter can be understood as an expression of their agreement with a joke's comedic premise, here their responses
expressed agreement with the jokes' *moral* premise. Like the breathless, endless
news coverage and the quasi-pornographic Starr Report, these jokes tapped
into the simultaneous desires for titillation and self-righteous outrage.

Politically Incorrect's Bill Maher, an odd man out among late-night's uptight tut-tutters, was almost alone in critiquing, rather than parroting, the puritanical logic of Clinton's prosecutors. Opening his show one night in character as Trent Lott (then the Senate majority leader and a leading Clinton opponent), he launched into an insightful, if unsubtle, tirade:

> We [congressional Republicans] think Clinton deserves hate, because
> he's sexy and likes sex, and we aren't and don't. Oh, it's true, we have a
> lot of mistresses, sure, but that's just to show off to each other. It's a
> status thing. They're not attractive women, and frankly, we're not
> attractive men. . . . But Clinton, he likes sex. That man had to go.[27]

O'Brien's "Clutch Cargo" pieces also took a somewhat less judgmental tone toward the president than Letterman, Leno, and his own monologues. The Clinton he "interviewed" via video monitor, reveled in his bad-boy behavior, and the audience loved him for it. In effect, they were invited not only to laugh at the president but to laugh *with* him. "Clutch" Clinton is a Rabelaisian figure: an earthy, lusty hero-king whose outsized appetites bespeak joie de vivre and reject puritan shame.

But most of late-night's category three gross-out jokes assumed the audience was as appalled by the spectacle of human sexuality as Kenneth Starr—or Cotton Mather. The jokes I have identified as category four pointed to an even uglier strain of puritanism: gynophobia—a pathological fear and hatred of the female.

Devil with the (Stained) Blue Dress On

Misogyny, from mild (Henny Youngman's "Take my wife . . . *please*") to brutal (the entire oeuvre of Andrew Dice Clay, comedic poster boy for the eighties post-feminist backlash), has long been a source of tendentious humor, one that blurs Freud's neat distinction between the hostile and the obscene. Stand-up has always been a male-dominated field—a fact that helps explain both the prevalence of wife and mother-in-law jokes heard on *The Ed*

Sullivan Show in years past and the all-male late-night hosts' response to the Lewinsky matter.

This is not to say that the mainstream hosts are "alpha" males. The Diceman wasn't in the running for *The Tonight Show*. In fact, though he didn't mention Clay by name, Jay Leno might very well have had the then well-known provocateur in mind when he said, in a 1992 interview:

> You know, comedy has sort of turned around. . . . Years ago, you had Carlin or Pryor, they were the little guy versus the establishment. They were fighting the police, corporate America. Now when you see these comedians, suddenly the majority of white men are bashing the minority. When I watch some of these cable shows, they look like Nazi bund rallies—angry white teenagers going "Yeah! Yeah!"
>
> What is that in a comedy show? What is that all about? It's not anger against the system that's oppressing, it's anger towards oppressing the oppressed. It's waiting at the dock with sticks to beat these people up. And I don't like that. It's like fascist comedy.[28]

Leno seems to have learned since then that the "angry white teenagers" he once disparaged are known in the television industry as "white males, age 18–34." This is the key demographic he, Letterman, O'Brien, and network executives covet most, and—it doesn't seem too speculative to say—an audience that might be particularly receptive to jokes about oral sex and "fat chicks." In any event, Leno now appears to pander to an audience he once disdained. The crudeness and misogyny that began to surface in his Monica material (and have continued to color his once squeaky-clean monologues ever since) are hard to reconcile with the carefully tended "nice guy" persona he once projected, to say nothing of the comedic philosophy he laid out in 1992. Apparently, he's joined the "bund"—or perhaps women just don't count as "little guys."

Leno, always more of a salesman than an artiste, seems willing to stoop to almost anything to win the ratings war. Letterman had for some time refused to tell O. J. Simpson jokes. "Double homicides just don't crack me up the way they used to," he said.[29] But when Monicagate broke, he showed no hesitation in leaping into the muck. Perhaps he had learned something from having lost the Nielsen race to Leno's "Dancing Itos." O'Brien, who in his previous career as a writer for *SNL* wrote a sketch that featured the word "penis" forty-two times, attracts a younger demographic, with a show that is probably more consistently "dirty" than the 11:30 shows. Still, he too seems circumspect about catering to the *Jackass* crowd, aptly describing the "woo"-prone audiences he finds so distasteful as "too frat."[30]

Still, none of the mainstream late-night comics seemed too troubled by the chauvinistic cheap shots they were taking, night after night. As unsavory as the president's adulterous affair was, what the country's news and entertainment media made of it was far uglier. It would be asking a lot of mere comedians to resist that tide, or to handle it with restraint—though Leno's comments back in 1992 seemed like a reason to hope.

Politically Incorrect

None of this is to suggest that sex jokes and satire are mutually exclusive: there is a rich tradition of bawdy humor aimed at powerful persons dating back to Aristophanes. Nor are dirty jokes incompatible with the higher aspirations of art: think not only of Rabelais but of Dante and Shakespeare, who had their own scatological and smutty moments.

The question is not whether sexually explicit or scatological humor can have aesthetic merit—a dirty joke can be a good one—but whether it has any intrinsic *political* meaning. There is a widespread assumption that challenging taboos is "liberating," and thus inherently "liberal." The fact that "liberty," "liberate," "liberal," and "libertine" share the common root *liber*—Latin for "free"—has led to no end of confusion, and rhetorical manipulation.[31] Many of the complaints about "the liberal media" have less to do with the perception of bias on the *CBS Evening News* than with the smutty jokes on *Two and a Half Men*. Conflating the latter with the former—something of a specialty for organizations like Brent Bozell's—is fundamentally dishonest. Plenty of Americans who favor things like universal health care and affirmative action have never partaken of a ménage à trois and are not moved to laughter by references to excrement.

Nor is any assault on societal conventions inherently "liberal," in the politically progressive sense of the word. It depends on which conventions are being attacked. Since the end of the civil rights era, the idea that people ought to be judged, in the words of the Rev. Martin Luther King Jr., "not by the color of their skin, but by the content of their character," has been widely accepted as an American ideal—which is to say, a societal convention.[32] Ditto for the notions that men and women deserve the same pay for the same work, that those with physical handicaps deserve the same educational and occupational opportunities as the able-bodied, and that it is not only impolite but immoral to verbally or physically harass people because of their race, ethnicity, gender, or sexual orientation.

Moreover, many of the attitudes and sensitivities mocked as "politically correct" have only the faintest connection to politics. Despite the presence of the word "political," this overused phrase generally indicates a set of social taboos, more than an ideology. (Sometimes "politically incorrect" is used as a euphemism for simple rudeness or cruelty.) Yet despite its conceptual and ideological vagueness, professional iconoclasts from the libertarian center-left (Bill Maher) to the misogynist and crypto-racist right ("Dice" Clay, Colin Quinn, FOX News's *Half-Hour Newshour*) all proclaim their opposition to PC, regardless of what they might like to see happening in D.C.

When Parker and Stone mock homosexuals on *South Park*, or depict the violent deaths of Michael Moore, Janeane Garofalo, and other Hollywood lefties (in puppet form) in their film *Team America,* they are certainly attacking convention—that is, "political correctness." But this does not make them satirists, and despite all the confusion over *liber* and its suffixes, it certainly doesn't make them "liberal." In fact, right-wing author Brian C. Anderson has approvingly called Parker and Stone's foul-mouthed TV show "the most hostile to liberalism in television history," celebrating, in a book titled *South Park Conservatives,* what he sees as an emergent "anti-Left ethos" exemplified by Cartman and company's attacks on rampant media "liberalism" and PC sensitivity.[33] Before there were *South Park* conservatives, there were "pants-down Republicans," a libertine but anti-liberal cadre founded by former *National Lampoon* editor P. J. O'Rourke. The "pants-down" manifesto proclaimed,

"We Are in Favor of: Guns, Drugs, Fast Cars, Free Love (if our wives don't find out). We Are Opposed to: Taxes, Kennedys, Motorcycle Helmet Laws, Being a Pussy About Nuclear Power" and "Busing Our Children Anywhere Other Than Yale." A self-styled rebel who throws stones from the balcony of his penthouse, O'Rourke has continued his assault on PC "pussies" in such books as *Give War a Chance, Age and Guile Beat Youth, Innocence, and a Bad Haircut,* and *Republican Party Reptile.*[34]

Four-letter words have no particular political weight. Scatological humor, in the narrow, lavatorial sense, is "small-d" democratic, in that it reduces its human targets to the lowest-common denominator of their physicality. After all, as the title of a popular children's book puts it, *Everyone Poops.*[35] Beyond this general leveling tendency, however, bodily-function humor has no political valence. It might be revolutionary to suggest that some larger-than-life authoritarian strongman has to defecate, just like everybody else—depicting Stalin on the toilet would have been a brave act in the Soviet Union sixty years ago. But the United States doesn't have that kind of system. There is nothing to be gained for "liberalism"—in the politically progressive sense—from a parody of the Lincoln Memorial in which the Great Emancipator's pants are down around his ankles.[36] What would be the point? We already knew Lincoln was a common man, from a lowly background. That, indeed, is one of his, and America's, glories.

The violation of PC rules regarding race, gender, sexuality, and physical handicaps is more complicated. It is worth investigating the insincerity of our commitments to the ideals of equality to the extent that they go no deeper than the self-conscious use of euphemistic labels, such as "differently abled" for "handicapped" or "alternative lifestyle" for "gay." Certainly we should not allow politicians, bosses, landlords, or garden-variety bigots to paper over their racist pandering, hiring policies, or attitudes just because they have adopted the "politically correct" terminology to refer to those they otherwise despise or fear.

However, the "sensitivity" felt by African Americans regarding the use of the N-word, by women regarding sexist remarks in the workplace, and by minorities striving to triumph over discrimination arises not from some overweening and fundamentally dishonest prudery but from a real and in many cases horrible history of abuses. In such cases, words and jokes are suppressed not just because they are *politically* incorrect but because they are *actually* incorrect—and truly harmful.

The question of what should or should not be said is more difficult to determine, though, when viewed through the fog of comedy. When Carlos Mencia stages a "Stereotype Olympics," featuring such events as a watermelon-eating contest and a looting competition, is this an opportunity to critique stereotypes or an excuse to revive them? When Sarah Silverman "observes" in one of her faux-homilies at the end of *The Sarah Silverman Program* that "old black women are wise beyond their years; and young black women are . . . prostitutes," is she mocking such attitudes or merely exploiting them?[37]

Without a clearly defined, progressive agenda, opening such previously closed avenues for comic exploration is merely opening Pandora's box. By making "political correctness"—rather than bigotry, homophobia, sexism, and cruelty—the primary target, "edgy" comedy has moved our discourse in a mostly *illiberal* direction. The critical—or rather *uncritical*—praise that has been heaped upon the mostly mindless and often irresponsible iconoclasm of Silverman, *Family Guy,* Parker and Stone, et al. has not only inflated the reputations of a fair number of artists insufficiently talented to succeed without shock, it has also helped enable a revival of a much uglier kind of humor by providing the pretense that merely violating taboos is a worthy end in itself.

The Imus affair illustrated the shallowness of this view. Don Imus had for years enjoyed the imprimatur of legitimacy, owing to the frequent guest appearances by heavy hitters from the worlds of politics and journalism—Senators John Kerry, Joe Lieberman, and John McCain, as well as NBC's Tim Russert and *Newsweek*'s Howard Fineman were frequent guests—on his radio show. But it all came crashing down when he referred to the Rutgers women's basketball team (which included a large proportion of African American players) as "nappy-headed hos."

Imus, roundly condemned by the nation's editorial pages and abandoned by many of his former friends, was off the air in two weeks. Yet the slur that broke the camel's back was no worse than many of Imus's other "politically incorrect" remarks over the years—among other examples, Imus and his sidekicks referred to Gwen Ifill as "the cleaning lady," Barack Obama as "a young colored fella," and CBS management as "cheap Jewish bastards."[38] The innocence of his victims—college athletes who could be considered "public figures" only by virtue of their inspiring achievement in reaching the NCAA final—had something to do with the outrage in this instance. But it is possible that the shock jock's comeuppance marked a turning point in the public's tolerance for intolerant humor.

Washington Post media columnist Howard Kurtz revealed much about the extent to which "political incorrectness" has come to be legitimized as a worthy end in itself (not least by the Beltway press Kurtz represents) when he rather carelessly proclaimed, "Imus made fun of blacks, Jews, gays, politicians. He called them lying weasels. This was part of his charm."[39] (What is more charming than bigotry and cynicism?) Imus's defenders, and a few of his detractors, took the opportunity to equate his outrageous remarks to the politically incorrect parlance of rappers, provocateurs like Coulter, shock comics like Silverman, and satirists like Chris Rock. Offensive is offensive, right? The N-word is the N-word, no matter who says it.

This is specious reasoning, of course, but it is the inevitable corollary of the celebration of outrageousness for its own sake. What distinguishes Chris Rock's use of racist language from Imus's is political intent: Imus's political leanings are a mugwump mixture of xenophobic conservatism and humanist-liberal, but his "politically incorrect" remarks have nothing to do with his politics—they are entirely gratuitous. Rock's shocks are not just politically incorrect but *political*, and progressive.

But the celebration of "edge" pays no heed to intent; and without imposing some kind of *real* standard of political (that is, ideological) correctness—unthinkable in a pluralistic democracy—how can we enforce any standard that takes intent into account? When Rush Limbaugh refers to Senator Barack Obama as "Halfrican-American," how is he different than Mencia? When Fox News's "comedy" show, *The Half-Hour News Hour*, claims that, if elected president, Hillary Clinton will appoint "a diverse group . . . of angry lesbians," how can those who celebrate Silverman's "outrageousness" complain? When self-proclaimed "Red-State Comedian" Brad Stine titles his stand-up DVD *Tolerate This,* who are we not to tolerate it?[40]

FRONTIER BRIS

In 1893, historian Frederick Jackson Turner proclaimed that the closing of the frontier marked the end of the first chapter in the development of the American character. Up to that point, Turner argued, we had been defined as a people by continually advancing the "edge" of civilization. Now that that edge had disappeared, we would have to discover a new paradigm.

American comedy, too, has been defined by its pursuit of the "edge"— at least since the rise of "boomer humor" dawned with the 1950s debut of Mort Sahl, Lenny Bruce, *MAD* magazine, and the Second City. But the frontier those pioneers faced—a post-war society rife with conformism, a squeaky-clean popular culture, entrenched racial discrimination, and pre-Aquarian attitudes toward sex—is long gone. A lot of today's allegedly "edgy" comedy aims to colonize territory where Lenny Bruce already broke the sod fifty years ago. Some of it even threatens to let loose the lawless villains run off the range by Sheriffs Dick Gregory, Richard Pryor, and Norman Lear back when racism, sexism, and homophobia shot up the saloon every Saturday night.

Critics who define "edginess" as an end in itself, and laud "meanness" as a worthy comedic goal, need to orient themselves to a New Frontier. There is plenty of untamed territory for comedians brave enough to explore it. But it requires appealing to the audience's highest intelligence and their deepest humanity, not their lowest physical commonality and their most shameful fears and hatreds—which are not justified simply by coating them with a layer of irony.

Most of all, it requires embracing a sense of mission and purpose beyond the easy nihilism that, in different ways, makes the comedy of both the late-night mainstream and the officially sanctioned "edge" so toothless. "It may ridicule, parody, or caricature its target," writes Charles E. Schutz, "but the purpose of satire with its negative approach is positive change."[41]

In the meantime, we are awash in comedy that has almost reached the peak of pointless offensiveness predicted by Judge's *Idiocracy*. Worse, the critical establishment seems bent on preparing us to accept *Ow, My Balls!* upon its foreordained actual premiere, as the height of wit. Andrew Corsello rightly complains that "instead of regarding *South Park* as the poo-poo-joke repository it surely is, *Rolling Stone* declares it 'an uncompromisingly hilarious and curiously affecting show . . . [with a] bluntly smart *fin de siècle* comedic sensibility.'" When even the *New Yorker* asks us to contemplate the brilliance of Silverman's lyric, "If I find a stick I'll put it in your mama's butt / And pull it out and stick / The doody in her eye!" we have strayed a long way from what Lenny Bruce hoped comedy could accomplish, to say nothing of Steve Allen.[42] Ask not for whom the bell dings. It dings for us.

LAUGHING ALL THE WAY
TO THE WHITE HOUSE

The present blurring of the line between politics and entertainment was foreshadowed, long before Comedy Central or the Pew Center poll, in a very silly 1934 film called *Stand Up and Cheer*.[1] The plot concerns a Flo Ziegfeld–type producer (Warner Baxter), who is summoned to the nation's capital on a mission of the greatest urgency. As the president (presumably FDR, though we see only the back of his head) explains to this patriotic showman, all that is really necessary to restore the nation's confidence—and thus its prosperity—is a healthy dose of all-singing, all-dancing entertainment. Toward this end, Our Hero has been selected to fill a newly created cabinet post: Secretary of Amusement.

Though Jay Leno's Senate confirmation hearings would undoubtedly represent a ratings bonanza for C-SPAN, we probably won't be seeing the creation of such a post anytime soon. However, the road between the green room and the White House that brought Stephen Colbert to Washington, D.C., is a two-way street: presidential aspirants now routinely show up on late-night shows to demonstrate their comedic chops. They come seeking not only votes but—given the American public's relative respect for entertainers as compared to politicians—legitimacy. In fact, the biggest difference between *Stand Up and Cheer*'s vision of showbiz/government collaboration and the contemporary spectacle of John McCain or Hillary Clinton visiting *The Tonight Show* lies in who plays the host and who the eager-to-please guest. (Perhaps this power relationship should be conveyed by showing Letterman only from the back.)

The phenomenon of the late-night campaign stop is not entirely a new one. Both John F. Kennedy and Richard Nixon appeared on Jack Paar's *Tonight Show* in 1960.[2] But from Paar's relatively staid and respectful interviews to contemporary candidates' elaborate stunts and obligatory Top Ten Lists, the showbiz quotient of such meetings has increased considerably.

Even if they risk looking ridiculous, though, it's easy to understand why presidential aspirants would want to visit Jay, Dave, or Conan. The guest seat on a widely viewed entertainment program is a forum from which to reach an audience beyond the beltway and political-junkie demographic that follows developments on the *New York Times* op-ed page or the Sunday public affairs shows. But a late-night guest shot also affords a candidate the chance to demonstrate that he or she has a sense of humor, just like a regular person.

This can be a tricky business, however. In a 1952 essay titled "The Humor Paradox," E. B. White noted that "every American, to the last man, lays claim to a 'sense' of humor and guards it as his most significant spiritual trait, yet rejects humor as a contaminating element wherever found". With sardonic precision, White goes on to point out that "almost the only first-string Amerian statesman who managed to combine high office with humor was Lincoln, and he was murdered finally."

White's ruminations were prompted by the presidential campaign then under way. "Adlai Stevenson has been reprimanded by General Eisenhower for indulging in humor and wit, and Mr. Stevenson has very properly been warned of the consequences by his own party leaders, who are worried," wrote White. "Their fears are well grounded." Though Stevenson's two losses to Eisenhower were certainly attributable to more than the candidates' relative wittiness, it seems safe to concede that White had a point—at least in 1952.[3]

Yet eight years later, witty John F. Kennedy defeated (albeit narrowly) the humorless Richard M. Nixon. And twenty years after that, the comedically adept challenger Ronald Reagan trounced the earnest incumbent Jimmy Carter. Now candidates routinely seek to distinguish themselves as not only more honest and qualified but funnier than their foes. What has become of White's paradox over the last half century? Has the rise of the pseudo-satire industry turned a good sense of humor from a political liability to an asset—even a necessity? Is it still even possible for a candidate to be, in Morris Udall's memorable phrase, "too funny to be president"?[4]

The Mount Rushmore of Funny

Though Congress has had its share of jokers (Senator Udall being one of the most renowned), and the White House walls have doubtless echoed with private wit, only a few U.S. presidents have been publicly known as funny men. Three in particular—Abraham Lincoln, John F. Kennedy, and Ronald Reagan—stand out, not just because they were funny, but because they understood how to use humor to their political advantage.

Legend treats Lincoln's humor as just another facet of his folksy authenticity: like his honesty, his great physical strength, and his homely/wise visage. But the real Lincoln was less a backwoods naïf than a shrewd politician. His humor was not just a personal trait, but a tool he used consciously, and with considerable guile. Far from a badge of his humble sincerity, Lincoln's comic facility was the secret weapon of a master manipulator.

John Ford's 1939 film *Young Mr. Lincoln* portrays the future president as more stand-up comedian than lawyer, able to charm a jury or calm a lynch mob simply by keeping them in stitches. Though the plot's details are fictionalized, this characterization has considerable foundation in fact. Lincoln often used humor to move an audience, whether in the courtroom or on the dais during his celebrated debates with Stephen A. Douglas.

As president, though, Lincoln had little occasion to coax laughter from a crowd; jokes would have seemed distinctly out of place in the Gettysburg Address or the Second Inaugural. But in more intimate settings he continued to use humor to soothe, to cajole, even to misdirect. While Lincoln's love of anecdotes was genuine, "he also knew how to use storytelling to deflect criticism, to avoid giving an answer to a difficult question, and to get rid of a persistent interviewer," according to biographer David Herbert Donald. "Lincoln used this technique throughout his presidency, to the bafflement of those who had no sense of humor and the rage of those who failed to get a straight answer from him."[5]

It's not surprising that Lincoln is the only nineteenth-century president widely remembered for being funny. Before the dawn of the age of mass communication, humor had limited political value. It was one hundred years before the United States had its second really funny president, John F. Kennedy—who, not coincidentally, is also remembered as the first "television president". In fact, thanks to his mastery of the new medium, Kennedy had opportunities to use humor on a public scale Lincoln could not have imagined. Kennedy's smooth repartee and spontaneous wit (which his decision to broadcast live press conferences let shine) charmed the public and press corps alike. In Lincoln's day, one might seek an audience with the president; now the president *had* an audience—and by playing to them he could assure that, to a large extent, those few killjoys "enraged" and "baffled" by his flippant remarks would be drowned out in a sea of chuckles. Though some undoubtedly did disdain his breezy manner as a sign of elitism or frivolity, many more could not get enough of "the Kennedy wit," even after his death—as evinced by sales of Bill Adler's 1967 book of that title.[6] (E. B. White, still on the scene in 1963, was not so sardonic as to suggest a pattern of funny presidents being assassinated.)

As a Hollywood-trained performer, Reagan was poised to take the stand-up presidency to the next level, and in the two decades that separated his election from JFK's, television and the entertainment-based culture it enabled had spread across the land like crabgrass. In 1960, wit and charisma—even glamour—had helped Kennedy triumph over an unimpressive résumé and a more experienced opponent, as demonstrated by the famous televised debate in which the fit, tanned, and rested senator had "won" by debating the haggard, pasty vice president to a draw. In 1980, an ease and rapport with the camera had become such a vital and accepted prerequisite for leadership of the free world that a résumé that included starring roles in *Hellcats of the Navy* and *Bedtime for Bonzo,* far from being an embarrassment, was a positive boon. If Kennedy was a politician with an entertainer's facility, Reagan represented the next logical step: the entertainer as politician. Style had been a part of American politics since the beginning, but only with television could it come to so thoroughly trump substance. Consider the fact that while

Lincoln is memorialized as "The Great Emancipator," Reagan's moniker— "the Great Communicator"—alludes not to any political achievement, but to his rhetorical salesmanship.

As was true with Lincoln, Reagan's fondness for funny stories caused some to regard him as frivolous or disengaged. But whereas Lincoln was a melancholy workaholic who turned to humor as a means of political defense and personal escape, Reagan was a lazy and lighthearted fellow who saw in the presidency less a bully pulpit than a stage. According to biographer Lou Cannon, Reagan "was the resident humorist and gag writer in a White House where nearly everything else was done for him while he engaged in government by anecdote."[7] Reagan didn't need a Secretary of Amusement: that was one job he chose to handle personally.

It is difficult to overstate the importance of Reagan's humor to his political success. In both 1980 and 1984, his victories in the televised debates—and arguably, in the elections that followed—hinged on one-liners. "There you go again" was the zinger he used against Jimmy Carter. Though it failed to address Carter's point (regarding Reagan's past opposition to Medicare), Reagan's blithe bon mot struck many voters, in Cannon's words, as "funny, irrelevant—and thoroughly authentic."[8]

"Authentic" it may have been, but it was hardly substantive—nor was it spontaneous. Reagan had rehearsed the line in his debate prep and was just waiting for an opportune moment to unleash it.[9] In spite of its breezy irrelevance, Reagan's laugh line was instantly immortalized as a political masterstroke, while Carter's point, based as it was in mere matters of fact and policy, was quickly forgotten.

Four years later, the seventy-three-year-old incumbent faced rumors that he was fading into senescence, fueled by his fumbling performance in the first debate with Democratic challenger Walter Mondale. But Reagan came to their next face-off armed with another well-crafted quip. When the age question arose, Reagan parried it deftly, slyly insisting that he would not "exploit, for political purposes, my opponent's youth and inexperience."[10] Delivered flawlessly, the line got a good laugh even from Mondale. More important, it neutralized the "senility" issue by showing Reagan to be both aware of and untroubled by voters' misgivings about his age. His very blithe-ness effectively reassured the public that their concerns about his mental acuity were groundless. It was, as Jack Germond and Jules Witcover noted tersely in their chronicle of the 1984 election, "a hell of a one-liner."[11]

By and large, "the Reagan wit" (as Adler titled the 1998 "sequel" to his earlier bestseller) was perceived by the press, the public, and even many of his political opponents as a benign and endearing trait.[12] It served him well in a number of circumstances. After being wounded in an assassination attempt in 1981, Reagan was reported to have kept up a Henny Youngman– like stream of quips even as he was wheeled into surgery: "I hope all you fellas are Republicans," he supposedly said to the trauma team.[13] Reports of the presi-dent's display of grace under pressure smack of the apocryphal—being shot and sedated do not generally enhance one's ability to engage in good-natured banter. Nonetheless, the image of Reagan conducting an impromptu mono-logue from the operating table was completely—as they say in Hollywood—in character. Dubious though the details may be, news of Reagan's ER antics arguably reassured a nation shaken by the news of his shooting.

Reagan could also use his reputation as a joker to camouflage the darker aspects of his personality and worldview. When he claimed to have laryngi-tis to avoid reporters' Iran-Contra questions during a March 1987 photo oppor-tunity, reporters seemed more amused than outraged.[14] More disturbing was the "joke" the president told during the aircheck preceding his regularly scheduled radio broadcast in August of 1984. "My fellow Americans," the familiar voice began, "I am pleased to tell you I just signed legislation out-lawing Russia forever. The bombing begins in five minutes." This ghoulish remark elicited considerable outrage on the nation's editorial pages, and Reagan eventually offered a grudging apology. He also gave an intriguing, if unconvincing, rationale for the bombing bit: "I was sitting in a small room ready to do my radio broadcast with a few of my own people around me— and actually I meant it as a kind of a satirical blast against those who were trying to paint me as a warmonger."[15]

To which those convinced he *was* a warmonger might have replied, "Better a satirical blast than a real one." It seems more likely that the aircheck leak was deliberate, and that the "joke" was designed to send a message—or rather two messages, to two audiences: reassurance to Reagan's most ardently anti-Soviet supporters, intimidation and warning to the Soviets. As for everybody else, their outrage, their unease, and their offended sensibilities could all be dismissed with that disclaimer of last resort: "It was only a joke." There he goes again.

Gerald Ford versus Monkey Pus

With few exceptions, comedians are born, not made. Kennedy and Reagan had the gift—the presidents who served in the years between them did not. Lyndon Johnson, who sometimes displayed a lively, if crude, sense of humor in private, was, on television, as dour and ponderous as Ed Sullivan in a Stetson.[16] Richard Nixon was renowned for his humorlessness, his 1968 *Laugh-In* cameo notwithstanding.[17] Jimmy Carter, whose post-presidential public appearances (including a few late-night guest spots) have shown him to posses a surprisingly mischievous wit, while in office more often conveyed sanctimony.

Of course, America was a tough room in the 1960s and '70s. The cultural and political upheavals of those years opened up fissures all across the societal landscape: a "credibility gap" loomed between the people and their leaders, while a "generation gap" divided children from their parents. There was a humor gap, too. The "boomer humor" of the 1950s, exemplified by such figures as Mort Sahl and Lenny Bruce, had set the stage for George Carlin, Richard Pryor, and *National Lampoon*—the comedic equivalent of rock and roll.[18] ("Why such dirty language?" one can imagine perplexed elders asking. "Whatever happened to Jack Benny?")

The funny-president interregnum between Kennedy and Reagan coincided with an acceleration of comedy's stylistic transformation. For a time, in fact, it looked like a radical reconfiguration of the relationships between politics, public opinion, and laughter was under way. The sixties youth rebellion, after all, was directed not only against the war, the draft, racism, and capitalist excess but in some measure against seriousness itself. A good deal of countercultural satire was nihilistically absurd. The Yippies, not content to mock the existing parties and candidates in a manner that tacitly implied that *alternative* parties and candidates might be legitimate, attacked not only the social order but the whole *idea* of order through such outlandish actions as nominating a pig for president and attempting to levitate the Pentagon.[19]

Ultimately, the humor revolution would dissolve into the same miasma of co-optation, disillusionment, and decadence as most of the other "revolutions" of that era—as Woodstock spawned Altamont and eventually MTV, so did Pryor and Carlin lead to Andrew Dice Clay and Pauly Shore. But the deterioration from shock to schlock was gradual; and even commercialized, domesticated, and stripped of political purpose, "boomer humor" presented a bewildering challenge to politicians of an older generation.

As the first post-Vietnam and post-Watergate president, and the unelected successor of the first man ever to resign the office, Gerald Ford faced a number of daunting challenges. As it happened, he also had to face the comedic assaults of the burgeoning satire industry. In particular, he had to contend with *Saturday Night Live*, which debuted only months after he had been sworn in, and which, of course, featured Chevy Chase's clueless, stumbling impression of him. Ford may have been ill equipped to deal with such a barrage of ridicule, but he did seem to realize what he was up against—or at any rate, Press Secretary Ron Nessen, did, as he recounts in his memoir:

> One Saturday night in 1976 I was home in bed, flipping around the TV dial. . . . I stopped dead at Channel Four. I couldn't believe what I was seeing and hearing. A tall, young comedian named Chevy Chase was falling down, bumping into things, uttering malapropisms and misunderstanding everything said to him. . . . After that I watched with fascination every Saturday, wincing at Chase's portrayal of the president. I worried that the act could further damage Ford's public image, but stirring in the back of my mind was the notion that perhaps the popularity of "Saturday Night" might make it the vehicle to counteract the bumbler image.[20]

Step one was to arrange an invitation for Chase to perform at the 1975 Radio and Television Correspondents Association dinner, where he appeared in character as Ford, accompanied by "Secret Service Agents" John Belushi and Dan Ackroyd. By luring Chase onto the president's home turf, Ford would gain an opportunity to demonstrate his good sportsmanship. As Chase went through his repertoire of pratfalls and verbal blunders, the real Ford, seated just a few feet away on the dais, laughed indulgently. When Chase was finished, Ford launched into his own well-rehearsed bit, scattering silverware and the pages of his "speech" (actually a sheaf of blank paper). The president concluded his routine by pronouncing Chevy Chase "a very, very funny suburb."[21]

It all went very well for the administration, but the dinner was not, in those pre-C-SPAN days, much of a public affair. Soon Nessen got the chance to bring his co-optation offensive to a bigger stage. When he accepted Al Franken's half-joking invitation to host *SNL*, he did so with "a very specific political objective in mind," according to Hill and Weingrad.[22] The Correspondents Dinner had been merely an out-of-town tryout. *Saturday Night Live* would give the "good sport" plan a chance to work its magic on the public. The Ford administration would show it had nothing to fear from a bunch of punk kids and their silly sketch show. Nessen would share the stage with Chevy Chase, and the president himself would appear, via videotape, to introduce the show and the Chase-anchored "Weekend Update" segment.

Nessen's big mistake was trusting *SNL*'s writers and producers not to make fools of him and his boss. Here was the presidential press secretary handing an irreverent comedy show the opportunity, in the words of one of the show's writers, to "make [Ford] cringe and squirm."[23] *SNL*'s rebellion, as previously mentioned, stuck to the low road. The cringing and squirming would be induced not via brave or incisive political satire but by gross-out sketches like a commercial parody detailing the benefits of "Autumn Fizz . . . the douche with the effervescence of uncola." Another comic masterpiece took off on the Smucker's jam slogan ("With a name like Smucker's, it's got to be good!") with a list of randomly offensive product names, including Monkey Pus, Dog Vomit, and Painful Rectal Itch.[24] Presented with a unique opportunity to speak truth to power, Lorne Michaels and company responded with sketches based on juvenile wordplay and gratuitous ickyness.

Be that as it may, the administration's co-optation offensive had clearly backfired. Nessen's predecessor, Jerry terHorst, called his successor's decision to appear on *SNL* "a gross error of judgment," and in retrospect Nessen himself was hard-pressed to disagree.[25] But his error was tactical rather than strategic. While boomer-humor ridicule presented establishment types with a steep learning curve, co-optation could mitigate its effects, as favorable coverage of Ford's act at the Correspondents Dinner had demonstrated.

Like the advertisers of soft drinks and automobiles, politicians and their operatives will look for ways to use cultural (even countercultural) currents in order to better reach and influence the public. One can't begrudge them this; it is more or less their job. But for those who cling to the hope that satire might flourish on television—might even play some constructive political role—the more disheartening aspect of the Nessen affair is *SNL*'s failure to rise to the occasion. Considering his terrible judgment in the matter, perhaps Nessen deserved no better than carbonated douches and monkey pus—but the viewing (and voting) public most certainly did.

LEADING THE FREE WORLD IS EASY—*COMEDY* IS HARD

A sense of humor like Ronald Reagan's can no more be faked than a musician's sense of rhythm or an athlete's physical grace. Still, if Ford and Nessen's *SNL* misadventure provides a cautionary tale, Reagan presents a model for the politically effective use of humor in the television age. While his successor, George H. W. Bush, failed to follow his mentor's example, Bill Clinton showed that what was instinctual for the Gipper could be successfully emulated, even by one who lacked the Great Communicator's comic gift.

The elder Bush often seemed incapable of either making or taking a joke. Following *Newsweek*'s October 1987 cover story bearing the unflattering headline "Fighting the 'Wimp' Factor," he remained hypersensitive about any mention of what was thereafter referred to around the White House as the W-word. But as any past victim of playground taunting could have told him, letting on that it bothered him only made matters worse. Throughout Bush's presidency, journalists continued to invoke "the wimp factor." Again and again, one read either that it was finally being "put to rest" (as when the president sent troops to Panama or Iraq) or that it was coming back to haunt him (as when he backed down on his "no new taxes" pledge). No matter how many locker-room epithets he awkwardly salted his speech with, no matter how much country music he listened to, or how many pork rinds he ate, Bush could never entirely overcome the impression that he was an effete, effeminate fusspot. (Cartoonist Pat Oliphant always depicted Bush as carrying a purse.)[26]

Reagan's approach to personal criticisms operated on a sort of inoculation principle, in which a small, self-injected dose of the harmful pathogen induces immunity. Reagan's perceived personal flaws, such as advanced age and laziness, never took on the defining dimensions of the A-word or the L-word, because Reagan essentially beat his critics to the punch with a punch line. He was a master of defusing criticism through preemptive self-deprecation.

This was a strategy George H. W. Bush seemed incapable of following. Instead of humorously embracing his quirks and flaws, he worked earnestly to deny them. Rather than make light of his patrician background and manner, he went out of his way to convince the public that he was a Regular Joe who loved the Grand Old Opry and hated broccoli. Perhaps no amount of self-effacing humor would have persuaded Americans to accept Bush for the privileged, Ivy League preppy he was, and—unlike his equally well-born son—*seemed* to be. In any case, his attempts to impersonate John Wayne did little to dispel his effete image: Oliphant's purse remained, and so did the W-word.

Bush was somewhat more successful, though, in dealing with his term's Chevy Chase. It helped that Dana Carvey's impression of him was less cartoonishly broad than Chase's Ford. Whereas Chase had made no attempt to look or sound like Ford—he just acted confused and fell down a lot—Carvey captured the president's voice and (with some help from makeup and wardrobe) look. He also latched onto a couple of catchphrases ("Not gonna do it," "wouldn't be prudent") which—even if the real Bush had rarely if ever said them—seemed to capture the awkward emptiness of his rhetoric.

Bush's response to the impression was uncharacteristically good-natured and politically astute. He obliquely acknowledged Carvey's take on his speaking style at the 1990 Gridiron Dinner, with lines like "California earth-quake? Not my fault. San Andreas Fault."[27] It was a welcome moment of self-deprecation, though it was hard to get much political mileage out of it, since the Gridiron is a private affair, where even C-SPAN's cameras are not permitted and the details of what is said are officially off the record. Likewise, Bush's invitation for Carvey to perform the impression at the 1992 White House staff Christmas party showed great sportsmanship but a lousy political sense—like the Gridiron Dinner, it took place out of the public eye. What's more, the timing stank: by the time Bush cozied up to his doppel-ganger, the election was over, and he had lost. If he had learned anything about humor from Ford or the Gipper, he had learned it too late.

Bill Clinton's sense of humor may have been no better than Bush's, but he was a far more savvy and skillful politician. As a member of the post–World War II generation, he could also be expected to have a better understanding of boomer humor's underpinnings. He would need to draw on every advan-tage he could: not only was he in for a rocky eight years, but just as Ford's presidency coincided with the debut of *Saturday Night Live,* Clinton's aligned with another satire industry growth spurt, set off by the Leno/Letterman/Hall late-night "wars." He was in for a lot of mockery.

As a wit, Clinton was no Reagan or Kennedy, but he could be taught. Not that getting Clinton to use humor effectively wasn't a challenge. Mark Katz, the administration's more-or-less official joke-writer, describes his boss as a bit thin-skinned and reluctant to laugh at himself. Most of the jokes Katz wrote for his first assignment, the 1993 White House Correspondents Dinner, "were on the topic of [Clinton's] bumpy first hundred days in office. He leafed through my draft, his face unlit with enthusiasm. 'Enough jokes on me,' he said. 'We need to do more jokes on all of them'"—meaning the audi-ence full of reporters.[28]

Katz knew that self-deprecating humor was the best way for someone in a position of power to ingratiate himself to an audience. "From what I could tell," Katz writes, "this did not come naturally to Bill Clinton."[29] But Clinton did understand that the rise of infotainment culture meant that an effective politician had to be as much showman as statesman. It was Clinton, after all, who established late-night TV as an obligatory campaign stop with his appearance on *Arsenio* in 1992.

Before the end of his tumultuous tenure in the oval office, his political instincts would lead Clinton to see the wisdom of Katz's advice. By the time he made his final presidential appearance at the White House Correspondents Dinner in 2000, Clinton could deliver a comic monologue as skillfully as he did the State of the Union address (and in a fraction of the time).

Though it was a lame-duck event, and still only a semi-public affair (unlike the still off-the-record Gridiron gathering, the Correspondents Dinner now welcomed C-SPAN's cameras), Clinton still had a political purpose in mind: burnishing his post-presidential image. Following some suitably self-mocking remarks (and a handful of jabs at political opponents and reporters), he introduced a slickly produced—and quite funny—six-minute video presentation. Titled "The Final Days" (a tongue-in-cheek reference to Woodward and Bernstein's account of the twilight of the Nixon administration), the video showed Clinton suffering through the end of his term in lonely boredom, reduced to answering the White House phones, packing sack lunches for his wife (Hillary Clinton having just been elected the junior senator from New York), washing the limo, and playing Battleship with the chairman of the Joint Chiefs of Staff.[30] The film was a hit with the press corps, and on the Internet, where Peter Beckman of AdCritic.com reported two hundred thousand downloads in the first week.[31] The "Final Days" video may well be the funniest thing a United States president has ever done on purpose.

Not everyone approved of Clinton's emergence as an amateur sitcom star. Susan Silver, a writer for the *Mary Tyler Moore* and *Bob Newhart* shows, expressed her misgivings in an op-ed essay: "Now that the bar has been raised so high, America will be looking for a major laugh riot talent in the next president of the United States," she fretted. "Now all the candidates are yukking it up with Letterman and Leno. To prove what? That they're funny? That they're just like us? I don't want presidents to be just like me, and I don't care if they're funny."[32]

What Clinton had come to understand, however, was not so much that the American people demand their leaders be funny but that humor, used the right way, could be a valuable political tool. Moreover, he had shown that the proper use of this tool could be learned and that, in the television era, a certain kind of joking behavior was something a contemporary politician needed to master. Poor Adlai Stevenson—could it be he was just born forty years too soon?

A Funny Thing Happened on the Way to the White House

If it's true that a sense of humor has, since Stevenson's day, gone from being a political liability to an asset, this does not mean that the race always goes to the swiftest, or the election to the funniest. If a presidential candidate is now permitted—and even expected—to be funny, he must still be funny in the right way.

This is not just a matter of avoiding gaffes, though an ill-advised quip can hurt. John McCain raised some hackles with an off-the-cuff parody of the Beach Boys' "Barbara Ann," altering the lyrics to "Bomb Iran."[33] Hillary Clinton and Joe Biden, in separate incidents, invoked the stereotype of Indian immigrants running convenience stores (Clinton even managed to simultaneously insult India's greatest national hero, Mahatma Gandhi, introducing one of the great man's aphorisms by identifying him as the proprietor of "a gas station down in St. Louis").[34] But the political efficacy of humor depends not just upon good taste, or even comedic skill. It is also a matter of style.

If the 2000 election had been decided on the same basis as *Last Comic Standing,* Al Gore would have easily defeated George W. Bush. As vice president, he had already been a guest on Letterman's show in 1993—a funny turn, in which he smashed an ashtray with a hammer to demonstrate a ludicrous government regulation.[35] Gore possessed—in spite of his dull, "stiff" reputation—an ironic intelligence and an acute sense of comic timing. And, if needed, he could always count on advice from his daughter Kristin, a professional comedy writer.

Most important, Gore had demonstrated an ability to use his comic gifts to offset his perceived shortcomings. "Would you like to see me do the macarena?" he asked the crowd at the 1992 Democratic convention, who responded with cheers of encouragement. Gore stood for a moment, motionless and expressionless, then drawled, "Would you like to see it again?"[36] When the 2000 race got under way, he seemed eager to make further political use of his comic aptitude, and was soon seen holding Jay Leno's cue cards, and getting more laughs on *Letterman*.[37]

When it came to public displays of wit, it was George W. Bush who looked like the real stiff. His reluctance to follow Gore on the late-night trail seemed to indicate that he realized this. When Bush, after weeks of on-air taunting, finally agreed to a satellite interview with Letterman, the results were near disastrous. Bush's verbal clumsiness—a trait Letterman and his late-night peers had already singled out for ridicule—was exacerbated by the awkward satellite delay. Even worse was the candidate's charmless attempt to make sport of Letterman's recent open-heart surgery. (Letterman had undergone a quintuple bypass in January.) As recounted by Caryn James in the *New York Times*, "When Mr. Letterman asked what Mr. Bush meant by his phrase, 'I'm a uniter, not a divider,' the governor said, 'That means when it comes time to sew up your chest cavity, we use stitches as opposed to opening it up.' The audience booed; Mr. Letterman looked baffled; the camera turned to his producer, who shrugged as if to say, 'I don't know what it means either.'"[38]

Whatever he thought of Bush's "joke," Letterman appeared to be even more annoyed by the candidate's reluctance to pay his show a personal visit, as Gore had. In typical mock-hyperbolic manner, Letterman began lobbying on the air for Bush to show up on the stage of the Ed Sullivan Theater. "The road to the White House goes through me," he teased. At one point he issued an invitation for both candidates to face off in a *Late Show* debate. Gore immediately accepted, in spite of the ludicrous ground rules the comedian proposed. (Don Rickles was to moderate, and at some point, drop his pants and fire off a rocket.)[39] Bush ignored Letterman's entreaties to make a personal appearance, prompting further taunting from the *Late Show* host: "If you turn it down, see, it makes you look like you're scared, like you're a little girl," he said, purporting to address Bush personally.[40]

Finally, a few weeks before the election, Bush agreed to face Letterman. Things went considerably better for Bush this time, though it was far from

the lighthearted laugh-fest he and *Late Show* viewers may have been antici-
pating. Letterman was respectful but persistent, subjecting Bush to a fairly
serious grilling on a range of issues, from global warming to the Middle East
to the death penalty. "Letterman proved himself to be twice as tough as many
of the journalists who've covered Bush this year," wrote *Salon*'s Jake Tapper.[41]
Bush did not exactly wither under this interrogation, but he did appear
annoyed at times. When Letterman, pressing the then–Texas governor to
address Houston's worst-in-the-nation air pollution, said, "But listen to me,
Governor, here's my point," a grinning but clearly impatient Bush shot back,
"I am listening to you—I don't have any choice but to listen to you!"[42]

In the final segment, Letterman backed down long enough to let Bush
deliver his own Top Ten List, which got a few hearty laughs, despite Bush's
shouted, tone-deaf delivery and some awkward fumbling with his reading
glasses. (A revealing video clip, featured for weeks afterward on the show's
Web site, showed Bush casually grabbing the hem of producer Barbara
Gaines's blouse to clean his spectacles.)[43]

Still, if laughs were votes, Gore would have won hands down. That he lost
probably has a lot more to do with Ralph Nader, a politicized Supreme Court,
and the multifaceted chicanery that marred the Florida vote than with his and
Bush's respective comedy stylings. However, there is reason to believe that
while Bush's sense of humor may not have done him much good, Gore's did
measurable harm. This was not, as E. B. White might have expected, merely a
matter of frivolity versus gravitas: both candidates appeared on *Letterman*,
and they appeared jointly on *SNL*'s pre-election special. No, Gore was not too
funny to be president—he was just funny in the wrong way.

WIT AND POWER

The wittiest politicians are not necessarily the wisest in their political use of
humor. Stevenson, for instance, failed to take the American public's well-
known anti-intellectual bias into account when plying his gift for the erudite
bon mot. "Far from overcoming other handicaps in his public image,"
explained Richard Hofstadter in his 1962 history of *Anti-Intellectualism in*

American Life, "his wit seemed to widen the distance between himself and a significant part of the electorate."[44] With every quip, the public was reminded of Stevenson's reputation as an "egghead." On one occasion a voter purportedly told Adlai Stevenson that he had "the vote of every thinking American," to which Stevenson replied, "That's not enough, I need a majority!"[45]

Gore's sense of humor, like Stevenson's, often seemed to flaunt his intellect. But there was another problem as well. Though exercises in self-deprecation and appearances on late-night shows are often touted as ways of "humanizing" a candidate, it is somewhat risky for a would-be leader to appear *too* human—that is to say, too vulnerable. As the late German sociologist Hans Speier noted in his essay on wit and power, "A self-assured man is expected to tolerate some laughter at his expense. But why should the voter be impressed by the fact that the candidate seems to regard himself, and thus the office he seeks, less seriously than the office appears to the citizen? Humor directed at oneself requires a touch of melancholia, a quality more suitable to poets or philosophers than to heroes or to wielders of power."[46]

While "melancholia" is not the word that leaps to mind when one looks back on Gore's humorous forays, many of them do exhibit a kind of ironic and unheroic self-awareness, incompatible with the steely resolve many Americans seem to want from their presidents. Consider his macarena moment, or the opening line of his global-warming documentary, *An Inconvenient Truth*: "Hi, I'm Al Gore and I used to be the next president of the United States." Think also of the funny bit of business at 2007's Oscar ceremony, where, just as he appeared ready to announce another run for the White House, he was cut off by the "wrap it up" music.

Gore's self-deprecating tendencies, instead of merely making him seem down to earth, go so far as to make him seem almost pathetic. Moreover, his anything-for-a-laugh eagerness to please—his acceptance of Letterman's absurd invitation to debate, the *SNL* "hot tub" sketch—communicates not just wit but *want*.[47] His sense of humor, good as it is, suggests weakness. In a political sense, then, Gore's funny bone may be more of an Achilles' heel.

Different comic techniques can also convey strength or vulnerability. One of Gore's favorite shticks is the deadpan stare, which he employed to good effect during a 2002 *Late Show* appearance, when Letterman asked if he had recovered from the disappointment of losing the election. Gore's response was to stare—and stare—as if the effrontery of the question sent him into a state of shock.[48] The audience loved it. In purely theatrical terms, this is a risky technique, which in fact requires considerable confidence to pull off. Still, it trades on—and overtly communicates—the *appearance* of self-pity and passivity.

Even when it didn't make him look weak, his humor sometimes got Gore in trouble. He was actually blameless in what was supposedly his biggest gaffe: the Internet "boast," a talking point invented by the Republicans and parroted by comics and newspeople alike. "Invented the Internet" had become a phrase sensation that was sweeping the nation, and it was attached to Gore like an anchor.

Something had to be done. As the Democrats' go-to humor expert, Katz concocted a quip he thought might stem the rising tide of scorn and minimize the damage to Gore's campaign: "I was very tired when I said that. I was up late the night before, inventing the camcorder." It was a good line, and sounded like something Gore would say. The problem with this response was that it seemed to put Gore in the position of owning up to the Internet misquote. Katz anticipated as much, but if the truth were a sufficient defense, the videotaped evidence of Gore's actual words should have been answer enough, and it clearly was not. Feeling, perhaps, that he had nothing more to lose, Gore used Katz's line in a speech to the DNC. It got a laugh from this friendly audience, but as Eric Alterman writes, it also "gave the story further 'legs.'"[49]

More significantly, the Internet slur laid the foundation for the Serial Exaggerator Narrative the GOP—with the full compliance of both the news media and late-night—had begun to construct for Gore. From that point forward, just about any trivially inaccurate or even slightly ambiguous statement he made was seized upon as further "proof" of the candidate's mendacity. Even Gore's jokes could be turned against him in this way. Upon accepting the Teamsters' endorsement at a Las Vegas gathering in September, Gore chose to underline his longstanding pro-labor stance with a clever bit of hyperbole. "I still remember the lullabies I heard as a child," he told the crowd, whereupon he paused reverently before launching into a few bars of "Look for the Union Label." Gore's musical punch line brought applause—and, it is important to note, laughter—from the crowd, but critics were quick to point out that the song was not written until 1975, when Gore would have been twenty-seven years old.[50]

Mainstream journalists were quick to fit this lighthearted remark into the Exaggerator Narrative they had been constructing for the candidate. "So what are we to make of Gore's musical miscue?" asked *USA Today*'s Walter Shapiro. "Does it buttress his reputation as a candidate whose words come closer to the Tennessee tall-tale tradition than they do to the literal truth? Or was it an innocuous slip of memory that should not obscure the larger reality that Gore did indeed grow up in a pro-union family?"[51]

In fact, as Gore was forced to explain, it was a joke—as any reasonably astute person who was present or saw the videotape and heard the laughter must surely have known. This did nothing to prevent *U.S. News and World Report* from alluding to the musical gaffe in "The Al Gore Quiz," a snide piece that ran three weeks before the election. "If some 27-year-olds still need lullabies," the magazine chided, "who are we to judge?"[52]

Gore's claim about hearing the song in his crib is indisputably false, but it can hardly be called a lie. The crowd's laughter and the basic silliness of the claim (Who could "remember" such a detail from one's own infancy? Who lulls a child to sleep with agitprop union ditties?) make it clear that Gore's musical whimsy was not intended to deceive anyone. If such inconsequential departures from the strictly literal constitute "Tennessee tall tales," one can only note that Davy Crockett (like Gore, D, TN) was fortunate to have run for Congress in the 1830s, before the likes of Walter Shapiro and *U.S. News* roamed the earth.

While Gore's humor may have been too intellectual, too ironic, and—in the case of the "Union Label" fiasco—too subtle, George W. Bush's humor problem was that he just wasn't funny. Bush was so incompetent a quipster that, after he had been in office for some time, Letterman launched a recurring *Late Show* feature titled "The George W. Bush Joke That's Not Really a

Joke," comprised of videotaped snippets from what seemed to be an inex-haustible supply of the president's inept attempts at levity.[53]

But Bush's humor, such as it is, never detracts from his status. Take, for instance, his practice of bestowing nicknames: Secretary of State Colin Powell was "Balloonfoot"; political director Karl Rove was "Boy Genius" or "Turd Blossom," depending on how things were going that day. Members of Congress and the press corps are given presidential nicknames, too, which in some cases, no doubt, are worn with pride. But in *The Price of Loyalty,* Ron Suskind—interpolating former Treasury secretary Paul "Big O" O'Neill—calls the practice "a bully technique: I've given you a name, now wear it."[54]

Nicknaming, inflicting "jokes that aren't really jokes" upon groups com-pelled by protocol to laugh, even the vaguely threatening jest about Letterman's surgery—all are consistent with the ethos of a man in charge. Speier identi-fied this as *paternalistic* humor, a type of joking that "always buttresses the domination of the joking master over the servant."[55]

George W. Bush would not be caught holding anyone's cue cards. Even when he engages in self-deprecation, there is an aggressive edge. In the wake of the 5–4 Supreme Court decision that ended one of the most controversial elections in American history and put him in the White House, the president made a remark that was intended as conciliatory but carried an unmistakable hint of menace: "If this were a dictatorship, it would be a heck of a lot easier," he said, after meet-ing with congressional leaders of both parties, "just so long as I'm the dictator."[56]

Though less revealing than such extemporaneous witticisms, jokes pre-pared for Bush also manage to sound simultaneously self-deprecating and cocky. At the 2001 Radio-Television Correspondents Association Dinner, Bush—armed with a copy of *Bushisms*—took the opportunity to explain the hidden "wisdom" behind some of his more renowned malapropisms:

> Then there is my most famous statement: "Rarely is the question asked, is our children learning." [Laughter] If you're a stickler, you probably think the singular verb "is" should have been the plural "are." But if you read it closely, you'll see I'm using the intransitive plural subjunctive tense. [Laughter] So the word "is" are correct.[57]

Of the many lessons to be drawn from Bush versus Gore, the most perti-
nent, for our purposes, is that humor as an end in itself is useful only to the
professional comic. For the politician it must be looked at as a tool to achieve
other ends: to ingratiate or to obfuscate; to draw people in or throw them off
the scent. Even when he or she is not deploying it in such overtly manipulative ways, a politician should handle humor with care. One's humorous style
can communicate as subtly, but as decisively, as one's style of dress: by that
metaphorical measure, Bush's sense of humor brought out his steely eyes,
while Gore's made him look fat.

The Show Must Go On

If Clinton's 1992 *Arsenio* spot raised the showbiz quotient of presidential
politics, by 2000 the campaign had become, in the words of Frank Rich,
"full-fledged performance art." And the trend shows no sign of abating. The
2004 race saw all nine Democratic challengers appearing in late-night during
primary season, with Richard Gephardt, John Edwards, and Howard Dean
delivering Top Ten Lists, Al Sharpton hosting *SNL,* and John Kerry riding
his motorcycle onto the *Tonight Show* stage. Edwards, true to an earlier
promise, announced his candidacy on *The Daily Show.* In 2007, John McCain
announced his on Letterman. At this writing, no presidential campaigns
have been launched on *Last Call with Carson Daly,* but I'd keep my eye on
Dennis Kucinich.[58]

But while there is no question that humor, correctly used, can be a valuable tool for the Television Age politician, and while *Arsenio* probably did
help Bill Clinton back in 1992, the political benefit of late-night appearances
is far from clear. Any evidence that voters are impressed by the opportunity
to see a candidate's "human side" is based on the rather dubious assumption
that humanity has no better proving ground than Jay Leno's couch. What's
more, the risks to one's gravitas are considerable. John Kerry was so eager to
banter with Leno that he agreed to follow Robert Smigel's scatologically
inclined puppet character, Triumph the Insult Comic Dog (who was there to
promote his new album, titled *Come Poop with Me*). The press was quick to

equate Kerry's humiliating booking with his then-underwhelming showing in the polls. (So was Triumph. "The poop I made in the dressing room has more heat than John Kerry," Smigel's puppet told the audience awaiting the candidate's contrived Harley-Davidson entrance.)[59]

If the 2004 candidates showed little sign of having mastered late-night or the use of humor, there were further signs that even the most innocent moments of public lightheartedness could be turned against the politician who dared to indulge in a moment's unseriousness. Psychiatrist-turned-journalist Charles Krauthammer managed to simultaneously violate the ethics of both his current and former professions in a column that used the words of Howard Dean in a manner John ("Is Al Gore nuts?") Podhoretz might have appreciated. Broaching the subject of media consolidation, *Hardball* host Chris Matthews had asked Dean, in front of a live audience, "Would you break up Fox?" The crowd roared with laughter, and Dean, chuckling, answered "On ideological grounds, absolutely yes," a response that evoked further laughter. But Krauthammer's selectively edited version of this innocent exchange omitted any mention of the laughing audience to make it appear as if Dean's answer was given in earnest. (This absolutely reprehensible column was titled "The Delusional Dean.")[60]

Perhaps, as Ronald Reagan's example suggests, the balance of showmanship and statesmanship can be most successfully struck by those approaching the intersection from the Hollywood side. Arnold Schwarzenegger's gubernatorial announcement on *The Tonight Show* set a new high-water mark in the inundation of American politics by entertainment-world values.[61] It also raised important questions about what late-night's political guest shots mean, not only for the integrity of the electoral process but for the integrity of the comedian-hosts.

The California gubernatorial recall of 2003 was a bizarre free-for-all. Gray Davis, the unpopular Democratic incumbent, faced a field of 135 challengers.[62] The absurd number of candidates and the loose requirements of the state's recall statute meant that the winner would only need a small plurality of the vote. In such a situation, any amount of influence the L.A.-based *Tonight Show* exercised, even if it was minuscule, could be decisive.

Though his official position remained—as in any other election—"neutral," Leno had a professional and (inasmuch as such distinctions are bound to be blurry among show-folk) personal relationship with Schwarzenegger predating the latter's recent turn from big-budget action movies to politics. "Ahnuld" was, in the parlance of late-night, "a good friend of the show."

In practical terms, this meant not only that gubernatorial candidate Schwarzenegger got to announce on national television, but that he would receive almost absurdly gentle treatment in his friend's monologues as the campaign progressed. Despite the ludicrous spectacle of "the Terminator's" bid for public office, despite the dubious nature of his qualifications and the continuing revelations about his history of drug use and sexual harassment, the Center for Media and Public Affairs noted that Leno told only eighteen jokes about Schwarzenegger during the election and sixty-nine jokes about the other candidates. During the same period, David Letterman aimed forty jokes at Schwarzenegger (who was no "friend" of *The Late Show*) and only three at the other 134 contenders. As a gesture toward "equal time," Leno did invite ninety of the remaining candidates to appear as "guests" a few weeks later—though it would have been more accurate to call them a guest *audience,* since they occupied the studio's spectators' seats. Needless to say, none of the also-rans were given the kind of one-on-one attention Schwarzenegger received.[63]

Leno definitively crossed the line when he agreed to appear onstage at Schwarzenegger's victory celebration. This appearance alongside his "good friend"—now governor-elect of the nation's most populous state—caused a minor stir in the press. "Several longtime network executives and producers of late-night shows expressed surprise that Mr. Leno had been willing to take a step that Johnny Carson, David Letterman, Conan O'Brien and other late-night hosts have never taken," Bill Carter reported. Letterman, who usually avoided any mention of his rival, gleefully replayed a clip of Leno, surrounded by the balloons and confetti, looking uncomfortable and checking his watch.[64]

The California governor's mansion had been Ronald Reagan's first stop on the road from Hollywood to the White House, and soon Schwarzenegger was hinting that he would like to follow in the Gipper's footsteps—though, of course, the Constitution would have to be amended to allow the Austrian-born strongman to realize his dream. (Senator Orrin Hatch set to work on this project immediately, though the momentum behind this effort seems to have stalled.)[65] Whatever the implications of the whole affair for the future of American politics (one fervently hopes for a revival of Ahnuld's movie career), it's hard to call Leno's role anything other than unfortunate and embarrassing.

Integrity is often held to be an indispensable quality for political leaders, but it may be even more valuable to the comedian. It's harder to take shots at political lowlifes when one is down in the gutter with them. The satirist's natural habitat is the high moral ground: a lofty perch from which one may criticize but not socialize. While politicians' guest shots might provide a short-term ratings boost, in the final analysis the benefits for the shows are as questionable as for their distinguished visitors. As Ben Karlin, co-executive producer of *The Daily Show,* observes, "There's almost nothing genuine about a politician appearing on our show, including those we like. We're being used to bring them some associative hipness—so they can say, look at us, our guy can laugh at himself. We have no illusions about it. We're just another part of the media strategy."[66]

If there is anything to be said for the "nonpartisan" stance mainstream late-night hosts traditionally maintain, it is that it at least respects some notion of critical disinterest. But the late-night mainstream's increasingly chummy relationship with those it mocks exposes their "commentary" for the hollow product it is. As they continue to abet the conflation of show business and politics, these programs and their hosts may see short-term benefits, measured in high ratings and prestige, but risk losing their credibility. To maintain a balance between his roles as audience representative and privileged insider, the topical comedian must always keep one foot firmly planted on our side of the footlights—unless he's angling for an appointment as Secretary of Amusement.

CHAPTER 9

IRONY IS DEAD . . .
LONG LIVE SATIRE?

The silliest, yet most touching, thing about *Stand Up and Cheer* is that the Secretary of Amusement actually pulls it off. The musical extravaganza he stages is so full of boop-a-doop and pep—and, in her film debut, Shirley Temple—that the nation's confidence is restored. Just before the final number, a supporting character bursts into Warner Baxter's office to announce, "I've got great news for ya. The Depression's over!" Apparently, people had a lot more faith in the power of show business back in 1934. Instead of merely distracting us from our problems, it could—in the fantasy world of *Stand Up and Cheer*, anyway—actually solve them.

Today—at least in the world described by the Pew poll, and the journalists flogging the Usurper Narrative, and the cultural prognosticators fretting over our endangered youth—entertainment is itself part of the problem. Certainly the flippant comedy of late-night television would be no match for a crisis of the magnitude of the Great Depression or Pearl Harbor.

So as the smoke of September 11, 2001, began to clear, the one thing about which these sages seemed certain was that irony was dead. In fact, in the aftermath of that terrible day, those who could bear to think of such trivialities were practically tripping over each other to pronounce its eulogy. "I think it's the end of the age of irony," said Graydon Carter, who before becoming editor of *Vanity Fair* had helped define that age as the editor of *Spy*. "I think somebody should do a marker that says irony died on 9/11/01," agreed Gerry Howard of Broadway Books, publishers of *A Field Guide to the*

Urban Hipster and *The Dysfunctional Family Christmas Songbook*. Roger
Rosenblatt of *Time* saw irony's demise as the silver lining around ground
zero's dark clouds. "One good thing could come from this horror," he
declared. "It could spell the end of the age of irony." Robert Thompson,
director of Syracuse University's Center for the Study of Popular Television,
sounded a similar note: "The upside of this tragedy is that it might push the
culture out of the era of American irony and modern hip. How can you do
the wiseguy thing after September 11?"[1]

Well, it wasn't easy. Soon enough, though, it became clear that the reports
of irony's death had been greatly exaggerated. The late-night shows did stay off
the air for a week, preempted by news coverage of the attacks. When Letterman
returned to the air, it was hardly an immediate return to normal. September
17's *Late Show* opened in a subdued manner, with no theme song, no
announcement, no monologue, and very little of the host's usual cranky sarcasm. "We're told that [the hijackers] were zealots fueled by religious fervor,"
quavered the visibly shaken Letterman, "religious fervor—and if you live to be
a thousand years old, will that make any sense to you? Will that make any god-
damn sense?" His first guest was Dan Rather, who appeared even more dis-
traught, choking back tears at one point. Forgetting all pretense of journalistic
detachment—to say nothing of his alleged "liberal bias"—the CBS anchorman
declared, "George Bush is the president, he makes the decisions, and, you
know, as just one American, wherever he wants me to line up, just tell me
where."[2] Not only was irony apparently dead, it looked for the moment as if
even good old-fashioned American skepticism were on life support.

Leno returned the following night. (Irony might die, but network competition is eternal.) Eschewing his usual monologue, he offered instead a maudlin
and rather defensive opening statement about the necessity of humor in such
troubled times. "In a world where people fly airplanes into buildings for the
sole purpose of killing innocent people, a job like this seems incredibly irrelevant," Leno humbly said. "But, you know, we still have a job to do. And I
don't pretend that this is an important job. You know what this job is? This job
is like a cookie to those firemen. That's what we do. You know, we're standing there with a cookie. We're standing there with a glass of lemonade."[3]

An hour later Conan O'Brien was back, too, with an emotional and inter-mittently coherent set of opening remarks that veered from St. Patrick's Cathedral (across the street from the studio, where the host had gone to col-lect his thoughts before returning to the airwaves) to the novelty Eisenhower coffee mug on the host's desk (as if the terrorist attack had somehow trans-formed this kitschy artifact into a patriotic talisman) and ended with this rather remarkable plea:

> I—I also know that if I say anything else tonight, I know that we have a young audience that watches us. . . . There are a lot of young people watching, and there's a lot of cynicism among young people. And if I could say anything tonight to any of the people that watch our little show at 12:30 at night who are young, I would ask you not to be cynical. . . . We're an amazing country. There is a lot of goodness in the world, and I would ask young people to not give in to cynicism in any way and to try and rise above themselves. . . . Let's try and grow a little bit, let's try and accomplish something, let's try and make some sense out of what is a horrible, terri-ble, senseless act.[4]

The sentiments behind these sermonettes were probably sincere, though it wasn't long before Letterman recovered his sneer and Leno his swagger. O'Brien, too, soon forgot about stamping out cynicism and returned to stoking it. Still, the aftermath of 9/11 did reveal the limits of late-night's anti-political approach. Suddenly, glimmers of strident, showbiz patriotism kept popping up in what had previously been a no-reverence zone. Flag pins sprouted on hosts' lapels. O'Brien introduced the New York City police-men who worked security detail for the show (who had heretofore per-formed this duty off-camera and without acknowledgment) to hearty applause. Letterman took time at the top of the show to enumerate his new heroes, "'New York's bravest': the firefighters, 'New York's finest': the cops, and the United States Marine Corps."[5] Leno, three thousand miles from Ground Zero but not wishing to be left out, reserved a block of seats for Los Angeles firefighters, whom he introduced to reverent applause from the other members of that night's studio audience. In the weeks that followed, Letterman's Top Ten Lists were often delivered by carrier crews and fighter battalions. The patriotism was running so thick, it would have made Bob Hope blush.

It was understandable, however. In that time of fear, despair, and impotent rage, people really wanted to applaud firefighters—even if the ones on hand were mere proxies for those who had selflessly marched into those burning towers. What those nervous, post-9/11 crowds were less inclined to do was laugh. For the moment, reassurance, not irreverence, was what they craved; a little sentiment and a bit of flag-waving were perfectly welcome. More troublesome than the late-night hosts' excesses, though, was how quickly and how seamlessly those flag pins and paeans to the troops seemed to blend into pledges of fealty to the commander in chief. Even after they determined that it was okay to be funny again, they maintained a moratorium on jokes critical of President Bush. "It's not the time to pick on the president or the government or the military," Jay Leno asserted. Lorne Michaels, creator/producer of *Saturday Night Live* and alleged iconoclast, told a reporter, as the show prepared to return to the air, "We won't do anything that attempts to undermine President Bush's authority."[6]

This was supposed to reflect a spirit of nonpartisan unity—a higher, nobler manifestation of anti-politics: "You know, normally, I would be out here making fun of Democrats, making fun of Republicans, and you realize we don't have Democrats, Republicans anymore," said Leno on his first night back. "We only have Americans, and we have Americans united in one goal, for one reason."[7] Out in the real world, however, the unity he spoke of was fleeting; what's more, it soon became clear to a lot of Americans who *didn't* have their own TV shows that the post-9/11 goals of the Bush administration were anything but apolitical. The mainstream comedians, however (along with most of the mainstream news media), remained reluctant to question the president. The upshot was that just when the American public could have *used* a little skepticism, our late-night masters of disdain found something to believe in.

War Is Not Good for Comedians
and Other Living Things

The "irony" whose death pundits like Carter and Rosenblatt were rooting for was not the genuine article as a lit major would define it, but a cultural attitude best captured by Mark Crispin Miller's apt modifier, "prophylactic."[8] Prophylactic irony shields its wearers from the infection of involvement, and the contaminant of commitment. It is the dismissive "yeah, right" or "whatever," heard in the speech of sitcom singles and teenage mall-lingerers; the knee-jerk-skeptical ethos that had, by the close of the twentieth century, come to permeate American culture both high and low. What the silver-lining crowd hoped September 11 had banished from the land was this shrugging sense of detachment—a bargain-basement version of existentialism, in which not caring is the height of hip.

Late-night, as a wholesale distributor of this type of irony, could hardly be expected to give it up permanently, though an effort was made to soft-pedal the sarcasm for a while. The few weeks following September 11 saw the hosts gingerly testing the waters, reigning in their sarcasm, and hedging their bets with as many "serious" guests (journalists, preferably from their own networks, and politicians, preferably Senator John McCain) as they could book.

There was genuine irony (in the proper sense, this time) in the way the comedians' reluctance to criticize President Bush—which far outlasted their quasi-public affairs show piety—led them, by default, into taking sides in a way they had previously been careful to avoid. As of 9/10/01, the nation was as evenly and bitterly divided as it had been in years. Less than a year had passed since the too-close-to-call 2000 election ended in a controversial Supreme Court decision, and late-night, reflecting the public's lingering doubts, had kept questions about the "winner's" intelligence and legitimacy very much alive. After 9/11, though, all criticism of Bush was suddenly swept off the table. Indeed, the comics' post-attack treatment of the president went beyond kid-glove gentleness; Bush was virtually untouchable. It was almost as if they were apologizing for their earlier criticisms. Give Leno credit for at least recognizing the strain of maintaining this charade; when one of his innocuous, apolitical post-9/11 jokes bombed, he turned on the audience in mock exasperation, crying, "What do you want? Bush is *smart* now!"[9]

Not that all politicians were off-limits. With criticism of the current commander in chief now treated as tantamount to blasphemy, the comics turned once more to their favorite butt, former president Clinton. "I was thinking to myself today, you know what this country needs right now?" asked David Letterman. "A good old-fashioned Bill Clinton sex scandal."[10] The contrast in respect afforded the former and current presidents was made strikingly apparent in this Jay Leno joke:

> We might be on a little bit later than normal 'cause the president gave
> his speech. Obviously, we are taping this before he speaks, so we don't
> know what he said yet. But we have some of the transcripts, and it
> sounds inspiring. He's asking all Americans to pitch in, which, I
> think, is good. In fact, former President Bill Clinton, God bless him,
> did you see this? Wanting to show his patriotism, today Bill Clinton
> volunteered to be a judge at this Saturday's Miss America pageant . . .
> [laughter]. We're just being silly this week.[11]

The Center for Media and Public Affairs recorded eighty Clinton jokes between 9/11 and the end of 2001, compared to just twenty-five jokes about Bush—a remarkable discrepancy, given Bush's incumbency.[12]

One comic who refused to retreat into "silliness" in the wake of the attacks learned just how sensitive the television networks and the administration (if not the public) had become. For agreeing with a guest's rather sensible observation that, whatever else one could say about flying airplanes into buildings, it could hardly be called, as the president had called it, "cowardly," *Politically Incorrect*'s Bill Maher lost his network berth on ABC. His reckless truth-telling also earned him—along with any other potential wiseguys—a chilling warning from White House Press Secretary Ari Fleischer, who said Maher's fate should serve as a reminder "to all Americans that they need to watch what they say, watch what they do."[13] Questioning the administration was not only unfashionable but potentially hazardous to one's career.

That the Bush administration took advantage of the post-9/11 political climate to push their planned invasion of Iraq is now beyond any reasonable dispute. Members of the press and even of Congress concede that they should have been more skeptical of these machinations. But to the extent topical comedians have a similar watchdog function, they failed as well. None, save *The Daily Show*'s Jon Stewart, raised much of a yelp about a proposed course of action a good portion of the public—if opinion polls and the largest peace demonstrations since the Vietnam era mean anything—considered highly dubious.

Of course, many Americans supported the administration's plans, too, and the comics' failure to treat them with their customary skepticism could be rationalized away by their usual reluctance to alienate "half the room." The *Washington Post* explained that the network comics were "not exactly for [the war], nor are they solidly against it, either. They are, it seems, on both sides at once. They're the comedic equivalent of Switzerland."[14]

But to viewers wary of the administration's plans for "regime change" in Baghdad, Leno and especially Letterman seemed more Prussian than Swiss in the weeks leading up to the war. As the Afghanistan campaign (which most Americans understood as a response to the al-Qaeda attacks, and supported) blurred into the planned invasion of Iraq, there were far fewer jokes about Bush's attempts to sell his unprecedented, preemptive campaign than jingoistic (and at times racist) jokes about camels, burkas, and kefiyas. There were also plenty of jokes about Saddam Hussein (most of which could have been leftovers from the senior Bush's Iraq war), and jokes about America's uncooperative allies. "France wants more evidence" before supporting U.N. action against Iraq, sneered Letterman, in a joke that could have been written by Donald Rumsfeld. "And I'm thinking, you know, the last time France wanted more evidence, it rolled right through Paris with a German flag."[15]

Undoubtedly, war presents a unique challenge to the equal-opportunity offender credo mainstream late-night comics have pledged to uphold. The only way to remain "neutral" on Iraq was to ignore it altogether. This is essentially how Johnny Carson had treated the Vietnam War. Indeed, television viewers hungry for hard-hitting jokes about the most divisive foreign adventure in American history would have to look to *Laugh-In* or, briefly, to *The Smothers*

Brothers. But the boundaries of what televised political comedy is expected to address have broadened considerably since the Vietnam era. Though TV, for most of the 1960s, hid from "the '60s," it has since caught up with the world outside the box. These days, keeping mum on an event of such proportions on an ostensibly topical program—whether for reasons of taste or political sensitivity—would be as quaintly anachronistic as Rob and Laura Petrie's twin beds.

If ignoring the Iraq drumbeat was not an option, playing it "down the middle" was not as easy to do with a war as with an undertaking as neatly bipartisan (and purportedly inconsequential) as a presidential campaign. On the eve of invasion, public opinion on Iraq was almost as evenly divided as the Bush/Gore vote, but the comedians seemed disinclined to acknowledge the anti-invasion constituency, substantial though it was.[16] Those camel jokes were sure-fire, for one thing—the comedians had no more use for fine distinctions between one Middle Eastern country and another than the administration did. But there was also a question of which half of the room they were more reluctant to offend. "The number one thing the networks don't want is people booing and writing letters," explained Bill Maher—who had learned a hard lesson about angering the right. "But I think the networks and the media underestimate the appetite for contrarian points of view," he added. "It's certainly not the majority, but it is a sizable minority."[17]

Perhaps late-night's failure to find the middle ground on Iraq points to the inadequacy of the EOO paradigm when it comes to something as serious as war and peace. When the question is to bomb or not to bomb, it is not sufficient to shrug and say, as the comics routinely do when comparing parties and candidates, that it's six of one and half a dozen of the other. As it happened, in the case of Iraq, the late-night comics effectively endorsed the administration view, more or less by default.

Though they labor mightily to maintain the appearance of neutrality, the comics do in fact adhere to one definable political conviction, which 9/11 merely threw into sharper focus: namely, that in spite of the constant insinuations that our government is corrupt, our elections futile, and our democracy a sham, America is the greatest country in the world. Contradictory though it may be, this happens to be a popular view. Indeed, the cynical/patriotic paradox has been a feature of American national life since Andrew Jackson was a pup. It's a philosophy that has never lacked for adherents—what else could explain the prevalence of those who begrudge the government every penny taken in taxes but have no problem trusting the same government to spend the blood of their sons and daughters wisely?

The sizable percentage of the American population inclined to love their country in the abstract while despising its democratic system could be counted on to fall in line as soon as the administration started waving the flag. The mainstream late-night comics, unable to ignore the issue or finesse the controversy via their usual equivocations, fell in line with this faction, more or less by default, because it most closely conformed to their anti-political/pro-"patriotic" pattern.

Does this mean that late-night comedians enabled the administration's disastrous policy? Perhaps, in a small way—but they're toward the bottom of a very long list, below politicians of both parties, and a passel of print and broadcast journalists. Jay Leno is *not* the Secretary of Amusement, and comedians cannot be held to account by voters or taxpayers. And they certainly are not powerful enough to end a depression, or, probably, to prevent a war. But what role could comedy play?

Vote with Your Remote: The End of Consensus Comedy?

By embracing the idea of narrowcasting, a handful of political comics have been able to transcend the safe, "neutral" blandness of equal-opportunity offense and connect with the kinds of sizable minorities Maher claims the networks ignore. Indeed, the modestly sizable minority willing to spring for HBO can get a dose of left-libertarian satire from Maher's *Real Time*. The fact that *The Daily Show* qualifies as a hit with just over a million and a half viewers means that there is less pressure to please all of the people, all of the time. "You have a different charge when you're Jay Leno," explains *Daily Show* coexecutive producer Ben Karlin. "We're not a big network show, so we don't have to cater to the tastes of a massive audience. We like our nice little boutique audience."[18]

Between 9/11 and Abu Ghraib, viewers turned off by Letterman's celebration of all things military ("Here with tonight's Top Ten List, the members of the 103rd Bomber Squadron!") or Leno's "just silly" jingoism ("You know, there is now a $5 million bounty on Osama bin Laden's head, which marks the first time in history there's ever been a bounty on a guy's head who wears Bounty on his head") could turn to *The Daily Show* for what Frank Rich called "a much-needed comic counterpoint, or at least some comic relief, to the often oppressive triumphalism of the war weeks."[19] If their coverage of "Mess o'Potamia" stopped short of explicitly endorsing an *anti-war* position, Jon Stewart and company at least refused to join the Patriot Parade in which their competitors—in both the mainstream comedy and "real" news realms—seemed to be marching.

Having accepted their narrowcast, "boutique" status, Karlin, Stewart, and company could conceivably choose to cast off the limits of "objectivity" altogether, but for whatever reason, they have not taken the plunge. This may be for the best: though the equal-opportunity offensiveness of the late-night mainstream promotes cynicism, a comedy of outright advocacy might devolve into preachiness, or a set of talking points with a laugh track. Certainly this has been true on the right, where Dennis Miller and Fox News's *Half Hour News Hour* have plumbed new depths of labored unfunniness.

Polemical comedy can be funny, at least to a like-minded audience. The Internet has taken the possibilities of narrowcasting to the next level. Now, the choir can find someone to preach to them from the comfort of their own homes. Some of these sermons are pretty entertaining, too. In addition to the raunchy but clever Whitehouse.org, sites like Opinions You Should Have, Jesus' General, and *ScrappleFace* (a right-leaning version of the *Onion*), offer unabashedly one-sided comic invective that can be very satisfying, in occasional doses. Possibly the best satire on the web is provided by an anonymous genius who uses the name, and ironic technique, of Jonathan Swift, at http://jonswift.blogspot.com.

But comedy delivered over the Internet can't create a communion of laughing citizens to compare even with the scattered community of television viewers laughing along with the studio audience. More important, these completely self-selected sites, with their ideologically bounded humor, can offer little more than affirmation and reassurance for those who are already on their side. Not that that's nothing, but over the long run, even the choir will grow tired of the same old sermons.

There is something to the notion of the comedian as a detached, disinterested observer, who directs his ridicule to those people and policies that deserve it, without regard to party, ideology, or some arbitrary standard of "balance." But disinterest should not be confused with uninterest; democracy is not a spectator sport, especially to those whose words reach millions. Perhaps topical comedians should not be *in* the game, but they ought to act as referees, instead of just hurling insults from the sidelines.

A Moment of Zen

Jean Paul Sartre once observed, "If you begin by saying, 'Thou shalt not lie,' there is no longer any possibility of political action."[20] Dishonesty—or at any rate, something less than complete candor—is in a very real sense the very currency of political exchange. Smiling while taking less than one wants, fighting tooth and nail for a principle that may have to be cast aside tomorrow: these are the essence of compromise—the basis, even, of political pluralism. The government of the United States is called upon to represent *all* of the people: a bafflingly diverse group of citizens, holding often irreconcilable views. We—opponents of abortion and proponents of choice, free-traders and protectionists, red and blue staters—must keep fighting for what we believe in but accept that our victories and defeats will be partial and impermanent. That is not futility; just democracy.

Politics is not a holy quest, it is a dialectical process, in which thesis and antithesis must continually end in the imperfect but necessary synthesis of compromise. This is not to suggest that principles are not important; but because we *disagree* on principles, we must be prepared to temper them with pragmatism. Nor should this recognition of the necessity of compromise be taken as an appeal for calm, bipartisan consensus; it is a plain description of what is, and must be, an ongoing struggle.

That doesn't mean that we can't have a few laughs along the way. Comedy is not a holy quest, either—not exactly, anyway. But laughter is necessary, even if it serves—as it did for President Lincoln—no higher purpose than to keep us from crying. And in a society as rife with information and as dependent upon its efficient exchange as ours, I believe it can do much more.

Comedy and politics, like principle and pragmatism, are strange bed fellows. But, at their best, don't they share a common goal of making human society freer, fairer, and more just? Aren't politics and satire both, if undertaken in the spirit of Lincoln—or yes, the "Lincolnish" Stephen Colbert—profoundly moral undertakings?

The People's Thumb

The emergent field of what might be called "bullshit studies," inaugurated by Harry G. Frankfurt's best-selling little book *On Bullshit,* is undoubtedly a fertile one. Certainly there is a lot of it lying about nowadays. Yet it is far from clear how society—to say nothing of government—can survive without a certain amount of BS. It's fine for philosophers like Professor Frankfurt to pursue Ultimate Truth, but the rest of us have to live here. As Tennessee Williams's character Big Daddy observed in *Cat on a Hot Tin Roof,* "You've got to live with [mendacity]. There's nothing to live with but mendacity. Is there?"[21]

Whether we refer to it by Tennessee Williams's polite euphemism or Professor Frankfurt's earthier term, we ought to consider—carefully— whether mendacity or bullshit may be something a bit nobler than just a nec- essary evil. As Freud argued, without the repression of base instincts—a kind of truth, after all—civilized life would be impossible. A world in which we all went around punching or kissing whoever we felt like, whenever we wanted to—a world where everyone said whatever was on his or her mind at all times without fear of consequence—would be ungovernable, and unlivable. As Sartre suggests, without some tolerance for mendacity, politics would be impossible. For those who earnestly embrace the anti-political vision that mainstream late-night comics tacitly endorse, a world without politics might sound pretty good. But what would replace it? The only historically plausible alternatives are chaos, brute force, and tyranny.

Politics cannot be cleansed of bullshit. Comedy cannot tolerate it. That's why we need both. But it's important that comedy targets the *right* bullshit, in the right way. Partisan satirists like Dennis Miller and the Air America crew are diligent about sniffing out their opponents' BS but likely to hold their fire (and their noses) when it comes to their own heroes' impurities. The late-night mainstream's utterly anti-political, pseudo-satirical approach proposes that *everything* is bullshit—which is no help, either.

Neither the one-sided nor the no-sided approach is ultimately satisfactory, because each aims at dismissing, rather than engaging with, political arguments. If comedy is to have any positive effect on politics, it must be understood as taking *part* in politics, keeping it on track, and nudging it toward its ostensible goal of improving the common good. Late-night's traditional, pseudo-satirical approach amounts to nothing more than negation: its premise insists that since politics is inherently impure, elections, deliberation, and democracy itself are all futile. However, genuine, politically engaged satire, motivated by a passionate belief in democracy, equality, justice—all those corny things the age of irony has encouraged us to roll our eyes at—can play a vital role in telling the people what is going on, and why they should care. At their best, Colbert, Stewart, Maher, and a few others provide this vital service.

If politics invariably pits principle against pragmatism, the best satire can do is to help keep those forces in balance. Lobbyists, interest groups, and the overfunded, never-ending campaign season press down, like a dishonest butcher's thumb, on the side of expediency. It's up to satire to act, then, as the people's thumb—restoring some weight to the "principles" side of the scale. The results will rarely be as dramatic or apparent as Thomas Nast's exposure of Boss Tweed—or even *Crossfire*'s suspiciously timely cancellation in the wake of Jon Stewart's scathing smack-down. But though Mark Twain may have overestimated its lethality, the assault of laughter *is* a potent weapon—and one of the few we, the people, have.

"If men were angels," James Madison famously observed, "no government would be necessary."[22] And if politicians were angels, no satire would be necessary. That they are not is only to be expected—the people they represent aren't angels, either. But our representatives' foibles and our system's flaws—like our own human imperfection—are no cause for despair, or for cynicism. They are, and ever will be, cause for humility, for vigilance, and—whether as a corrective or merely a balm—for laughter.

ACKNOWLEDGMENTS

My first expression of gratitude is due to the members of my PhD committee at the University of Iowa's American Studies Department: Corey Creekmur, Lauren Rabinovitz, John Raeburn, David Redlawsk, and the late Ken Cmiel, a tireless mentor and endlessly entertaining curmudgeon who showed me and so many of my peers that scholarship can be a moral, not merely an intellectual, pursuit. And although I have been fortunate to encounter many other fine teachers, I would have had neither the confidence nor the ability to write a book without the encouragement I received early on from Alma Reinecke, Lorraine Norman, and the late D. J. Cline.

My agents—Nicholas Ellison, along with Sarah Dickman, and Marissa Matteo—showed a great deal of patient faith in my ability to translate an academic text into a book people might actually want to read. Leslie Mitchner, my editor at Rutgers University Press, was similarly patient and supportive in helping me realize the potential of the project (and another thanks to Lauren for putting us in touch with one another). Copy editor India Cooper proofed the manuscript with meticulous care and sensitivity to authorial intent and the spirit of the project.

The deepest and most heartfelt thanks to my wife, Becky. I can say, without indulging in the least hyperbole, that this book would not exist without her inspiration, encouragement, and her screenwriter's eye for clarity, thematic unity, and narrative coherence. My name is on the cover, but this is our book, and I dedicate it to you, with all my love.

NOTES

TV SHOWS AND MOVIES MENTIONED

All in the Family, CBS, 1971–1992, produced by Norman Lear.

Amos 'n' Andy, CBS, 1951–1953.

The Arsenio Hall Show, syndicated, 1989–1994.

Bedtime for Bonzo, directed by Frederick de Cordova, Universal, 1951.

The Bernie Mac Show, Fox, 2001–2006, co-created by *The Daily Show*'s Larry Wilmore.

Borat: Cultural Learnings of America for Make Benefit Glorious Nation of Kazakhstan, directed by Larry Charles, written by Sacha Baron Cohen et al., 20th Century Fox, 2006.

The Brady Bunch Movie, directed by Betty Thomas, Paramount, 1995; *A Very Brady Sequel,* directed by Arlene Sanford, Paramount, 1996.

Bulworth, directed by Warren Beatty, screenplay by Beatty and Jeremy Pisker, 20th Century Fox, 1998.

Cedric the Entertainer Presents, Fox, 2002–2003.

Chappelle's Show, Comedy Central, 2003–2006

The Chris Rock Show, HBO, 1997–2000.

Clutch Cargo, syndicated, 1959.

Countdown with Keith Olbermann, MSNBC, 2003–present.

Dateline NBC, NBC, 1992–present.

Family Guy, Fox, 1999–present.

Fat Actress, Showtime, 2005 (series). Produced by Scott Butler and starring Kirstie Alley.

Fear Factor, NBC, 2001–2006.

The Flip Wilson Show, NBC, 1970–1974.

The Goldbergs, CBS, 1949–1951; NBC, 1952–1953; Dumont, 1954.

Good Times, CBS, 1974–1979.

Hellcats of the Navy, directed by Nathan Juran, Columbia, 1957.

The Honeymooners, CBS, 1955–1956.

House, M.D., Fox, 2004–present.

The Hughleys, UPN, 1998–2002.

I Love Lucy, CBS, 1951–1961.

Idiocracy, directed by Mike Judge, written by Judge and Etan Cohen, 20th Century Fox, 2006.

In Living Color, Fox, 1990–1994.

An Inconvenient Truth, directed by Davis Guggenheim, Paramount, 2006.

It's Garry Shandling's Show, Fox, 1986–1990.

Jackass, MTV, 2000–2002.

The Jeffersons, CBS, 1975–1985.

The Jerry Springer Show, syndicated, 1991–present.

The King of Queens, CBS, 1998–present.

The Larry Sanders Show, HBO, 1992–1998, created by Dennis Klein and Garry Shandling.

Last Comic Standing, NBC, 2003–2006.

Lateline, NBC, created by Al Franken, 1998–1999.

Man of the Year, written and directed by Barry Levinson, Universal, 2006.

Married . . . with Children, Fox, 1987–1997.

Maude, CBS, 1974–1978.

Meet the Press, NBC, 1947–present, hosted by Tim Russert.

Mind of Mencia, 2005–present, Comedy Central,

Mr. Smith Goes to Washington, directed by Frank Capra, Columbia, 1939.

My Name Is Earl, NBC, 2006–present.

A Night at the Roxbury, directed by John Fortenberry, starring Will Ferrell and Chris Kattan, Paramount, 1998.

The Original Kings of Comedy, 2000, directed by Spike Lee, written by and starring Steve Harvey, Cedric the Entertainer, Bernie Mac, and D. L. Hughley.

The Pat Sajak Show, CBS, 1989–1990.

Patch Adams, directed by Tom Shadyac, MCA/Universal, 1998.

Politically Incorrect, Comedy Central, 1994–1997; ABC, 1997–2003.

Real Time with Bill Maher, HBO, 2003–present.

Road to Rio, directed by Norman Z. McLeod, Paramount, 1947.

RV, directed by Barry Sonnenfeld, Columbia, 2006.

The Sarah Silverman Program, Comedy Central, 2006.

Saturday Night Live, Oct. 11, 1975–present, produced by Lorne Michaels.

Seinfeld, NBC, 1990–1998, created by Larry David and Jerry Seinfeld.

The Simpsons, Fox, 1989–present.

The Smothers Brothers Comedy Hour, CBS, 1967–1969 (original run)

Stand Up and Cheer, directed by Hamilton MacFadden, dialogue by Ralph Spence, story by Lew Brown, from an idea by Will Rogers, 20th Century Fox, 1934.

The Stephanie Miller Show, syndicated, September 1995–January 1996.

The Steve Harvey Show, WB, 1996–2002.

Stuart Saves His Family, directed by Harold Ramis, written by Al Franken, Paramount, 1995.

That Was the Week That Was, NBC, 1964–1965.

30 Rock, NBC, 2006–present.

Two and a Half Men, CBS, 2003–present.

The West Wing, NBC, 1999–2006.

Young Mr. Lincoln, directed by John Ford, written by Lamar Trotti, 20th Century Fox, 1939.

INTRODUCTION

1. *The Tonight Show with Jay Leno,* NBC, week of Feb. 19–25, 2006. Retrieved from About.com Political Humor, comp. Daniel Kurtzman, http://politicalhumor .about. com/library/bllatenightjokes2006.htm (accessed March 14, 2007).

2. *Late Show with David Letterman,* CBS, week of Feb. 19–25, 2006, ibid.

3. *Anderson Cooper 360,* CNN, first broadcast on Feb. 22, 2006, http://transcripts. cnn.com/TRANSCRIPTS/0602/22/acd.01.html (accessed 14 March 2007).

4. *The Colbert Report,* Comedy Central, Feb. 22, 2006.

5. *Nightline,* ABC, Feb. 23, 2006.

6. Pew Center for the People and the Press, "Cable and Internet Loom Large in Fragmented Political News Universe," http://people-press.org/reports/print.php3? PageID=776 (accessed Oct. 23, 2004).

CHAPTER 1 — LOSING OUR RELIGION

1. The 2006 White House Correspondents Association Dinner was first broadcast on C-SPAN, April 29, 2006.

2. Elisabeth Bumiller, "A New Set of Bush Twins Appear at Annual Correspondents' Dinner," *New York Times,* May 1, 2006, Lexis-Nexis, via Infohawk, http://web.lexis-nexis.com.proxy.lib.uiowa.edu. On "followed suit," see Dan Froomkin, "The Colbert Blackout," *Washington Post,* May 2, 2006, http://www.washingtonpost.com/wp-dyn/content/blog/2006/05/02/BL2006050200755.html (accessed March 14, 2007). See also Josh Kalven and Simon Maloy, "Media Touted Bush's Routine at Correspondents' Dinner, Ignored Colbert's Skewering," *Media Matters,* May 1, 2006; Julie Millican, "For Third Day in a Row, Good Morning America Touted Bush's White House Correspondents Dinner Skit While Ignoring Colbert's Routine," *Media Matters,* May 3, 2006, both available at http://mediamatters.org.

3. Froomkin, "The Colbert Blackout"; "Thank You, Stephen Colbert" Web site, http://thankyoustephencolbert.org.

4. Joan Walsh, "Making Colbert Go Away," *Salon,* May 3, 2006, http://www.salon. com/opinion/feature/2006/05/03/correspondents/index_np.html (accessed June 1,

2006), including Grove, Lehman, and Cox quotes; Mike Allen and Chris Matthews, *Hardball with Chris Matthews,* MSNBC, May 1, 2006.

5. Dan Froomkin, "Why So Defensive?" *Washington Post,* May 4, 2006, http://www.washingtonpost.com/wp-dyn/content/blog/2006/05/04/BL2006050400967.html (accessed June 1, 2006).

6. Richard Cohen, "So Not Funny," *Washington Post,* May 4, 2006, http://www.washingtonpost.com/wp-dyn/content/article/2006/05/03/AR2006050302202.html (accessed June 1, 2006).

7. Letterman, retrieved from About:com Political Humor, "Late-Night Jokes about President Bush from 2004," comp. Daniel Kurtzman, http://politicalhumor.about.com/library/blbush2004jokes.htm (accessed June 1, 2006); Leno and O'Brien, retrieved from About.com Political Humor, "Late-Night Jokes about John Kerry," comp. Daniel Kurtzman, http://politicalhumor.about.com/library/bljohnkerryjokes.htm (accessed June 1, 2006).

8. Center for Media and Public Affairs (CMPA), "Joke Archive, through August 24, 2004," http://www.cmpa.com/politicalHumor/archiveapril16th.htm (accessed March 14, 2007). President Bush held a commanding lead over Kerry for the year to date, but when Kerry became the presumptive and then official nominee, the numbers started to even out. Unfortunately, data for the months leading up to the election are unavailable, but in examining this and the other years' joke counts, the trend is clear.

9. Alex Strachan, "Maher Targets Left and Right in Comedy Special," *Montreal Gazette,* Nov. 1, 2003; Doug Moore, "Williams' Act Has St. Louis Laughing at Itself," *St. Louis Post-Dispatch Everyday Magazine,* March 21, 2002; Gary Budzak, "Outspoken Honduras Native an Equal-Opportunity Offender," *Columbus Dispatch,* Jan. 6, 2005; Debra Pickett, "Middle East Duo Bets That Misery Loves Comedy," *Chicago Sun-Times,* June 6, 2003; Duane Dudek, "Blinded by the Bite; Silverman Skewers All with a Smile in 'Jesus,'" *Milwaukee Journal Sentinel,* Dec. 16, 2005; Bruce Westbrook, "Provocative Comedy: No Magic in Silverman's 'Jesus,'" *Houston Chronicle,* Dec. 9, 2005, Lexis-Nexis, via Infohawk, http://web.lexis-nexis.com.proxy.lib.uiowa.edu.

10. Jason Zengerle, "The State of the George W. Bush Joke," and Sharon Waxman, "The Boys from 'South Park' Go to War," *New York Times,* Aug. 22, 2004, national ed., Arts and Leisure, 1.

11. Marshall Sella, "The Stiff Guy vs. the Dumb Guy," *New York Times Magazine,* Sept. 24, 2000, 74.

12. *Tonight Show* viewership 6.4 million viewers, per Toni Fitzgerald, "Sunrise Surprise: The CBS Early Show," *Media Life,* March 1, 2007, http://www.medialifemagazine.com/artman/publish/article_10482.asp (accessed March 15, 2007); *Colbert Report* viewership approximately 1.2 million, *Daily Show*'s 1.6 million, per Julie Bosman, "Serious Book to Peddle? Don't Laugh, Try a Comedy Show," *New York Times,* Feb. 25, 2007, Lexis-Nexis, via Infohawk, http://web.lexis-nexis.com.proxy.lib. uiowa.edu.

13. In his first debate with Al Gore in 2000, Bush said, "I fully recognize I'm not of Washington. I'm from Texas." See Richard L. Berke, "Bush and Gore Stake Out Differences in First Debate," *New York Times,* Oct. 4, 2000. Reagan's "government is the problem" remark is from his First Inaugural speech, as printed under the headline "Let Us Begin an Era of National Renewal," *New York Times,* Jan. 21, 1981, Lexis-Nexis, via Infohawk, http://web.lexis-nexis.com.proxy.lib.uiowa.edu.

14. Will Rogers, quoted in *Bartlett's Familiar Quotations,* 15th ed., ed. Emily Morrison Beck (Boston: Little, Brown, 1980), 765.

15. Will Rogers, *The Best of Will Rogers,* ed. Bryan B. Sterling (New York: Crown Publishers, 1979), 55; Leno, *Tonight,* Nov. 6, 2000; *South Park,* episode 808, "Douche and Turd," first aired Oct. 27, 2004.

16. Louis D. Rubin, "The Great American Joke," in *What's So Funny? Humor in American Culture,* ed. Nancy A. Walker (Wilmington, DE: Scholarly Resources, 1998), 109–110.

17. Sigmund Freud, *Jokes and Their Relation to the Unconscious,* trans. James Strachey (New York: W. W. Norton, 1963).

18. Henri Bergson, *Laughter: An Essay on the Meaning of the Comic,* trans. Cloudesley Brereton and Fred Rothwell (Los Angeles: Green Integer Books, 1999), 176.

19. Freud, *Jokes,* 105.

20. Abbie Hoffman (a.k.a. "Free"), *Revolution for the Hell of It* (New York: Dial Books, 1968). For a useful overview of the history of American anti-political sentiment, see Garry Wills, *A Necessary Evil: A History of American Distrust of Government* (New York: Simon & Schuster, 1999).

21. Marc Peyser, "The Truthiness Teller," *Newsweek,* Feb. 13, 2006, Lexis-Nexis via Infohawk, http://web.lexis-nexis.com.proxy.lib.uiowa.edu.

22. Zengerle, "The State of the George W. Bush Joke," 1.

CHAPTER 2 — "SHOWMEN IS DEVOID OF POLITICS":
THE ROOTS OF PSEUDO-SATIRE AND THE RISE OF THE
COMEDY-INDUSTRIAL COMPLEX

1. See, for example, John Dillin, "Perot Puts Spotlight on Free-Trade Issue," *Christian Science Monitor,* July 3, 1992, Lexis-Nexis via Infohawk, http://web.lexis-nexis.com.proxy.lib.uiowa.edu.

2. See, for example, "57 Varieties, One Last Name," *Washington Post,* March 7, 2003, Lexis-Nexis via Infohawk, http://web.lexis-nexis.com.proxy.lib.uiowa.edu.

3. George S. Kaufman quoted in *Bartlett's,* 15th ed., 813.

4. Al Franken, *The Truth, with Jokes* (New York: Dutton, 2005). Actually, Andy Borowitz's books include *The Borowitz Report: Big Book of Shockers* (New York: Simon & Schuster, 2004) and *The Republican Playbook* (New York: Hyperion, 2006), which is uncharacteristically partisan in its title, though not particularly so in its humor.

5. "President's Ruminations on the Three Year Anniversary of America's Super-Successful Freedomizationizing of Vietraq," http://www.whitehouse.org/news/2006/031906.asp (accessed March 15, 2007); http://www.jibjab.com.

6. "ABC Campaign '88," *Saturday Night Live,* show 14.1, first broadcast Oct. 8, 1988.

7. Dan Balz, "Resident Thinker Given Free Rein in White House; Official Promotes Role of Ideas in Politics," *Washington Post,* Dec. 13, 2004, Lexis-Nexis via Infohawk, http://web.lexis-nexis.com.proxy.lib.uiowa.edu; Bill Sammon, *Strategery: How George W. Bush Is Defeating Terrorists, Outwitting Democrats, and Confounding the Mainstream Media* (Washington: Regnery Publishing, 2006).

8. Biographical information on Larry the Cable Guy can be found at Answers.com, http://www.answers.com/topic/larry-the-cable-guy, and more notoriously in comedian David Cross's "Open Letter to Larry the Cable Guy," Dec. 1, 2005, http://www.boband-david.com/david.asp?artId=183 (accessed March 17, 2007).

9. See Constance Rourke, *American Humor: A Study of the National Character* (Tallahassee: University Presses of Florida, 1986).

10. E. B. White, "Preface," in *A Subtreasury of American Humor,* ed. E. B. White and Katherine White (New York: Coward-McCann, 1941), xiv.

11. James C. Austin, *Artemus Ward* (New York: Twayne Publishers, 1964).

12. Artemus Ward (Charles Farrar Browne), "Interview with President Lincoln," in *The Assault of Laughter: A Treasury of American Political Humor,* ed. Arthur P. Dudden (New York: Thomas Yoseloff, 1962), 94–99.

13. Ward, "The Show Is Confiscated," in *The Assault of Laughter,* 103.

14. James C. Austin, *Petroleum V. Nasby* (New York: Twayne Publishers, 1965).

15. Petroleum V. Nasby (David Ross Locke), "The Assassination," in *The Assault of Laughter,* 132–134.

16. Former Speaker of the House Tom DeLay, or the staff running his legal defense fund's Web site, apparently did not understand that Colbert was not a fellow conservative. When Robert Greenwald appeared on *The Colbert Report* to promote his documentary, *The Big Buy: Tom DeLay's Stolen Congress,* the site posted Colbert's supposed "takedown" of the filmmaker under the headline "Hollywood Pulls Michael Moore Tactics on Tom DeLay; Colbert Cracks the Story on Real Motivations behind the Movie." Nico Pitney, "Desperate for Supporters, DeLay Turns to Stephen Colbert." Think Progress blog, May 24, 2006, http://thinkprogress.org/2006/05/24/delay-colbert/ (accessed May 3, 2007).

17. See Austin, *Petroleum V. Nasby.*

18. William Marcy "Boss" Tweed, quoted in Jerry Robinson, *The Comics: An Illustrated History of Comic Strip Art* (New York: Berkley Windhover Books, 1974), 20.

19. Will Rogers's longest-running radio stint was as host of *The Gulf Headliners Show* from 1933 to 1935 on NBC. John Dunning, *On the Air: The Encyclopedia of Old-Time Radio* (New York: Oxford University Press, 1998), 722–723. Fred Allen hosted

Texaco Star Theater on CBS radio, 1940–1944, and *The Fred Allen Show* on NBC radio, 1945–1949. Senator Claghorn was played by Kenny Delmar. When Delmar had an opportunity to reprise the role years later on television, he had to get permission from Warner Bros., due to their copyright on the animated chicken. Ibid., 268.

20. "The first and most important thing to know about Mort Sahl is that he was, in every way, the first. He came from nowhere, out of left field, with no warning and few antecedents. . . . He worked clubs that had previously booked only music, and he was the first man to put spoken funny words on the hitherto musical twelve-inch LP. He probably invented the comedic 'riff,' that extended free-form metaphor that explores all the possibilities of a preposterous premise or paints the details of a verbal picture based on one, a technique which became an indispensable creative tool of all modern comedians—indeed, which has passed into everyday conversation." Tony Hendra, *Going Too Far* (New York: Dolphin Books, 1987), 30.

21. For a historical analysis of television comedy, including the eclipse of "vaudeo" by the sitcom, see David Marc, *Comic Visions: Television Comedy and American Culture* (Boston: Unwin Hyman, 1989). For a general history of network television, see J. Fred MacDonald, *One Nation Under Television: The Rise and Decline of Network TV* (Chicago: Nelson-Hall Publishers, 1994); on *Tonight*, see 112.

22. See Marc, "Planet Earth to Sitcom, Planet Earth to Sitcom," chap. 4 of *Comic Visions*, 121–156.

23. "In the course of [a 1967 *Playboy* interview], Carson attacked the C.I.A. for hiring students to compile secret reports on campus subversives . . . supported the newly insurgent blacks in demanding 'equality for all.' . . . Moreover, he summed up the war in Vietnam as 'stupid and pointless.' He seldom voiced these opinions with much vehemence on the show." See Kenneth Tynan's profile of Carson, "Fifteen Years of the Salto Mortale," in *Life Stories: Profiles from the New Yorker,* ed. David Remnick (New York: Modern Library, 2001), 331.

24. Aniko Bodroghkozy cites, among others, Neil Vidmar and Milton Rokeach, "Archie Bunker's Bigotry: A Study in Selective Perception and Exposure," *Journal of Communication* (Winter 1974). *Groove Tube* (Durham, NC: Duke University Press, 2001), 298, n. 59.

25. The definitive story of Watergate is told in Bob Woodward and Carl Bernstein, *All the President's Men* (New York: Warner Books, 1975) and *The Final Days* (New York: Simon & Schuster, 1976).

26. "Watergate Wit," *Time,* June 25, 1973, 94; "A Day That Will Live in Infamy," *Newsweek,* June 25, 1973, 20.

27. John Leonard quoted in Laurence Leamer, *King of the Night: The Life of Johnny Carson* (New York: William Morrow, 1989), 267.

28. Doug Hill and Jeff Weingrad, *Saturday Night: A Backstage History of Saturday Night Live* (New York: Beech Tree Books, 1986), 179–180, 184–187.

29. Steven D. Stark, *Glued to the Set: The 60 Television Shows and Events That Made Us Who We Are Today* (New York: Free Press, 1997), 194; Hill and Weingrad, *Saturday Night,* 183.

30. A thorough and fascinating treatment of both Meader and Frye can be found in Gerald Nachman, *Seriously Funny: The Rebel Comedians of the 1950s and 1960s* (New York: Pantheon Books, 2003).

31. Hill and Weingrad, *Saturday Night,* 15–18.

32. "Rising Number of Uninsured Tops Health News for 2006," *Health Day,* Dec. 29, 2006, http://www.nlm.nih.gov/medlineplus/news/fullstory_43252.html (accessed March 15, 2007).

CHAPTER 3 — FILM AT 11:00, JOKES AT 11:30: TOPICAL COMEDY AND THE NEWS

1. For "nearly a quarter," Karla Peterson, "Late-Night Becomes Must-See-Me TV for Presidential Candidates," *San Diego Union-Tribune,* Feb. 21, 2004, Lexis-Nexis, via Infohawk, http://web.lexis-nexis.com.proxy.lib.uiowa.edu. For "under-30 crowd," Stephen Battaglio, "The Anti-Anchor: How Jon Stewart Is Stealing TV's Political Clout," *New York Daily News,* Jan. 13, 2004, Lexis-Nexis, via Infohawk, http://web.lexis-nexis. com.proxy.lib.uiowa.edu. For "core campaign coverage," "The Big Three," *Sacramento Bee,* March 11, 2004, and for "primary vehicle," "Young Americans Get Their News from 'The Daily Show,'" *Chicago Sun-Times,* Jan. 13, 2004, Lexis-Nexis, via Infohawk, http://web.lexis-nexis.com.proxy.lib.uiowa.edu. For "sole source," Wendy Melillo, "Are Late-Night Jokes No Laughing Matter?" *Adweek,* March 29, 2004. For "young genera- tion," "Young Americans," *Chicago Sun-Times,* Jan. 13, 2004, Lexis-Nexis, via Infohawk, http://web.lexis-nexis.com.proxy.lib.uiowa.edu. For "form political opinions," Dusty Saunders, "Stewart Makes Politics Fun," *Rocky Mountain News,* Jan. 13, 2004. For "vot- ing under the influence," J. Kelly Nestruck, "Voting Under the Influence: Campaign Jokes Are No Laughing Matter," *Montreal Gazette,* Oct. 30, 2004.

2. Pew Center for the People and the Press, "Cable and Internet Loom Large," 2004. Capitalization in original.

3. Alicia C. Shepard, "Gatekeepers without Gates," *American Journalism Review* 21 (March 1999): 22.

4. Howard Kurtz and Lisa De Moraes, "ABC News Rallies behind 'Nightline,'" *Washington Post,* March 2, 2002, C1, C7; Jody Baumgartner and Jonathan S. Morris, East Carolina University, "The Daily Show Effect: Candidate Evaluations, Efficacy, and American Youth," *American Politics Research* 34, no. 3 (2006): 341–367; Richard Morin, "Jon Stewart, Enemy of Democracy?" *Washington Post,* June 23, 2006, Lexis-Nexis, via Infohawk, http://web.lexis-nexis.com.proxy.lib.uiowa.edu; *Scarborough Country,* MSNBC, June 27, 2006.

5. Marshall Sella, "The Stiff Guy vs. the Dumb Guy," *New York Times Magazine,* Sept. 24, 2000; 72–73 quoted below.

6. James Bennet, "Did You Hear the One about the '96 Campaign?" *New York Times,* July 9, 1996, A17.

7. "Like the nation's leading anchorman, Carson delivered his version of the news each day through his celebrated monologue. . . . And like an anchorman (or a president), Carson was one of the few performers whom TV etiquette allowed to address the camera directly—the culture's ultimate sign of respect and authority." Stark, *Glued to the Set,* 183.

8. "By addressing the audience directly and demanding its personal response, the stand-up comedian may appear to be a formal cousin to the feared circle of TV news reporters . . . who daily address the viewership-citizenry as the voices of information, authority, power, and connection." Marc, *Comic Visions,* 17.

9. This is based on Anthony Downs's "economic" model, in which voters may transfer to the news media the functions of *procurement, analysis,* and *evaluation* (210). Anthony Downs, *An Economic Theory of Democracy* (New York: Harper, 1957).

10. "Well, as you probably know, tensions mount, accusations continue, and the rhetoric heightens. Boy, that Delta Burke's got a big mouth."

11. Letterman, retrieved from About.com Political Humor, "Post-War Iraq Jokes," comp. Daniel Kurtzman, http://politicalhumor.about.com/library/bllatenightjokes 2006–2.htm (accessed March 16, 2007); Leno, *Tonight,* retrieved from About: Political Humor, "Jokes for the Week of April 2–8, 2006," Kurtzman, http://politicalhumor.about.com/library/bllatenightjokes2006.htm (accessed March 16, 2007).

12. Leno, *Tonight,* Sept. 25, 2001.

13. *The Dick Cavett Show* ran on ABC, 1969–1972 (he may be better remembered for his 1975–1982 PBS series). Merv Griffin's eponymous late-night show was on CBS from 1969 through early 1972. *The Joey Bishop Show* preceded Cavett in the same time slot on ABC, 1967–1969. The HBO parody, *The Larry Sanders Show,* was created by Dennis Klein and Garry Shandling and ran 1992–1998.

14. In 1980, the year before his retirement, Cronkite's *CBS Evening News* averaged twenty million viewers nightly: Michael Socolow, "A Fuzzy Picture," *Boston Globe,* April 28, 2005, Lexis-Nexis, via Infohawk, http://web.lexis-nexis.com.proxy.lib.uiowa.edu. For the week ending April 22, 2007, the three network newscasts had a combined audience of about twenty-four million: *Media Life,* April 26, 2007. http://www.medialifemagazine.com/artman/publish/article_11678.asp (accessed May 3, 2007). For the week ending May 27, 2007, Leno averaged 5.7 million viewers to Letterman's 3.8 and Kimmel's 1.9 million viewers: Toni Fitzgerald, "For ABC, Gains Extend into Late-Night," *Media Life,* June 7, 2007, http://www.medialifemagazine.com/artman2/publish/Dayparts_update_51/dayparts.asp (accessed July 27, 2007). For Carson's fifteen-million-viewer peak, see Adam Bernstein, "For Decades, Comic Ruled Late-Night TV," *New York Times,* Jan. 24, 2005, Lexis-Nexis, via Infohawk, http://web.lexis-nexis.com.proxy.lib.uiowa.edu. The *Daily Show* figure is cited in Julie Bosman,

"Serious Book to Peddle? Don't Laugh, Try a Comedy Show," *New York Times,* Feb. 27, 2007, Lexis-Nexis, via Infohawk, http://web.lexis-nexis.com.proxy.lib.uiowa.edu. The O'Reilly number is cited in Tim Cuprisin, "Outfoxing Other News Channels: Fox News Celebrates 10 Years of Knowing Its Audience," *Milwaukee Journal Sentinel,* Oct. 15, 2006, Lexis-Nexis, via Infohawk, http://web.lexis-nexis.com.proxy.lib.uiowa.edu.

15. *This Week'*s sister ABC News program, *Prime Time Live,* even experimented with a revival of *That Was the Week That Was* as a regular segment. Peter Johnson, " 'Primetime Live' Struggles with Ratings Plunge, Staff Unrest," *USA Today,* Feb. 9, 2005, http://www.usatoday.com/life/columnist/mediamix/2005-02-09-media-mix_x.htm (accessed May 3, 2007).

16. The *Times* runs selected quips in its Week in Review section. Until the magazine's recent redesign, *Time* also ran a regular recap of late-night jokes.

17. Raymond Williams, *Television: Technology and Cultural Form* (New York: Schocken Books, 1975); Roderick P. Hart, *Seducing America: How Television Charms the Modern Voter* (New York: Oxford University Press, 1994), 93.

18. Annenberg Public Policy Center, "National Annenberg Election Survey: Daily Show Viewers Knowledgeable about Presidential Campaign," http://www.Annenberg publicpolicycenter.org (accessed Oct. 28, 2004).

19. Warren St. John, "The Week That Wasn't," *New York Times,* Oct. 3, 2004, Lexis-Nexis, via Infohawk, http://web.lexis-nexis.com.proxy.lib.uiowa.edu.

20. Colbert quoted in Steve Murray, "Critic's Notebook: Comedy Phenomenon Deconstructs TV News," *Atlanta Journal-Constitution,* Oct. 3, 2004, Lexis-Nexis via Infohawk, http://web.lexis-nexis.com.proxy.lib.uiowa.edu. Leno quoted in Bennet, "Did You Hear?"

21. William Shakespeare, *Julius Caesar,* Act I, Scene 1, in *The Annotated Shakespeare,* ed. A. L. Rowse (New York: Greenwich House, 1988), 1677; "Russian Jokes," Wikipedia, http://en.wikipedia.org/wiki/Russian_joke (accessed March 16, 2007).

22. Quoted in Bennet, "Did You Hear?"

23. "Laughter is, above all, a corrective. By laughter, society avenges itself for the liberties taken with it. It would fail in its object if it bore the stamp of sympathy or kindness. . . . Laughter punishes certain failings somewhat as disease punishes certain forms of excess, striking down some who are innocent and sparing some who are guilty. . . . In this sense, laughter cannot be absolutely just." Bergson, *Laughter,* 176–177.

24. "Vice President Al Gore on CNN's Late Edition," CNN, March 9, 1999, http://www.cnn.com/ALLPOLITICS/stories/1999/03/09/president.2000/transcript. gore/ (accessed March 16, 2007). The Gore Internet story is recounted in Eric Alterman, *What Liberal Media? The Truth about Bias and the News* (New York: Basic Books, 2003), 163–164; Richard Wiggins, "Al Gore and the Creation of the Internet," *First Monday* 5, no. 10 (Oct. 2000), http://www.firstmonday.org/issues/issue5_10/wiggins. It's difficult to trace the precise path from Gore's defensible claim to the outrageous and oft-repeated

"boast," but Bob Somerby sums it up nicely in the headline "Dick Armey [then House GOP leader] Faxed Out Some Internet Spin. The Press Corps Typed It Up," Daily Howler blog, March 26, 1999, http://www.dailyhowler.com/h032699_1.shtml (accessed May 4, 2007).

25. The cue card reference stems from Gore's Sept. 19, 2000, appearance on *The Tonight Show with Jay Leno*. The other references are from Letterman's "Top Ten Other Achievements Claimed by Al Gore," first broadcast Dec. 3, 1999.

26. "If it's true that Al Gore created the Internet, then I created the 'Al Gore created the Internet' story," claims journalist (and avowed libertarian) Declan McCullagh. "I was the first reporter to question the vice president's improvident boast, way back when he made it in early 1999. . . . That statement was enough to convince me, with the encouragement of my then-editor James Glave, to write a brief article that questioned the vice president's claim. Republicans on Capitol Hill noticed the *Wired News* writeup and started faxing around tongue-in-cheek press releases—inveterate neatnik Trent Lott claimed to have invented the paper clip—and other journalists picked up the story too. My article never used the word 'invented,' but it didn't take long for Gore's claim to morph into something he never intended." Declan McCullagh, "The Mother of Gore's Invention," *Wired News,* Oct. 17, 2000, http://web.archive.org/web/20001027190912/http://www.wired.com/news/politics/0,1283,39301,00.html (accessed May 4, 2007). McCullagh's claim of primacy might be technically correct, but to say the story "morphed" minimizes the role played by Republican politicians and campaign personnel in embellishing what Gore said, and by the compliant (or plain lazy) members of the media who accepted and disseminated their (and McCullagh's) deliberate mischaracterizations.

27. " 'Yo Blair!' Bush Drops His Guard," *Toronto Star,* July 18, 2006, Lexis-Nexis via Infohawk, http://web.lexis-nexis.com.proxy.lib.uiowa.edu.

28. Cynthia Grenier, "Late Night Gurus," *The World & I,* Aug. 1, 1999, 103. http://www.elibrary.com/education (accessed Nov. 14, 2001).

29. Twain's positive assessment of laughter's power is offset by the fact that the line is spoken by Satan, in the course of berating mankind for failing to adequately appreciate it. "Against the assault of laughter, nothing can stand. You are always fussing and fighting with other weapons. Do you ever use that one? No; you leave it lying rusting. As a race, do you ever use it at all? No; you lack sense and the courage." Mark Twain, "The Mysterious Stranger," in *The Complete Short Stories of Mark Twain* (New York: Bantam Books, 1983), 674.

30. Freud, *Jokes,* 133.

31. Leno quoted in Bennet, "Did You Hear?" Vickers quoted in Richard Zoglin, "Politics, Late-Night Style: Talk-Show Hosts Are Looking to the Headlines for Laughs," *Time,* June 12, 1989, http://www.time.com/time/magazine/article/0,9171,957930-2,00.html (accessed March 15, 2007).

32. Charles R. Gruner, *Understanding Laughter: The Workings of Wit and Humor* (Chicago: Nelson-Hall, 1978), 201.

CHAPTER 4 — THE PERSONAL AND THE POLITICAL

1. Talk about getting news from unconventional sources. The 2000 "beer poll" was conducted by the brewers of Samuel Adams. See Julie Mason, "Campaign 2000: Campaign Notebook," *Houston Chronicle,* Oct. 19, 2000, Lexis-Nexis via Infohawk, http://web.lexis-nexis.com.proxy.lib.uiowa.edu. But in 2004, the question was adopted by a more serious polling organization. "A recent Zogby/Williams Identity Poll reflected that. It found that 57% of undecided voters would rather have a beer with Bush than Kerry," noted Richard Benedetto. "(In Bush's case, it would be a nonalcoholic beer.)" Richard Benedetto, "Who's More Likeable: Bush or Kerry?" *USA Today,* Sept. 17, 2004, http://www.usatoday.com/news/opinion/columnist/benedetto/2004–09–17-benedetto_x.htm (accessed March 16, 2007). The idea has also been casually asserted many times. See Michael Saul, "Gore Is Not Bridging the Guy Gap, Polls Show: Men Relate to Bush's Down-Home Image," *Dallas Morning News,* July 30, 2000: " 'There is a comfort level that men have with Bush. He seems like the kind of guy you can have a beer with,' Allyn said. 'Al Gore is the kind of guy who wants you to drink light beer, and then he'll lecture you on the dangers of alcohol.' "

2. Chris Matthews, *Hardball* transcript cited in Simon Malloy, "Matthews on Bush and the Port Deal," *Media Matters,* Feb. 27, 2006, http://mediamatters.org/items/200602270010 (accessed March 16, 2007); Patrick Healy, "For Clintons, Delicate Dance Of Married and Public Lives," *New York Times,* May 23, 2006, Lexis-Nexis via Infohawk, http://web.lexis-nexis.com.proxy.lib.uiowa.edu.

3. Tonya Reiman and Bill O'Reilly, *The O'Reilly Factor,* transcript cited in AI, "O'Reilly: 'Hillary Just Looks Like a Zombie' during SOTU," *Media Matters,* Jan. 31, 2007, http://mediamatters.org/items/200701310004 (accessed March 16, 2007); Elisabeth Bumiller, "Running on a Campaign Trail Paved in Comfy Feathers," *New York Times,* March 22, 2004, Lexis-Nexis via Infohawk, http://web.lexis-nexis.com.proxy.lib.uiowa.edu.

4. Josh Kalven, "Media Ignored Context of Kerry's Remarks and Acknowledgments by Prominent Republicans That Kerry Did Not Mean to Insult Troops," *Media Matters,* Nov. 1, 2006, http://mediamatters.org/items/200611010012 (accessed March 16, 2007).

5. Ibid.

6. R. M., "Broadcast Networks All Led with Kerry's 'Botched Joke,' Entirely Ignored Bush's Statement That a Democratic Victory Means 'Terrorists Win and America Loses,' " *Media Matters,* Nov. 1, 2006, http://mediamatters.org/items/200611010009 (accessed March 16, 2007); Simon Malloy, "LA Times, Network News Hyped Kerry Comments, Downplayed Story about Kidnapped U.S. Soldier," *Media Matters,* Nov. 1, 2006, http://mediamatters.org/items/200611020004 (accessed March 16, 2007).

7. Kalven, "Media Ignored." Armey told Chris Matthews, "Well, it's pretty standard fare in political discourse. You misconstrue what somebody said. You isolate a statement, you lend your interpretation to it and then feign moral outrage." DeLay's defense of Kerry was a bit more back-handed: "I don't think he intended to insult the troops at a campaign event, but he did," said DeLay on Fox's *Hannity and Colmes*. "I don't think he intended to call them stupid, but he did."

8. Leno, *Tonight*, Nov. 4, 2006, Letterman, *Late Show*, Nov. 2, 2006, and O'Brien, *Late Night*, Nov. 2, 2006, all retrieved from About.com Political Humor, "2006 Late-Night Joke Archive," comp. Daniel Kurtzman, http://politicalhumor.about.com/library/bllatenightjokesarchive.htm (accessed March 16, 2007).

9. Jon Stewart, *The Daily Show with Jon Stewart*, Comedy Central, Nov. 2, 2006.

10. Jon Stewart, interview by Maureen Dowd, "Jon Stewart and Stephen Colbert: America's Anchors," *Rolling Stone*, Nov. 16, 2006, 56.

11. Retrieved from About.com Political Humor, "Jokes for the Week of March 12–18," comp. Daniel Kurtzman, http://politicalhumor.about.com/library/bllatenight jokesarchive.htm .

12. Leno, *Tonight*, Sept. 27 and Dec. 11, 2006, and O'Brien, *Late Night*, Dec. 4, 2006, all retrieved from About: Political Humor, "2006 Late-Night Joke Archive," comp. Daniel Kurtzman, http://politicalhumor.about.com/library/bllatenightjokesarchive.htm (accessed March 16, 2007).

13. Robert McKee, *Story* (New York: Regan Books, 1997), 375.

14. "Every comic character is a type. . . . And what is most comic of all is to become a category oneself into which others will fall, as into a ready-made frame; it is to crystallize into a stock character." Bergson, *Laughter*, 134.

15. Ibid., 145.

16. Ibid., 147.

17. See Phyllis Hartnoll, *The Concise History of Theatre* (New York: Harry N. Abrams, 1968), 60–70.

18. "Humours," *The Concise Oxford Dictionary of Literary Terms,* ed. Christopher Baldick (Oxford University Press, 1996), Oxford Reference Online, http://www.oxfordreference.com.proxy.lib.uiowa.edu/views/ENTRY.html?subview=Main&entry=t56.e468 (accessed May 4, 2007).

19. "The attitudes, gestures and movements of the human body are laughable in exact proportion as that body reminds us of a mere machine," Bergson, *Laughter*, 32. Bergson sees the theme of mechanical rigidity and "automatism" at work not only in what is physically laughable but also in the behavior of single-minded or absentminded characters.

20. Gerard Mulligan quoted in Sella, "Stiff Guy vs. Dumb Guy," 77.

21. Ibid.

22. Bob Elliot and Ray Goulding, *Write If You Get Work: The Best of Bob and Ray* (New York: Random House, 1975), 27–29.

23. Picasso quoted in Gertrude Stein, *The Autobiography of Alice B. Toklas*, 1933, e-book available at http://gutenberg.net.au/ebooks06/0608711.txt (accessed March 18, 2007).

24. Michael Wines, "White House Wraps Christmas in Laughs," *New York Times*, Dec. 8, 1992, B12.

25. Bergson, *Laughter*, 39.

26. Will Jordan quoted in Nachman, *Seriously Funny*, 519.

27. Ibid.

28. *The Columbia World of Quotations*, no. 44191, 1996, http://www.bartleby.com/66/91/44191.html (accessed March 18, 2007).

29. Susan T. Fiske and Shelley E. Taylor, *Social Cognition*, 2nd ed. (New York: McGraw-Hill, 1991), 13.

30. "The pleasure in jokes has seemed to us to arise from an economy in expenditure upon inhibition. . . ." Freud, *Jokes*, 236.

31. For a useful overview of schema theory, see Fiske and Taylor, *Social Cognition*, chaps. 4–6, 96–241.

32. Leno, *Tonight*, Nov. 27, 2000.

33. Leno, *Tonight*, retrieved from About.com Political Humor, "Republican Jokes: Late-Night Jokes and Funny Quotes about Republicans," comp. Daniel Kurtzman, http://politicalhumor.about.com/library/blrepublicanjokes.htm.

34. Letterman, *Late Show*, retrieved from About.com Political Humor, "Democrat Jokes," comp. Daniel Kurtzman, http://politicalhumor.about.com/library/bldemocratjokes.htm.

35. Leno on Bush, *Tonight*, Nov. 3, 2000; on Bob Livingston, *Tonight*, quoted in John McQuaid, "Livingston Confession Adds to Atmosphere; Latest Dirt-Digging Pushes Washington Further into Bottomless Pit of Sex, Lies and Politics." *New Orleans Times-Picayune*, Dec. 19, 1998, Lexis-Nexis via Infohawk, http://web.lexis-nexis.com.proxy.lib.uiowa.edu.

36. Letterman, *Late Show*, Dec. 20, 2000.

37. Leno, *Tonight*, Dec. 18, 2000.

38. Fiske and Taylor, *Social Cognition*, 118.

39. Letterman, *Late Show*, Dec. 20, 2000.

40. "John C. Average Reporting for Duty," *St. Petersburg Times* (Florida), June 12, 2005, Lexis-Nexis via Infohawk, http://web.lexis-nexis.com.proxy.lib.uiowa.edu.

41. Leno, *Tonight*, Oct. 25, 2000.

42. Jimmy Kimmel, *Jimmy Kimmel Live*, ABC, retrieved from About.com Political Humor, "The Week's Best Late-Night Jokes," comp. Daniel Kurtzman, http://politicalhumor.about.com/b/a/256841.htm.

43. Leno, *Tonight*, week of Oct. 29–Nov. 4, 2004, ibid.

44. "Reagan the Mastermind," *SNL*, Dec. 6, 1986.

45. See the "Comedy Central" entry in Tim Brooks and Earle Marsh, *The Complete Directory to Prime Time Network and Cable TV Shows, 1946-Present,* 6th ed. (New York: Ballantine Books, 1995), 205–206.

46. Peter W. Kaplan, "David Letterman's Shtick Shift." *Rolling Stone,* Nov. 3, 1998, 70–75. Another article in the same issue noted that there were "now more than 300 full-time comedy clubs in America, nearly a hundredfold increase from the early Seventies." Duncan Strauss, "The Clubbing of America," 89–90.

47. Quoted in Paul Brownfield, "Cheap Shots at a Steep Price?" *Los Angeles Times,* Aug. 27, 2000, Calendar, 3.

48. Quayle on "mind," quoted in *What a Waste It Is to Lose One's Mind: The Unauthorized Autobiography of Dan Quayle,* by the editors of the *Quayle Quarterly* (Bridgeport, CT: Quayle Quarterly, 1992), xi; on "embargo," quoted in *Esquire,* Aug. 1992.

49. The autobiography is *What a Waste It Is to Lose One's Mind* (see the previous note). The *Quayle Quarterly* and 1–900–USA–DANNY were the creations of Gary Cohn. See Susan Trausch, "Quayles of Laughter," *Boston Globe,* Feb. 22, 1991, Lexis-Nexis via Infohawk, http://web.lexis-nexis.com.proxy.lib.uiowa.edu.

50. Dan Quayle, *Standing Firm: A Vice-Presidential Memoir* (New York: Harper Collins Publishers, 1994), 188.

51. Robert Lichter quoted in Scott Shepard, "Political Humor: So Who's Laughing?" *St. Louis Post-Dispatch, Everyday Magazine,* Dec. 24, 1991, Lexis-Nexis via Infohawk, http://web.lexis-nexis.com.proxy.lib.uiowa.edu; "Will the Jokes Ever Stop?" *Newsweek,* Nov. 28, 1988, 39.

52. Quoted in Jonathan Alter, "Curbing the Quayle Hunt," *Newsweek,* Nov. 18, 1991, 37.

53. Quoted in Brownfield, "Cheap Shots."

54. *The Simpsons,* "Treehouse of Horror VII," show 4F02, first aired Oct. 27, 1996, written by Ken Keeler, Dan Greaney, and David S. Cohen.

55. Sella, "Stiff Guy vs. Dumb Guy."

56. See Sam Howe Verhovek, "The Nation: What Makes Ralph (and Pat) Run?" *New York Times,* Oct. 29, 2000, Lexis-Nexis via Infohawk, http://web.lexis-nexis.com.proxy.lib.uiowa.edu.

57. From Maureen Dowd's column following the 2000 GOP candidates' debate in December 1999: "When the Republican candidates were asked to name their favorite political philosophers, Mr. Bush replied: 'Christ, because he changed my heart.' Pressed to elaborate, the Texas governor again showed his inability to go deep. . . . His mouth curled down into that famous smirky look. 'Well, if they don't know, it's going to be hard to explain,' he said. 'When you turn your heart and your life over to Christ, when you accept Christ as the Savior, it changes your heart. It changes your life. And that's what happened to me.'" Maureen Dowd, "Playing the Jesus Card," *New York Times,* Dec. 15, 1999, Lexis-Nexis via Infohawk, http://web.lexis-nexis.com.proxy.lib.uiowa.edu.

58. Letterman, *Late Show,* Nov. 8, 2000; Leno, *Tonight,* Nov. 13, 2000.

59. O'Brien, *Late Night,* Nov. 10, 2000.

CHAPTER 5 —— PAY NO ATTENTION TO THAT MAN IN FRONT OF THE CURTAIN

1. An Internet rumor that Kerry had been involved in an extramarital affair with for-mer staffer Alexander Polier was picked up by Matt Drudge and Rush Limbaugh before being duly reported *as a rumor* by a few more mainstream media outlets. Polier and Kerry both declared that there was no truth to the allegations of an affair. See Mark Memmott, "Kerry Rumor Tests Media's Standards," *USA Today,* Feb. 20, 2004, Lexis-Nexis via Infohawk, http://web.lexis-nexis.com.proxy.lib.uiowa.edu. During the 2000 South Carolina Republican primary campaign, leaflets were distributed claiming that Senator McCain's wife, Cindy, was a drug addict, and that McCain had a "black baby." In fact, the McCains' adopted daughter, Bridget, then eight years old, was born in Bangladesh. Though no evidence has been discovered to prove the allegation, the Bush campaign was suspected to have played a role in spreading this morsel of thinly dis-guised race-baiting. See Melinda Henneberger, "The Other McCain: Unexpectedly, Cindy McCain Basks in a New Political Role," *New York Times,* March 3, 2000, Lexis-Nexis via Infohawk, http://web.lexis-nexis.com.proxy.lib.uiowa.edu.

2. Quoted in Randy Kennedy, "Hey, That's (Not) Funny," *New York Times,* April 15, 2007, Lexis-Nexis via Infohawk, http://web.lexis-nexis.com.proxy.lib.uiowa.edu.

3. "Two decades ago, an official Family Hour was established for prime-time televi-sion. As a result of prodding from Congress and the Federal Communications Com-mission, the networks formally agreed in 1975 to set aside the first hour of prime time (eight to nine P.M. on the coasts, seven to eight P.M. in the heartland) for programming suitable for all ages. The Writers Guild of America and other groups challenged the restriction on First Amendment and anti-trust grounds, and won. The Family Hour was struck down in 1976. In a sense, though, eight to nine P.M. always has been the unofficial family hour, the home of such wholesome series as 'Little House on the Prairie,' 'Happy Days,' 'The Cosby Show,' and 'Full House.' In turn, more adult-oriented fare, such as 'The Golden Girls,' 'Designing Women,' 'L.A. Law,' 'thirtysomething,' and 'Knots Landing,' was broadcast between nine and 11 P.M. . . . This understanding began to crumble a few years back and now is largely in ruins." Thomas Johnson, "The Decline of Television's Family Hour," *USA Today Magazine,* Nov. 1996, Academic Search Elite via Infohawk, http://web.ebscohost.com.proxy.lib.uiowa.edu.

4. Joan Rivers hosted *The Late Show,* Fox, 1986–1988, from its debut in October 1986 until mid-May 1987, when she was replaced by Arsenio Hall, who later returned with *The Arsenio Hall Show,* 1989–1994. *The Joey Bishop Show* lasted from April 1967 to December 1969 on ABC. *The Merv Griffin Show* only ran from August 1969 to February 1972 on CBS late-night; of course, he was a daytime presence for many more years. Sammy Davis Jr.'s *Sammy and Company* managed fifty-five syndicated episodes

between 1975 and 1977, but did inspire SCTV's *Sammy Maudlin Show. The Chevy Chase Show* ran only six weeks on Fox, in September and October 1993. Alan Thicke's *Thicke of the Night* lasted from 1983 to 1984, in syndication. The Quincy Jones–produced *Vibe* debuted in 1997 with Chris Spencer as host; Sinbad took over in 1998. *The Pat Sajak Show* lasted fifteen months after its January 1989 premiere on CBS.

5. Shaw quoted in Will Kaufman, *The Comedian as Confidence Man: Studies in Irony Fatigue* (Detroit: Wayne State University Press, 1997),194. Hans Speier referred to "the special case in which the narrator is inferior in power to the victim but enjoys immunity from retaliation, because, as client to a powerful master, he is protected from the victim's revenge. This is the case of the court jester who entertains his master with jokes at the expense of the master's courtiers whose power exceeds that of the jester but does not equal that of the lord. In a more modern situation, one sees professional comedians working for gain and public applause with impunity because the mighty defer to the power of public opinion, which protects the storyteller. If the mighty censor or punish the comedian, as they do in oppressive regimes, the power and freedom of public opinion is curtailed or abolished altogether. . . . [O]nly fools and professional humorists may laughingly say the truth in the presence of the mighty." Hans Speier, "Wit and Politics: An Essay on Laughter and Power," trans. Robert Jackall, *American Journal of Sociology* 103, no. 5 (March 1998): 1386, 1393.

6. Though George W. Bush likes to refer to himself as "Forty-three" (to distinguish himself from his father, "Forty-one"), he is actually one of only forty-two men to hold the office to date. Grover Cleveland's two non-consecutive terms make him both the twenty-second and twenty-fourth presidents.

7. Marc, *Comic Visions,* 17.

8. Lawrence Mintz, "Stand-up Comedy as Social and Cultural Mediation," *American Quarterly* 37, no. 1 (1985): 71–80.

9. Marc, *Comic Visions,* 26.

10. See Paul Farhi, " 'Seinfeld' Comic Richards Apologizes for Racial Rant," *Washington Post,* Nov. 21, 2006, Lexis-Nexis via Infohawk, http://web.lexis-nexis.com.proxy.lib. uiowa.edu. Amateur video taken at the comedy club where Richards lost it is widely available online.

11. Ben Alba, *Inventing Late Night: Steve Allen and the Original Tonight Show* (Amherst, NY: Prometheus Books, 2005), 116–120.

12. See the chapters on Paar in Robert Metz, *The Tonight Show* (New York: Playboy Press, 1980), 108–167.

13. Richard Zoglin, "And What a Reign It Was," *Time,* March 16, 1992: 66; "tight as an egg," Harry F. Waters, with Lynda Wright and Jeanne Gordon, "Stranger in the Night," *Newsweek,* May 25, 1992, Lexis-Nexis via Infohawk, http://web.lexis-nexis.com.proxy. lib.uiowa.edu; Carson quoted in B. Zehme and D. Cowles, "A Sad Day for Comedy," *Rolling Stone,* May 28, 1992, 63.

14. Carson once said, "I don't think I've ever been political. I don't think most people could tell you really whether I'm a Republican or Democrat. I've always tried to distance myself (from politicians) because I want to keep an open mind when I go out and do a monologue. . . . I picked on (John) Kennedy as much as I picked on Nixon or Agnew or Lyndon Johnson or Reagan, all the way along. And I like it that way." Rick DuBrow, "This Is It . . . Maybe, Says Johnny Carson," *Los Angeles Times*, April 23, 1991, F1.

15. Carson's *Life* interview quoted in Virginia Mann, "King of Late Night Leaves Us Laughing," *Record* (Bergen Co., NJ), May 17, 1992, Lexis-Nexis via Infohawk, http://web.lexis-nexis.com.proxy.lib.uiowa.edu.

16. Wuoted in Eirik Knutzen, "Last Curtain Call," *Toronto Star*, May 16, 1992, Lexis-Nexis via Infohawk, http://web.lexis-nexis.com.proxy.lib.uiowa.edu.

17. See Leamer, *King of the Night*, 38.

18. Waters, "Stranger in the Night."

19. Robert Balkin quoted in Colin McEnroe, Jon Lender, and Donna Larcen, "Yessss, It's . . . Goodnight, Johnny! No Mere Comedian, Johnny Influenced Show Careers, Political Opinion," *Hartford Courant*, May 22, 1992, Lexis-Nexis via Infohawk, http://web.lexis-nexis.com.proxy.lib.uiowa.edu.

20. Andy Edelstein, "Say Good Night, Johnny," *Newsday*, May 10, 1992, Lexis-Nexis via Infohawk, http://web.lexis-nexis.com.proxy.lib.uiowa.edu.

21. On extremes, see Lawrence Goodwyn, *The Populist Moment: A Short History of the Agrarian Revolt in America* (New York: Oxford University Press, 1978). On Milwaukee, see Melanie Hupfer, "Bridge Warriors, Abolitionists, and 'Sewer Socialism': Important Facts to Know about the History of Milwaukee," *UMW Post*, http://www.uwmpost.com/article/c58b6a040bf450fc010bfc2963b80007 (accessed March 17, 2007).

22. "As a people, [midwesterners] are extraordinarily reticent, secretive even, about personal matters. If decency and good manners are part of this reticence, a shade of hypocrisy is there too. Appearance is the truth that matters. . . . To learn the truth about a person, one did not ask baldly for the facts. As often as not, humor was the vehicle of truth. Even today, if one sits in the coffee shops or the American Legion halls, one hears a sly, subtle humor. When a man leaves the table, he is sometimes knifed in the back." Leamer, *King of the Night*, 31.

23. See especially Bernard Timberg, "Television Talk and Ritual Space: Carson and Letterman," *Southern Speech Communication Journal* 52 (Summer 1987): 390–402.

24. *Our American Cousin*, by Tom Taylor, 1858. The prototypical Yankee play is Royall Tyler's *The Contrast*, 1787.

25. Rourke, *American Humor*, 30.

26. Kaplan, "David Letterman's Shtick Shift," 71.

27. Alex Ross writes that "every component" of *Late-Night with David Letterman* "was a deliberately inadequate echo of Carson's show-biz juggernaut." Alex Ross, "The Politics of Irony," *New Republic*, Nov. 8, 1993, 26.

28. See Matthew Gilbert, "On TV: Bringing Up Daddy: Dave Delivers the Goods on His New Life," *Boston Globe,* Nov. 13, 2003, Lexis-Nexis via Infohawk, http://web.lexis-nexis.com.proxy.lib.uiowa.edu.

29. Diane Werts, "A Regular Guy Ascends the Throne," *Newsday,* May 20, 1992, Lexis-Nexis via Infohawk, http://web.lexis-nexis.com.proxy.lib.uiowa.edu.

30. Eric Idle, *The Road to Mars* (New York: Pantheon Books, 1999), 7.

31. Among White Face comics, Idle lists Carson, Letterman, O'Brien, Bill Maher, Woody Allen, Mort Sahl, and his old Python colleague, John Cleese. Red Nose comics include Leno, John Belushi, Robin Williams, Danny Kaye, Mel Brooks, and Jerry Lewis. Idle, *Road to Mars,* 145.

32. Paul Brownfield, "It's Not Just 'Tonight.' It's Every Night," *Los Angeles Times,* July 9, 2000, Calendar, 4, Electric Library, http://www.elibrary.com/education (accessed Nov. 14, 2001); Leno quoted in Tom Shales, "Jay Leno, Laughing Last: The Comedian's Bumpy Road to the Top of 'Tonight,'" *Washington Post,* June 27, 1991, Lexis-Nexis via Infohawk, http://web.lexis-nexis.com.proxy.lib.uiowa.edu.

33. Quoted in Ross, "The Politics of Irony," 30.

34. Werts, "A Regular Guy Ascends the Throne."

35. "Leno Leans on Politicians," *USA Today,* May 26, 1992, Lexis-Nexis via Infohawk, http://web.lexis-nexis.com.proxy.lib.uiowa.edu.

36. Tom Shales, "Jay Leno Missing His Funny Bone," *Washington Post,* July 30, 1992, Lexis-Nexis via Infohawk, http://web.lexis-nexis.com.proxy.lib.uiowa.edu.

37. *Late Show with David Letterman,* March 1, 2007.

38. Former *Late Show* writer Chris Kelly quoted in Sella, "Stiff Guy vs. Dumb Guy." Letterman's denial, *Late Show,* Sept. 26, 2000.

39. John Limon, *Stand-up Comedy in Theory, or, Abjection in America* (Durham, NC: Duke University Press, 2000), 68–69.

40. O'Brien quoted in Sella, "Stiff Guy vs. Dumb Guy," 74.

41. See Jacqueline Cutler, "Believe in Yourself, and 'Late Night' Is Possible: Conan O'Brien Celebrates 10 Years of Talking and Following in His Heroes' Footsteps," *Times-Picayune* (New Orleans, LA), Sept. 14, 2003, Lexis-Nexis via Infohawk, http://web.lexis-nexis.com.proxy.lib.uiowa.edu. Also, "Conan O'Brien Biography," Biography.com, http://www.biography.com/search/article.do?id=9542192 (accessed March 17, 2007).

42. Bill Carter writes, "The offices of Letterman's *Late Night* constituted a kind of unofficial Harvard Club." Bill Carter, *The Late Shift* (New York: Hyperion, 1994), 240.

43. Tom Shales, "Better Never than Late: Conan O'Brien Not Worth a Hoot to the Night Owl," *Washington Post,* Sept. 15, 1993, Lexis-Nexis via Infohawk, http://web.lexis-nexis.com.proxy.lib.uiowa.edu.

44. *Late Night,* Feb. 23, 2007.

45. Nathan Rabin, "Interview: Conan O'Brien," *Onion AV Club,* Aug. 30, 2006, http://www.avclub.com/content/node/52144 (accessed March 17, 2007).

46. Rivers claimed that when she called Carson to explain her decision to defect from *Tonight*, he hung up on her. See George Hackett, "Can We Talk? (Crash, Click, Buzz)," *Newsweek*, May 19, 1986, Lexis-Nexis via Infohawk, http://web.lexis-nexis.com.proxy.lib.uiowa.edu.

47. TV's *The Stephanie Miller Show* (syndicated) aired from September 1995 through January 1996. Miller's syndicated radio program, also titled *The Stephanie Miller Show*, debuted in September of 2004.

48. Fey's association with *SNL* lasted from 2000 to 2006.

49. Dave Itzkoff, "The All Too Ready for Prime Time Players," *New York Times*, Jan. 2, 2005, Lexis-Nexis via Infohawk, http://web.lexis-nexis.com.proxy.lib.uiowa.edu.

50. A letter from *Times* reader Joe Andrews, responding to Itzkoff's story, made this point: "When a show has been dominated by men with a strong focus on political satire, what is it to do when its strongest contributors, behind and in front of the camera, are women? In other words, if "Saturday Night Live" is to leverage the best collection of female talent it has ever had, what will the source material be? Beyond Maya Rudolph's brilliant send-up of Condoleezza Rice, who else might they satirize? Barbara Boxer? Dianne Feinstein? (Of course there's Hillary Clinton, but best to wait until 2008 for that.) Should they ignore the female cast altogether and do traditional male-centric political satire in spite of the missing gender-appropriate talent?" *New York Times*, Jan. 9, 2005, Lexis-Nexis via Infohawk, http://web.lexis-nexis.com.proxy.lib.uiowa.edu.

51. Pre-Bee female correspondents on *The Daily Show* include Stacey Grenrock-Woods, Rahael Harris, Laura Kightlinger, and Nancy Walls.

52. Christopher Hitchens, "Why Women Aren't Funny," *Vanity Fair*, Jan. 2007, http://www.vanityfair.com/culture/features/2007/01/hitchens200701 (accessed March 17, 2007).

53. Carter, *Late Shift*, 84.

54. Harry F. Waters and Michael Reese, "Arsenio Hall's Late Arrival," *Newsweek*, April 10, 1989, Lexis-Nexis via Infohawk, http://web.lexis-nexis.com.proxy.lib.uiowa.edu.

55. "We all know by now that Johnny Carson will end his 30-year run as 'The Tonight Show' host on May 22. Out of respect, Arsenio Hall will air reruns of his talk show during Carson's last week. 'Arsenio's going to be home watching Carson,' said a spokeswoman. 'We're taking the week down. It's a show of respect to Carson by Arsenio.' Comedy Central, the cable channel, plans to 'go dark.' Hall, in classic one-upmanship, says that 'as a personal tribute to Mr. Carson, I'm going to stay dark the rest of my life.' " Michael Blowen, "Out of Respect for Johnny," *Boston Globe*, May 11, 1992, Lexis-Nexis via Infohawk, http://web.lexis-nexis.com.proxy.lib.uiowa.edu.

56. "Arsenio Hall Says He's Ready to Take on Leno in TV War and 'Kick Jay's Ass,' " *Jet*, May 4, 1992.

57. Mike McDaniel and Louis B. Parks, "CBS Fires First Shot in Late-Night War: Station Eagerly Awaits Letterman," *Houston Chronicle*, Jan. 15, 1993, Lexis-Nexis via Infohawk, http://web.lexis-nexis.com.proxy.lib.uiowa.edu.

58. Carter, *Late Shift*, 86.

59. See Denene Millner, "Standup Sensation: Four Black Jokers—Subject of Spike Lee's New Movie—Put On the Most Successful Comedy Tour in History. How Come Mainstream America Didn't Notice?" *New York Daily News*, Aug. 6, 2000, Lexis-Nexis via Infohawk, http://web.lexis-nexis.com.proxy.lib.uiowa.edu.

60. "In July [1989], during the ratings sweeps, Hall's audience was 53 percent white, 45 percent black and 2 percent other." Michael Norman, "TV's Arsenio Hall: Late-Night Cool," *New York Times*, Oct. 1, 1989, Lexis-Nexis via Infohawk, http://web.lexis-nexis.com.proxy.lib.uiowa.edu.

61. Lawrence Christon, "Grand Illusionist," *Los Angeles Times*, May 17, 1992, Lexis-Nexis via Infohawk, http://web.lexis-nexis.com.proxy.lib.uiowa.edu.

62. *Vibe* (syndicated) debuted in August 1997 with Chris Spencer as host. Spencer lasted until October, after which the better-known Sinbad took over until the show ended in May 1998.

63. *The Bernie Mac Show*, Fox, 2001–2006, co-created by *The Daily Show*'s Larry Wilmore. *Cedric the Entertainer Presents*, Fox, 2002–2003. (Cedric had previously been a cast member on Harvey's show.) *The Steve Harvey Show*, WB, 1996–2002, was already under way when Lee's movie came out. Hughley had also established a television presence as the star of *The Hughleys*, UPN, 1998–2002.

64. "Black George Bush," *Chappelle's Show*, episode 27, first aired April 14, 2004.

65. Larry Wilmore, *Daily Show*, Aug. 22, 2006 ("Macaca"), and Oct. 18, 2006 (Madonna).

66. Quoted in Phil Reeves, "Excuse Me, George Herbert. . . ." *Independent* (London), June 21, 1992, Lexis-Nexis via Infohawk, http://web.lexis-nexis.com.proxy.lib.uiowa.edu.

67. Ibid.

68. Limon, *Stand-up Comedy in Theory*, 1.

69. Frank Rich, "So Long to Johnny, America's Sandman," *New York Times*, May 10, 1992, 5.

70. Limon, *Stand-up Comedy in Theory*, 80.

71. "Since 1995, when Paramount canceled his 1-year-old syndicated talk show, an off-shoot of the one he started for MTV in 1993, Stewart has been mentioned as a replacement for Conan O'Brien in the early years, for [Tom] Snyder (for whom he was a fill-in host), and most memorably, for Garry Shandling's Larry Sanders on The Larry Sanders Show on HBO." Kurt Jensen, "Stand-Up Veteran Is No Longer a Stand-In," *USA Today*, Jan. 11, 1999, Lexis-Nexis via Infohawk, http://web.lexis-nexis.com.proxy.lib.uiowa.edu.

72. See David Segal, "The Seriously Funny Jon Stewart: Cable's 'Daily Show' Host Delivers Satire with Substance," *Washington Post*, May 2, 2002, Lexis-Nexis via Infohawk, http://web.lexis-nexis.com.proxy.lib.uiowa.edu.

73. Cool Papa Bell quote cited in Dick Kreck, "ESPN Classic Re-Creates Negro League Baseball Game," *Denver Post*, Feb. 23, 2006, Lexis-Nexis via Infohawk, http://web.lexis-nexis.com.proxy.lib.uiowa.edu.

74. " 'The Daily Show' prides itself on its bipartisanship. 'People ask, "Why aren't you really making fun of Democrats right now?" ' Mr. Stewart says, 'and we say we'd love to if we knew where they were.' . . . In Mr. Stewart's view, 'Liberals and conservatives are two gangs who have intimidated rational, normal thinking beings into not having a voice on television or in the culture.' " Frank Rich, "Jon Stewart's Perfect Pitch," *New York Times*, April 20, 2003, Lexis-Nexis via Infohawk, http://web.lexis-nexis.com. proxy.lib.uiowa.edu.

75. Stewart, *Daily Show*, Nov. 1, 2004.

76. Carson quoted in Stephen Cox, *Here's Johnny: Thirty Years of America's Favorite Late Night Entertainment* (New York: Harmony Books, 1992), 174; "Johnny Carson Sets Us Straight," *Nation*, June 18, 1977, 746.

77. James Poniewozik, "The American Bald Ego," *Time*, Nov. 6, 2005, http://www. time.com/time/magazine/article/0,9171,1126747,00.html (accessed March 17, 2007).

CHAPTER 6 — TRUTH VERSUS TRUTHINESS; OR, LOOKING FOR MR. SMITH

1. Bernard Timberg remarks that "the talk show host is as much a representative of the people as an elected official." Timberg, "Television Talk and Ritual Space," 402.

2. Jason Horowitz, "Senator McCain Worked Blue on New York Stage," *New York Observer*, May 29, 2006, http://observer.com/20060529/20060529_Jason_Horowitz_pageone_newsstory1.asp (accessed Marchch 17, 2007).

3. Steven Wright, *I Have a Pony* [CD], Rhino Flashback, 2005 (originally released 1985).

4. George Orwell, "Funny, but Not Vulgar," in *The Collected Essays, Journalism and Letters of George Orwell: As I Please, 1943–1945*, vol. 3, ed. Sonia Orwell and Ian Angus (New York: Harcourt, Brace & World, 1968), 284.

5. Quoted in Kaufman, *Comedian as Confidence Man*, 13.

6. Ibid., 12.

7. Quoted ibid., 35.

8. Ibid, 187.

9. Mark Twain, *The Tragedy of Pudd'nhead Wilson: And the Comedy, Those Extraordinary Twins* (1894). See also Kaufman, *Comedian as Confidence Man*, 217–229.

10. Twain's late writings are, writes Kaufman, "notorious in their misanthropic savagery." *Comedian as Confidence Man*, 189.

11. Kaufman (ibid.) uses this famous phrase as the title of his chapter on Bruce.

12. See Hendra, *Going Too Far*, 170–171. See also *The Lenny Bruce Performance Film*, a low-budget recording of a late-period club date, produced by John Magnuson and available on DVD from KOCH Vision, 2005.

13. Robert Rice, "The Fury," *New Yorker*, July 30, 1960, 31–52.

14. Mort Sahl quoted in Hendra, *Going Too Far*, 39.

15. Nachman, *Seriously Funny*, 80.

16. Mort Sahl, *Heartland* (New York: Harcourt Brace Jovanovich, 1976), 93.

17. Nachman, *Seriously Funny*, 53; 80–86.

18. Bambi Haggins, *Laughing Mad: The Black Comic Persona in Post-Soul America* (New Brunswick, NJ: Rutgers University Press, 2007), 230–231; "dancing, not shuffling," quoted in Lola Ogunnaike, "Dave Chappelle, Alive and Well," *New York Times,* May 16, 2005, Lexis-Nexis via Infohawk, http://web.lexis-nexis.com.proxy.lib.uiowa.edu; "Everyone around me," quoted in Christopher John Farley, "Dave Speaks," *Time,* May 14, 2005, http://www.time.com/time/magazine/article/0,9171,1061512-3,00.html; *Anderson Cooper 360,* CNN, July 7, 2006, http://transcripts.cnn.com/TRANSCRIPTS/0607/07/acd.01. html (accessed March 17, 2007).

19. See Haggins, *Laughing Mad,* 14–24.

20. Howard Kurtz, "No Kidding: On Iraq, Janeane Garofalo Fights to Be Taken Seriously," *Washington Post,* Jan. 27, 2003, Lexis-Nexis via Infohawk, http://web.lexis-nexis.com.proxy.lib.uiowa.edu.

21. Al Franken, *Rush Limbaugh Is a Big Fat Idiot (and Other Observations)* (New York: Delacorte Press, 1996).

22. Al Franken, *Lies and the Lying Liars Who Tell Them: A Fair and Balanced Look at the Right* (New York: Dutton, 2003).

23. Al Franken, *The Truth, with Jokes* (New York: Dutton, 2005), cover copy quoted.

24. Maher interviewed by Paul Begala and Tucker Carlson on *Crossfire,* CNN, Nov. 27, 2002, http://transcripts.cnn.com/TRANSCRIPTS/0211/27/cf.00.html (accessed March 17, 2007).

25. The polygraph image was also featured on the show's Web site: http://www.hbo.com/billmaher/?ntrack_para1=leftnav_category0_show6 (accessed May 5, 2007).

26. Maher interviewed by Larry King, *Larry King Live,* July 31, 2003, http://transcripts.cnn.com/TRANSCRIPTS/0307/31/lk1.00.html (accessed Marchch 17, 2007).

27. Zay N. Smith, "Whatever It Takes to Sell Those Books," *Chicago Sun-Times,* June 8, 2006, Lexis-Nexis via Infohawk, http://web.lexis-nexis.com.proxy.lib.uiowa.edu.

28. Quoted in Dave Kargol, "Chris Rock Speaks with Echo," *EchoOnline,* May 24, 2005, http://www.easternecho.com/cgi-bin/story.cgi?7260 (accessed March 17, 2007).

29. J. D. Salinger, *The Catcher in the Rye* (Boston: Little, Brown, 1951).

30. "Miller and his wife, Ali, have two children—six-month-old Marlon (named for Marlon Brando) and almost-four Holden (for 'Catcher in the Rye' protagonist Holden Caulfield)." Gail Shister, "Dennis Miller Preps for New HBO Series," *Philadelphia Inquirer,* April 7, 1994, Lexis-Nexis via Infohawk, http://web.lexis-nexis.com.proxy.lib.uiowa.edu.

31. Series writing credits for *Dennis Miller Live* obtained from the Internet Movie Database, http://www.imdb.com/title/tt0108742/fullcredits#writers (accessed March 17, 2007).

32. James Wolcott, *Attack Poodles and Other Media Mutants: The Looting of News in a Time of Terror* (New York: Miramax Books, 2004), 263–264.

33. "Say What You Want about Dennis Miller: But Is He Funny?" *Buffalo News,* Jan. 23, 2004, Lexis-Nexis via Infohawk, http://web.lexis-nexis.com.proxy.lib.uiowa.edu.

34. Dennis Miller on Leno, *Tonight*, Feb. 25, 2003, transcript retrieved from About. com Political Humor, http://politicalhumor.about.com/library/bldennismiller_rant. htm (accessed March 17, 2007).

35. Wolcott, *Attack Poodles,* 266.

36. Miller on *The O'Reilly Factor,* Jan. 25, 2007, transcript retrieved from http://www.foxnews.com/story/0,2933,246742,00.html (accessed March 17, 2007).

37. Quoted in Wolcott, *Attack Poodles,* 267–268.

38. Associated Press, "Dennis Miller: '9/11 Changed Me': Comedian Defends Bush, Will Open Fire on Others on New Show," CNN.com, Monday, Jan. 26, 2004, http://www.cnn.com/2004/SHOWBIZ/TV/01/26/tv.dennismiller.ap/ (accessed March 17, 2007).

39. On Murphy, see Justin Cole, "Daily Ror-Shocked: Is CNBC's Dennis Miller Funny?" *Media Matters,* July 7, 2004, http://mediamatters.org/items/200407070004 (accessed March 17, 2007). On Alterman, see Catherine Seipp "Dr. D & DM," *National Review Online,* May 12, 2004, Lexis-Nexis via Infohawk, http://web.lexis-nexis. com.proxy.lib.uiowa.edu. On cancellation, see "CNBC Cancels 'Dennis Miller,' " CNN Money.com, May 12, 2005, http://money.cnn.com/2005/05/12/news/newsmakers/ cnbc_miller/ (accessed March 17, 2007).

40. "Funnyman Dennis Miller Returns to FNC!" Fox.com, Friday, Sept. 22, 2006, http://www.foxnews.com/story/0,2933,215178,00.html (accessed March 17, 2007).

41. *The Dennis Miller Show,* CNBC, April 30, 2004, interview with Amy Goodman, transcript, http://book.democracynow.org//articles/miller.html (accessed March 17, 2007).

42. "Biography for George Burns," International Move Database, http://imdb.com/ name/nm0122675/bio (accessed March 17, 2007).

43. Jon Stewart, *Daily Show,* April 24, 2007; Leno quoted in Sella, "Stiff Guy vs. Dumb Guy," 74.

44. See Philip Shenon, "Five Senators Struggle to Avoid Keating Inquiry Fallout," *New York Times,* Nov. 22, 1989, Lexis-Nexis via Infohawk, http://web.lexis-nexis.com. proxy.lib.uiowa.edu.

45. Ann McFeatters, "Politicos' Finances Full of Surprises: Abstemious Ralph Nader Wonders Why His Assets Aren't Bigger," *Pittsburgh Post-Gazette,* June 25, 2000, Lexis-Nexis via Infohawk, http://web.lexis-nexis.com.proxy.lib.uiowa.edu.

46. David Sanford, *Me & Ralph: Is Nader Unsafe for America?* (Washington: New Republic Books, 1976), 23–26.

47. ". . . Ralph Nader, who frittered away the thirty years of credibility he had earned for good causes by indulging his ego. His premise that there was no difference between the two major parties and their candidates was ridiculous, as Bush demonstrated as soon as he took office. (Does anyone really believe Gore would have chosen a John

Ashcroft for attorney general?)" Jack W. Germond, *Fat Man in a Middle Seat: Forty Years of Covering Politics* (New York: Random House, 2002), 278.

48. Senator William Fessenden of Maine complained that the proclamation "did not and could not affect the status of a single negro." Quoted in Doris Kearns Goodwin, *Team of Rivals: The Political Genius of Abraham Lincoln* (New York: Simon & Schuster, 2005).

49. See Doris Kearns Goodwin, *No Ordinary Time: Franklin and Eleanor Roosevelt: The Home Front in World War II* (New York: Simon & Schuster, 1994), 190–195.

50. Clinton construed "sexual relations" as referring only to intercourse, not oral sex. See J. M. Lawrence, "Clinton's 'Slick' Statement Circumvents Legal Definition," *Boston Herald*, Jan. 27, 1998, Lexis-Nexis via Infohawk, http://web.lexis-nexis.com.proxy.lib.uiowa.edu.

51. *The Colbert Report*, Jan. 16, 2007.

52. Nathan Rabin, "Interview: Stephen Colbert," *Onion AV Club*, Jan. 25, 2006, http://www.avclub.com/content/node/44705 (accessed March 17, 2006).

53. Frank Rich, "Truthiness 101: From Frey to Alito," *New York Times*, Jan. 22, 2006, Lexis-Nexis via Infohawk, http://web.lexis-nexis.com.proxy.lib.uiowa.edu.

CHAPTER 7 — FOR WHOM THE BELL DINGS

1. The quote is attributed to Harlan Howard, co-writer (with Hank Cochran) of "I Fall to Pieces" and other country hits: http://www.quotegarden.com/music.html (accessed March 18, 2007).

2. George Carlin, *Class Clown* (sound recording), Little David/Atlantic Records, released Sept. 1972.

3. Ed Ames's great moment is preserved on *The Tonight Show Starring Johnny Carson: The Ultimate Collection*, Volume 1, DVD, R2 Entertainment.

4. "It is our belief that civilization and higher education have a large influence in the development of repression," writes Freud. "The repressive activity of civilization brings it about that primary possibilities of enjoyment, which have now, however, been repudiated by the censorship in us, are lost to us. But to the human psyche all renunciation is exceedingly difficult, and so we find that tendentious jokes provide a means of undoing the renunciation and retrieving what was lost." Freud, *Jokes*, 101.

5. Tad Friend, "Hostile Acts," *New Yorker*, Feb. 5, 2007, 76.

6. Ibid.

7. Sarah (to a room full of elementary school kids): "If we can put a man on the moon, then we can put a man with AIDS on the moon. And then someday . . . we can put everyone with AIDS on the moon." *The Sarah Silverman Program*, "Positively Negative," Comedy Central, first aired Feb. 15, 2007.

8. Anthony Corsello, "There's Something about Morons," *GQ*, June 1999, 230; Miller quoted in Warren Berger, "Where Have You Gone, Standards and Practices?" *New York Times*, Sept. 20, 1998, Lexis-Nexis via Infohawk, http://web.lexis-nexis.com.proxy.lib. uiowa.edu.

9. For a history of the audience/performer relationship in American culture, see Laurence Levine, *Highbrow/Lowbrow: The Emergence of Cultural Hierarchy in America* (Cambridge, MA: Harvard University Press, 1988).

10. "The first major adjustment all stage comedians faced in radio was the empty studio. All their performing lives they had learned to play to live audiences, responding to laughs, adjusting their timing and material, and catching the audience up in the infectious quality of laughter. So, in early radio, comedians demanded live studio audiences, which allowed comics . . . to assume that if they made the studio audience laugh they would also make the folks at home laugh. . . ." Robert Toll, *The Entertainment Machine* (New York: Oxford University Press, 1982), 227–228, quoted in Marc, *Comic Visions*, 12.

11. Keith Phipps, "Interview: Conan O'Brien," *Onion AV Club,* May 9, 2001, http://www.avclub.com/content/node/22745 (accessed March 17, 2007).

12. See Marshall McLuhan, *Understanding Media: The Extensions of Man* (New York: McGraw-Hill, 1964).

13. "Jay Leno's Greatest Hits," Center for Media and Public Affairs (CMPA) press release, April 30, 2002, http://www.cmpa.com/pressReleases/JayLenosGreatestHits.htm (accessed March 17, 2007).

14. "September 11th Joke Targets: Can We Go and Do Shows Now?" CMPA, April 30, 2002, http://www.cmpa.com/politicalHumor/September11Jokes.htm (accessed March 17, 2007).

15. Letterman, *Late Show,* Jan. 28, 2000.

16. Tynan, "Fifteen Years," 343.

17. Werts, "A Regular Guy."

18. "Washington Wire," *Wall Street Journal,* Jan. 30, 1998, Lexis-Nexis via Infohawk, http://web.lexis-nexis.com.proxy.lib.uiowa.edu.

19. Leno, *Tonight,* March 1, 1999.

20. President Clinton ordered airstrikes on a suspected chemical weapons plant in Sudan that was believed to be under the control of Osama bin Laden. The immediate provocation was the al Qaeda attacks on the U.S. embassies in Kenya and Tanzania on August 7, 1998. The airstrikes took place on August 20, just three days after Clinton's videotaped deposition in the Lewinsky inquiry. In 2004, the 9/11 Commission, in chronicling the government's failure to prevent the growth of al-Qaeda, noted that "at the time [of the airstrikes], President Clinton was embroiled in the Lewinsky scandal, which continued to consume public attention for the rest of that year and the first months of 1999. . . . As it happened, a popular 1997 movie, 'Wag the Dog,' features a president who fakes a war to distract public attention from a domestic scandal. Some Republicans in Congress raised questions about the timing of the strikes. . . . The failure of the strikes, the 'wag the dog' slur, the intense partisanship of the period and the nature of the al Shifa evidence, likely had a cumulative effect on future decisions about

the use of force against Bin Ladin.' " Deb Reichman, "Monica and Osama: Two Separate Issues," *Newark Star-Ledger* (AP), July 25, 2004, Lexis-Nexis via Infohawk, http://web.lexis-nexis.com.proxy.lib.uiowa.edu.

21. Leno, *Tonight,* Jan. 28, 1998.

22. Leno, *Tonight,* March 2, 1999.

23. Aldous Huxley, *Brave New World* (New York: Harper & Brothers, 1946).

24. Letterman, *Late Show,* Oct. 26, 1999.

25. Leno, *Tonight,* Nov. 10, 1999; Oct. 25, 2000; Nov. 3, 2000.

26. Kenneth Anderson, "The American Inquisition," in *Left Hooks, Right Crosses: A Decade of Political Writing,* ed. Christopher Hitchens and Christopher Caldwell (New York: Thunder's Mouth Press, 2002), 301.

27. Bill Maher, *Politically Incorrect,* ABC, Nov. 3, 2000.

28. Werts, "A Regular Guy."

29. Quoted in Neal Justin, "Horror or Humor? Whoever Tells the Joke Decides," *Minneapolis Star Tribune,* July 3, 1994, Lexis-Nexis via Infohawk, http://web.lexis-nexis.com.proxy.lib.uiowa.edu.

30. Nathan Rabin, "Interview: Conan O'Brien (Part 2)," *Onion AV Club,* Aug. 30, 2006, http://www.avclub.com/content/node/52144/3 (accessed March 18, 2007); "too frat" quoted in Phipps, "Interview."

31. *Oxford English Dictionary* online, http://dictionary.oed.com.proxy.lib.uiowa.edu (accessed May 5, 2007).

32. Martin Luther King Jr., "Address at the March on Washington, August 28, 1963," in *A Patriot's Handbook: Songs, Poems, Stories, and Speeches Celebrating the Land We Love,* ed. Caroline Kennedy (New York: Hyperion, 2003), 323.

33. Brian C. Anderson, *South Park Conservatives: The Revolt against Liberal Media Bias* (Washington, DC: Regnery Publishing, 2005), 88.

34. P. J. O'Rourke, *Republican Party Reptile: Essays and Outrages* (New York: Atlantic Monthly Press, 1987), xiii on "pants-down Republicans"; *Give War a Chance: Eyewitness Accounts of Mankind's Struggle against Tyranny, Injustice and Alcohol-Free Beer* (New York: Atlantic Monthly Press, 1992); *Age and Guile Beat Youth, Innocence, and a Bad Haircut: Twenty-five Years of P. J. O'Rourke* (New York: Atlantic Monthly Press, 1995).

35. Taro Gomi, *Everyone Poops,* trans. Amanda Mayer Stinchecum (Brooklyn, NY: Kane/Miller Publishers, 1993).

36. In the academic world, the principal touchstone of the liberating potential of scatological and sexual humor is the Soviet literary theorist Mikhail Bakhtin (1895–1975). Bakhtin celebrated the egalitarian subtext of Rabelaisian comedy, which focused on the "lower bodily stratum." "Degradation digs a bodily grave for a new birth; it has not only a destructive, negative aspect, but also a regenerating one . . . [not] merely hurling [what it mocks] into the void of nonexistence, into absolute destruction, but to hurl it down to the reproductive lower stratum, the zone in which conception and a new birth take

place . . . the fruitful earth and the womb." Mikhail Mikhailovich Bakhtin, *Rabelais and His World,* trans. Helene Iswolsky (Cambridge, MA: MIT Press, 1968), 21. But Bakhtin spent his adult life under the thumb of an oppressive Soviet regime, serving a stretch in Stalin's gulag and coming close to being executed for his unorthodox intellectual activities. One can see how Rabelaisian humor would penetrate, at least symbolically, the inhuman carapace of a Stalin; in a society like ours, it is more of a challenge to take government seriously *enough,* without focusing unduly on our leaders' private parts.

37. *Mind of Mencia,* "Stereotype Olympics," season 2, episode 11, first aired July 23, 2006, http://www.imdb.com/title/tt0833779/ (accessed March 18, 2007); *The Sarah Silverman Program,* "Batteries," Comedy Central, first aired Feb. 1, 2007.

38. Nick Madigan, "Imus' Lucrative Franchise Could Be in Peril," *Baltimore Sun,* April 11, 2007, Lexis-Nexis via Infohawk, http://web.lexis-nexis.com.proxy.lib.uiowa.edu.

39. Andrew Ironside, "Kurtz: 'Imus made fun of blacks, Jews, gays, politicians. He called them lying weasels. This was part of his charm,'" *Media Matters,* April 13, 2007, http://mediamatters.org/items/200704140001 (accessed Aug. 31, 2007).

40. Limbaugh transcript excerpted in Adam H. Shah, "Limbaugh on Obama: 'Halfrican American,'" *Media Matters,* Jan. 24, 2007, http://mediamatters.org/items/200701240010 (accessed March 18, 2007); *The Half Hour News Hour,* Fox News Channel, Feb. 18, 2007; Brad Stine, *Tolerate This,* DVD, Word Distribution, 2005.

41. Charles E. Schutz, *Political Humor: From Aristophanes to Sam Ervin* (London: Associated University Press, 1977), 50.

42. Corsello, "Something about Morons," 231; on Silverman, Friend, "Hostile Acts," 76.

CHAPTER 8 — LAUGHING ALL THE WAY TO THE WHITE HOUSE

1. *Stand Up and Cheer,* directed by Hamilton MacFadden, dialogue by Ralph Spence, story by Lew Brown, from an idea by Will Rogers, 20th Century Fox, 1934.

2. After losing the California gubernatorial race in 1962, Nixon appeared on *The Jack Paar Show,* playing a piano piece of his own composition, and foreshadowing Clinton's sax solo on *Arsenio.* Steven Winn, "Jack Paar: Affable, Emotional TV Host Turned Viewers On to Late-Night Talk," *San Francisco Chronicle,* Jan. 28, 2004. Lexis-Nexis via Infohawk, http://web.lexis-nexis.com.proxy.lib.uiowa.edu.

3. E. B. White, "The Humor Paradox," in *Writings from the New Yorker: 1927–1976,* ed. Rebecca Dale (New York: Harper Perennial, 1991) 35.

4. Morris K. Udall, *Too Funny to Be President* (New York: Henry Holt, 1988).

5. David Herbert Donald, *Lincoln* (New York: Touchstone, 1996), 259.

6. *The Kennedy Wit,* ed. Bill Adler (New York: Carol Pub Group: 1991).

7. Cannon, Lou. *President Reagan: The Role of a Lifetime* (New York: Simon & Schuster, 1991), 120.

8. Ibid, 141.

9. Ibid.

10. Quoted ibid., 550.

11. Jack Germond and Jules Witcover, *Wake Us When It's Over: Presidential Politics of 1984* (New York: Macmillan, 1985).

12. *The Reagan Wit: The Humor of the American President,* ed. Bill Adler and Bill Adler Jr. (New York: William Morrow, 1998).

13. Germond and Witcover, *Wake Us When It's Over,* 32.

14. "For the second day in a row, Reagan smiled broadly Wednesday and whispered, 'I've lost my voice,' when reporters asked him during a brief photo session with congressional leaders about the Iran arms scandal and prospects for further U.S. aid to Nicaragua's Contra rebels. However, Reagan quickly found his voice when one reporter asked why there were no women at the meeting. 'It's just our bad luck,' the President replied." "Reagan Gets 'Laryngitis,'" *St. Petersburg Times* (Florida), March 12, 1987, Lexis-Nexis via Infohawk, http://web.lexis-nexis.com.proxy.lib.uiowa.edu.

15. For Reagan's "joke," see Germond and Witcover, *Wake Us When It's Over,* 468–469; for his rationale, see Lou Cannon, "Reagan Eyes Sweep, Visits Minnesota," *Washington Post,* Nov. 5, 1984, Lexis-Nexis via Infohawk, http://web.lexis-nexis.com.proxy.lib.uiowa.edu.

16. Historian Robert Dallek recounts a famous Johnson anecdote: visiting West German chancellor Ludwig Erhhart allegedly teased Johnson by saying, "I understand you were born in a log cabin," to which Johnson replied, "No, no, you have me confused with Abe Lincoln. I was born in a manger." Jerry Krupnik, "What It Takes to Be President Subject of 'Character' Forum," *Newark Star-Ledger,* May 29, 1996, Lexis-Nexis via Infohawk, http://web.lexis-nexis.com.proxy.lib.uiowa.edu.

17. Nixon intoned the catchphrase, "Sock it to me?" on *Rowan and Martin's Laugh-In,* NBC, Sept. 16, 1968.

18. The phrase "boomer humor" was coined by Tony Hendra in *Going Too Far.*

19. See Paula Span, "Abbie Hoffman's Radical Cheek: The Eternal Revolutionary As Comedian of Conscience," *Washington Post,* April 14, 1989, Lexis-Nexis via Infohawk, http://web.lexis-nexis.com.proxy.lib.uiowa.edu.

20. Ron Nessen, *It Sure Looks Different from the Inside* (Chicago: Playboy Press, 1978), 172–173.

21. An account of President Ford's comedy routine can be found in Hill and Weingrad, *Saturday Night Live,* 180–184.

22. Ibid., *Saturday Night,* 180.

23. Ibid., 184.

24. Ibid., 185–186.

25. Quoted in Nessen, *It Sure Looks Different,* 176.

26. "Fighting the 'Wimp' Factor," *Newsweek,* Oct. 19, 1987, cover.

27. See Hank Burchard, "Caricature Assassination," *Washington Post,* April 6, 1990, Lexis-Nexis via Infohawk, http://web.lexis-nexis.com.proxy.lib.uiowa.edu.

28. Quoted in David E. Rosenbaum, "Capital Press and Officials Jab, but in Jest," *New York Times,* April 2, 1990, Lexis-Nexis via Infohawk, http://web.lexis-nexis.com. proxy.lib.uiowa.edu.

29. Mark Katz, *Clinton and Me: A Real Life Political Comedy* (New York: Hyperion Books, 2003), 181.

30. Ibid.

31. Katz has an interesting insider's account of how the video came to be. Among the details: the director and one of the co-writers was *Everybody Loves Raymond* co-creator Phil Rosenthal. Katz, *Clinton and Me,* 352–371.

32. Peter Beckman cited in David Cassel, "Up Close and Presidential?" AlterNet, posted May 16, 2000, http://alternet.org/story/9166/ (accessed March 18, 2007).

33. Susan Silver, "Funny Leaders Aren't So Funny," *Ottawa Citizen,* May 8, 2000, Lexis-Nexis via Infohawk, http://web.lexis-nexis.com.proxy.lib.uiowa.edu.

34. McCain was unapologetic about his off-the-cuff musical threat. When asked if he didn't think the remark insensitive, he replied, "Insensitive to what? The Iranians?" Karen Crummy, "Jokes in Hand, Politicians Work to Win in a Laugher," *Denver Post,* April 23, 2007, Lexis-Nexis via Infohawk, http://web.lexis-nexis.com.proxy.lib.uiowa.edu.

35. Clinton later apologized for this "lame attempt at humor." "Hillary Clinton 'Truly Regrets' Gandhi Joke," CNN.com, Jan. 6, 2004, http://www.cnn.com/2004/ALLPOLI-TICS/01/06/elec04.s.mo.farmer.clinton.ap (accessed May 4, 2007). True to form, Biden's comment was less a joke than a bout of logorrhea: "In a June 2006 appearance in New Hampshire, [Biden] commented on the growth of the Indian American population in Delaware by saying, 'You cannot go into a 7–11 or a Dunkin' Donuts unless you have a slight Indian accent. Oh, I'm not joking.' Xuan Thai and Ted Barrett, "Biden's Description of Obama Draws Scrutiny," CNN.com, Feb. 9, 2007, http://www.cnn.com/ 2007/POLI-TICS/01/31/biden.obama/ (accessed May 4, 2007).

36. Bill Nichols, "The Heir Apparent Has Solid Record and Stolid Image," *USA Today,* Aug. 29, 1996, Lexis-Nexis via Infohawk, http://web.lexis-nexis.com.proxy.lib.uiowa.edu.

37. Gore appeared on *Tonight* Sept. 19, 2000, and on *Late Show,* Sept. 14, 2000.

38. Caryn James, "Bush Flunks Letterman's Late-Night Examination," *New York Times,* March 2, 2000, Lexis-Nexis via Infohawk, http://web.lexis-nexis.com.proxy. lib.uiowa.edu.

39. Peter Marks, "The 2000 Campaign: The Comedian; Letterman Invites Candidates to Late-Night Debate," *New York Times,* July 21, 2000, Lexis-Nexis via Infohawk, http://web.lexis-nexis.com.proxy.lib.uiowa.edu.

40. "The 2000 Campaign: Bush to Appear Again on Letterman," *New York Times,* Oct. 3, 2000, Lexis-Nexis via Infohawk, http://web.lexis-nexis.com.proxy.lib.uiowa.edu.

41. Jake Tapper, "Meet the Press, with David Letterman," *Salon,* Oct. 20, 2000 (online).

42. *Late Show,* Oct. 19, 2000.

43. *Late Show,* Oct. 20, 2000.

44. Richard Hofstadter, *Anti-Intellectualism in American Life* (New York: Vintage Books, 1963), 225.

45. Attributed, but very much in character.

46. Speier, "Wit and Power," 1388.

47. *SNL,* season 28, episode 8, Dec. 14, 2002.

48. *Late Show,* Nov. 15, 2002.

49. Katz, *Clinton and Me,* 340–341. Katz also provides a timeline (347–348) headed "A Chronology of How Al Gore Invented the Internet," which serves as a useful illustration of the workings of the newsmaker/journalist/comedian echo chamber. For "legs," see Alterman, *What Liberal Media?* 164.

50. "Look for the Union Label," lyrics by Paula Green, music by Malcolm Dodds, was indeed composed in 1975, for the International Ladies' Garment Workers Union. For what it's worth, however, the song is obviously inspired by 1949's "Look for the Silver Lining," lyrics by Buddy G. DeSylva, music by Jerome Kern.

51. Walter Shapiro, " 'Untruthful' Label Could Dog Al Gore," *USA Today,* Sept. 20, 2000, Lexis-Nexis via Infohawk, http://web.lexis-nexis.com.proxy.lib.uiowa.edu.

52. "The Al Gore Quiz," *U.S. News and World Report,* Oct. 9, 2000, http://www.usnews.com/usnews/issue/001009/9john.htm.

53. The "Joke That's Not Really a Joke" debuted in 2003 and ran intermittently through 2005.

54. Ron Suskind, *The Price of Loyalty: George W. Bush, the White House, and the Education of Paul O'Neill* (New York: Simon & Schuster, 2004), 283.

55. Speier, "Wit and Power," 1388.

56. Quoted in Gene Lyons, "For Bush, Administration Powers Increasing," *Arkansas Democrat-Gazette* (Little Rock), Nov. 28, 2001,

57. Frank Bruni, "Word for Word/Bushspeak; The President's Sense of Humor Has Also Been Misunderestimated," *New York Times,* April 1, 2001, Lexis-Nexis via Infohawk, http://web.lexis-nexis.com.proxy.lib.uiowa.edu; *Bushisms: President George Herbert Walker Bush, in His Own Words,* comp. by the editors of *The New Republic* (New York: Workman, 1992).

58. Frank Rich, "Paar to Leno, J.F.K. to J.F.K.," *New York Times,* Feb. 8, 2004, AR1, 22. *Late Show* Top Ten Lists: Gephardt, Jan. 12, 2004; Edwards, Feb. 4, 2004; Dean, Jan. 22, 2004. Sharpton hosted *SNL* Dec. 6, 2003. Kerry rode his Harley onto the *Tonight* stage Nov. 11, 2003. Adam Nagourney, "In Newly Usual Way, McCain Says He'll Run," *New York Times,* March 1, 2007, Lexis-Nexis via Infohawk, http://web.lexis-nexis.com.proxy.lib.uiowa.edu.

59. Triumph, the Insult Comic Dog, *Come Poop with Me* (audio recording), Warner Bros., 2003; Triumph (Robert Smigel) on *Tonight,* Nov. 11, 2003.

60. Dean interviewed on *Hardball with Chris Matthews,* Dec. 1, 2003; Charles Krauthammer, "The Delusional Dean," *Washington Post,* Dec. 5, 2003, http://www.

washingtonpost.com/ac2/wp-dyn/A37125–2003Dec.4?language=printer (accessed March 18, 2007).

61. Schwarzenegger announced his candidacy on Leno's *Tonight,* Aug. 6, 2003.

62. Rick Lyman, "The California Recall: The Candidates; California Voters Wonder: Is Anyone Not Running?" *New York Times,* Aug. 16, 2003, Lexis-Nexis via Infohawk, http://web.lexis-nexis.com.proxy.lib.uiowa.edu.

63. David Bauder (AP), "The *Late Show* Joke's on Arnold," *Boston Globe,* Oct. 22, 2003, http://www.boston.com/news/globe/living/articles/2003/10/22/the_late_show_jokes_on _arnold (accessed July 25, 2007); Reuters, "Gubernatorial Guests," *Toronto Sun,* Aug. 14, 2003, Lexis-Nexis via Infohawk, http://web.lexis-nexis.com.proxy.lib.uiowa.edu.

64. Bill Carter, "NBC Supports Politically Partisan Leno," *New York Times,* Oct. 10 2003, Lexis-Nexis via Infohawk, http://web.lexis-nexis.com.proxy.lib.uiowa.edu; Letterman, *Late Show,* Oct. 8, 2003.

65. Edward Epstein, "Two Proposals in Congress Would Let Foreign-Born Become President; Constitutional Amendments Unlikely to Pass," *San Francisco Chronicle,* Aug. 12, 2003, Lexis-Nexis via Infohawk, http://web.lexis-nexis.com.proxy.lib.uiowa.edu.

66. Rich, "Paar to Leno."

CHAPTER 9 — IRONY IS DEAD . . . LONG LIVE SATIRE?

1. Carter quoted in Jeff Daniel, "Cynicism and Irony Have Fallen Out of Favor," *St. Louis Post-Dispatch,* Sept. 23, 2001; Howard quoted in Michiko Kakutani, "Critic's Notebook: The Age of Irony Isn't Over After All," *New York Times,* Oct. 9, 2001; Rosenblatt quoted in Sam Allis, "Irony's Death Greatly Exaggerated," *Boston Globe,* Sept. 29, 2001; Thompson quoted in Phil Kloer, "Edgy Pop Culture Will Be Right Back," *Atlanta Constitution,* Sept. 16, 2001, Lexis-Nexis via Infohawk, http://web.lexis-nexis.com.proxy.lib.uiowa.edu.

2. Letterman, *Late Show,* Sept. 17, 2001.

3. Leno, *Tonight,* Sept. 18, 2001.

4. O'Brien, *Late Night,* Sept. 18, 2001.

5. Letterman, *Late Show,* Sept. 18, 2001.

6. Michaels quoted in Gail Pennington, "People in the News," *St. Louis Post-Dispatch,* Sept. 29, 2001, Lexis-Nexis via Infohawk, http://web.lexis-nexis.com.proxy.lib.uiowa.edu.

7. Leno, *Tonight,* Sept. 18, 2001.

8. Mark Crispin Miller, *Boxed In: The Culture of TV* (Evanston, IL: Northwestern University Press, 1988), 15.

9. Quoted in Andy Seiler, "Are We Laughing Yet?" *USA Today,* Oct. 5, 2001, Lexis-Nexis via Infohawk, http://web.lexis-nexis.com.proxy.lib.uiowa.edu.

10. Letterman, *Late Show,* Oct. 1, 2001.

11. Leno, *Tonight,* Sept. 20, 2001.

12. "September 11th Joke Targets: Can We Go and Do Shows Now?" CMPA, http://www.cmpa.com/politicalHumor/September11Jokes.htm (accessed July 25, 2007).

13. Richard Reeves, "Patriotism Calls Out the Censor," *New York Times,* Oct. 1, 2001, Lexis-Nexis via Infohawk, http://web.lexis-nexis.com.proxy.lib.uiowa.edu.

14. Paul Farhi, "Take Iraq. Please: For Letterman, Leno and Company, the Mideast Is a Comedy Winner," *Washington Post,* March 13, 2003, Lexis-Nexis via Infohawk, http://web.lexis-nexis.com.proxy.lib.uiowa.edu.

15. Quoted ibid.

16. Four days before "Shock and Awe" commenced, 40 percent still opposed the invasion, despite the Bush administration's aggressive marketing campaign and Colin Powell's now infamous presentation before the U.N. Richard Benedetto, "Poll: Most Back War, but Want U.N. Support," *USA Today,* March 16, 2003, Lexis-Nexis via Infohawk, http://web.lexis-nexis.com.proxy.lib.uiowa.edu.

17. Quoted in Farhi, "Take Iraq."

18. Quoted ibid.

19. Leno, *Tonight,* Oct. 10, 2001.

20. Quoted in *The Great Thoughts,* ed. George Seldes (New York: Ballantine Books, 1996), 409.

21. Harry G. Frankfurt, *On Bullshit* (Princeton, NJ: Princeton University Press, 2005); Tennessee Williams, *Cat on a Hot Tin Roof* (New York: New Directions, 1955).

22. James Madison, "Federalist Fifty-one," in Alexander Hamilton, James Madison, and John Jay, *The Federalist Papers,* ed. Clinton Rossiter (New York: Signet, 1961), 322.

INDEX

ABOUT THE AUTHOR

Russell Peterson dabbled in both political cartooning and stand-up comedy before finding his calling in higher education. In 2005 he earned his PhD from the University of Iowa, where he is currently a visiting assistant professor of American Studies.